Caribbean Dispatches

Beyond the Tourist Dream

Compiled and edited by
Jane Bryce

MACMILLAN
CARIBBEAN

Macmillan Education
Between Towns Road, Oxford OX4 3PP
A division of Macmillan Publishers Limited
Companies and representatives throughout the world

www.macmillan-caribbean.com

ISBN-13: 978-1-4050-7136-9
ISBN-10: 1-4050-7136-2

Designed by Andy Magee
Typeset by EXPO Holdings, Malaysia
Illustrated by Ximena Maier
Cover design by Andy Magee
Cover illustration by Lennox Honychurch

Printed and bound in Thailand

2010 2009 2008 2007 2006
10 9 8 7 6 5 4 3 2 1

Contents

For Tumi -
at home in the in-between

Thanks and Acknowledgements

This book would not exist without the enthusiastic participation of its contributors. From the moment I started tentatively talking about the idea, almost all those I talked to were supportive and encouraging, excited and ready to commit themselves to the project. Not everyone who agreed to contribute has ended up in the book, but I appreciated their positive response. I want, especially, to thank the authors of the pieces collected here who withstood my relentless requests for drafts and the potentially bruising editing process with grace and good humour. This book owes everything to you.

Various people gave practical advice and shared professional expertise. For help and enthusiasm in its early stages, I want to thank Diana Loxley. As his literary executor, Jerome McElroy patiently unearthed different possible contributions from our mutual friend, Klaus de Albuquerque. Jeremy Taylor ran a publisher's eye over the project and made suggestions. And to Nick Gillard: thanks for getting it. Thanks too to Claire Bordewey, Ximena Maier, and all the people at Macmillan who worked to bring this book to light.

A very special personal thank you goes to Philip Nanton, who was part of the idea from its inception, read every draft of every piece and shared reactions with me, helped with the editing, and kept me company every step of the way. His perspective as a Caribbean person was invaluable.

The authors and publishers would like to thank the following rights holders for the use of copyright material:
Sheil Land on behalf of Jean Rhys Ltd for the extracts from *Wide Sargasso Sea* © 1966; *Smile Please: an unfinished autobiography* © 1979; 'Heat' and 'I used to live here once', short stories from *Sleep it off, Lady* © 1976; 'Mixing Cocktails', a short story from *Left Bank* © 1927, all by Jean Rhys.

The publishers have made every effort to contact the copyright holders, but, if they have inadvertently overlooked any, they will be pleased to make the necessary arrangements at the first opportunity.

List of Contributors

Klaus de Albuquerque (1946–1999): a sociologist who was internationally recognised for his seminal contributions in inter-island migration, island demography, sustainable tourism strategies, the socio-economic impact of political status change, and the link between tourism and crime. In 1998, his five-part series on drugs and the Caribbean, published in the largest Caribbean weekly, *Caribbean Week*, won The Distinguished Series Press Award. He taught at the University of Charleston, South Carolina.

Ian Bethell Bennett: of Bahamian origin, he wrote his PhD on Spanish-language literature of the Caribbean, and now teaches at the University of Puerto Rico. He is the editor of the journal *Sargasso*.

Stewart Brown: poet, editor and critic of Caribbean writing. His poems encompass the Caribbean, Africa, Wales and England as in *Elsewhere*, his latest collection. He co-edited the much-acclaimed *Oxford Book of Caribbean Short Stories* and the *Oxford Book of Caribbean Verse*. He has taught in Jamaica, Barbados and Nigeria, and is now Director of the Centre for West African Studies, University of Birmingham, England.

Jane Bryce (General Editor): worked for several years as a freelance journalist in Nigeria and London specialising in arts features, and currently contributes to the Nigerian newspaper, *New Age* as well as regional Caribbean journals. Since 1992, she has been a lecturer at the University of the West Indies, Cave Hill, Barbados specialising in African literature, film and creative writing. She has published in all these areas; *Chameleon*, a collection of short stories, is forthcoming with Peepal Tree Press.

Denise deCaires Narain: grew up in Guyana and has lived in Barbados and St Vincent. She teaches literature at the University of Sussex and is a critic specialising in contemporary Caribbean women's writing. She is the author of *Making Style: Caribbean Women's Poetry* and of a forthcoming book on Olive Senior.

Ian Craig: lived in Spain before moving to Barbados as a lecturer in Spanish at the University of the West Indies, Cave Hill campus. He is a frequent visitor to Cuba, where he has regularly attended the Havana Film Festival. He is a specialist in Latin American Cinema.

Annalee Davis: a Barbadian artist whose work has been exhibited widely across the Caribbean and in the USA. Her daring and provocative paintings and installations pursue a Creole aesthetic which syncretises the multiple visual traditions of the region.

James Ferguson: is a writer, editor and publisher based in England. He has written extensively on the Caribbean and Latin America, including books on Haiti, Grenada, Venezuela and the Dominican Republic, a history, and a literary companion to the Caribbean. He contributes a column on classic Caribbean books to *Caribbean Beat* magazine. His current publishing programme includes the 'Cities of the Imagination' series.

Lennox Honychurch: was born and grew up in Dominica in the Windward Islands and Barbados. He has been described by the fabled publisher Diana Athill as 'the region's best historian.' Among his many literary and academic publications is *The Dominica Story*, a history of the island.

Marie-Elena John-Smith: an Antiguan, who worked with non-profit organisations designing and implementing development and human rights programmes in Africa, before returning to Antigua to research and write her first novel, *Unburnable*, published in 2005.

Shake Keane (1927–1997): a noted Vincentian jazz musician and poet who contributed essays and poems to the literary magazines of the region. He published five collections of jazz poetry drawing on life in St Vincent, where he was briefly Director of Culture in the early Seventies, including *Volcano Suite*. His collection *One a Week With Water: Rhymes and Notes* won the Cuban Casas de Las Americas Prize in 1979. *The Angel Horn: Shake Keane 1922–1997 collected Poems* was published posthumously in 2005.

Oonya Kempadoo: was born to Guyanese parents in England. She has lived in Guyana, St Lucia, Trinidad and now lives in Grenada. Her first novel about growing up in Guyana, *Buxton Spice* was published to much acclaim. Her second novel, *Tide Running* is set in Tobago.

Simon Lee: was born in London and made his home in Trinidad, where he worked for 15 years as a freelance writer, travelling extensively in the Caribbean, covering culture, heritage and the environment for regional and international publications. Now based in London, he is writing a book on Caribbean music.

Rob Leyshon: is a theatre director and drama teacher. He is director of the Cave Hill Theatre Workshop in Barbados, and has a special interest in Shakespeare in the Caribbean. He has made a study of the Shakespeare Mas in Carriacou.

Ian McDonald: author of the poetry collections *Mercy Ward, Jaffo the Calypsonian, Essequibo* and *Between Silence and Silence*; and of the novel *The Humming-Bird Tree*; winner of the Guyana Prize for Literature in 1992 and 2004; Fellow of the Royal Society of Literature since 1970; Honorary Doctorate of Letters from the University of the West Indies. He is also the long-standing editor of *Kyk-over-al* in Guyana, the only one of the small but influential Caribbean literary journals of the 1950s still being published. He also worked for many years in the Guyanese sugar industry.

Mark McWatt: born in Guyana, he is Professor of West Indian Literature at the University of the West Indies, Cave Hill, Barbados, and a respected critic. A winner of the Guyana Prize, he has been publishing poems in anthologies and periodicals for many years and has two published collections: *Interiors* (1989) and *The Language of Eldorado* (1994). *Suspended Sentences*, a collection of short stories, is his most recent publication (2005). He co-edited the *Oxford Book of Caribbean Verse* (2005).

Philip Nanton: born in St Vincent, he lived for many years in England and now lives in Barbados. He has presented a number of programmes on aspects of Caribbean culture for BBC radio, and published in a variety of journals and regional literary magazines. He compiled and edited *Remembering the Sea*, the first critical book on Frank Collymore, founding editor of *Bim* and one of the pioneers of West Indian literature.

Opal Palmer-Adisa: Jamaican-born author of several books of poetry and stories for both adults and children, her most recent poetry collection is *Leaf-of-Life*, and her latest novel *It Begins With Tears*. She is also a professor at the University of California, Berkeley, and a conductor of community workshops.

Polly Pattullo: is a journalist with the *Guardian* newspaper, London. Her insightful book, *Last Resorts: the cost of tourism in the Caribbean*, now in its second edition, has been described as offering some of the most careful research and frank reporting of the Caribbean tourism industry. Having made a second home in Dominica, she is co-author of *The Gardens of Dominica* and also the co-founder of Papillote Press, publishers of *It Falls Into Place*, the short stories of Phyllis Shand Allfrey.

Kim Robinson: is editor of books and monographs at the Sir Arthur Lewis Institute of Social and Economic Studies at the University of the West Indies, Mona. She is also the editor of *Jamaica Journal* published by the Institute of Jamaica. She is the author of *Out of Order! Anthony Winkler and White West Indian Writing* and the children's book, *Dale's Mango Tree* (Kingston Publishers, 1992), which she also illustrated. Her critical essays, short stories and poems have appeared in a number of journals and anthologies. The short story, 'Spreeing in the SUV' was the regional winner at the Commonwealth Short Story Competition in 2005.

Marina Salandy-Brown: was born and grew up in Trinidad and emigrated to England in her late teens. She lived in Egypt, Spain and Mexico before joining the BBC where she earned a reputation as senior manager and programmes editor for Radio 4 and Five Live. She has now returned to live in Trinidad and contributes to various international periodicals.

Robert Edison Sandiford: is the author of two short story collections, *Winter, Spring, Summer, Fall* and, most recently, *The Tree of Youth*; the graphic story collections *Attractive Forces* and *Stray Moonbeams*; and a travel memoir, *Sand for Snow: A Caribbean-Canadian Chronicle*. He is a founding editor of Arts*Etc: The Premier Cultural Guide to Barbados*, and has worked as a book publisher and video producer.

Olive Senior: a Jamaican who currently lives in Toronto, is the author of the *Encyclopedia of Jamaican Heritage* and nine other books – poetry, fiction and non-fiction. Her latest poetry collection, *Over the Roofs of the World*, was shortlisted for the Canadian Governor-General's Literary Award 2005, while *Gardening in the Tropics* is on the CAPE syllabus for Caribbean schools. Her short story collection, *Summer Lightning*, won the 1987 Commonwealth Writers Prize.

Hazel Simmons-Macdonald: was born in St Lucia. She teaches at the University of the West Indies, Cave Hill, Barbados and researches in applied linguistics, specialising in language acquisition, vernacular literacy and bilingualism in Creole contexts. Her poetry has been published in many regional magazines, and she is the author of the collection, *Silk Cotton and Other Trees*.

Andy Taitt: former travel editor of *Caribbean Week*, a regional fortnightly newspaper which covered the anglophone Caribbean. He is Chairman of the Frank A. Collymore Literary Award Fund which awards an annual prize for creative writing in Barbados.

Jeremy Taylor: was born in England, married a Trinidadian and has lived in Port of Spain since 1971, working first as a teacher, then as a journalist, editor and publisher. He is the founding editor of *Caribbean Beat*, the highly regarded BWIA in-flight magazine which covers art and culture around the region. He is author of two books about Trinidad and Tobago, *Masquerade* and *Going to Ground*.

Marina Warner: novelist, critic, historian and mythologian, she is from an English family with historical connections to the Caribbean. She is the author of several prize-winning novels, including *Indigo*, set in an imaginary Caribbean island.

Anthony Winkler: a Jamaican full-time writer living in the USA. As well as co-authoring a number of English textbooks, he has published four very popular comic novels and an autobiographical work, all of which are set in his native Jamaica. One novel, *The Lunatic*, has been made into a highly successful film. His most recent publications are the short story collection *The Annihilation of Fish* and a fifth novel *Dog War*, both published by Macmillan.

Introduction

Tourism is the Caribbean's biggest industry, bringing thousands of overseas visitors every year to different parts of the region. Not all these visitors come in search exclusively of beaches and sunshine: many, if not most, want to experience something indefinable called 'culture' and are interested in history, art, music and whatever makes the local scene distinctive. Some will read Caribbean poetry or fiction, but most rely on guidebooks for the quick insight. Though there are innumerable travel guides of the 'where to go' variety, as well as a great deal of academic writing in the field of Caribbean studies, nothing has appeared in the last few decades comparable to *The Traveller's Tree*, Patrick Leigh Fermor's account of sailing round the Caribbean in the 1940s.

But Leigh Fermor was, after all, an outsider looking in. *Caribbean Dispatches* provides a well-written and idiosyncratic collection of personal views of Caribbean life by writers of mainly Caribbean origin, or who know it well, for readers who want to get beyond the exotic surface of the tourist experience. Rather than being strictly 'serious' – literary or sociological – or 'entertaining' – journalistic or popular – it occupies a space somewhere between the two. The painting on the cover by Dominican contributor Lennox Honychurch, which hangs on the wall of the Roseau General Post Office, shows how 'dispatches' – in the sense of words written and carried from one place to another by canoe, sailboat or amphibious plane – were an essential means of communicating for the Caribbean before modern technology took over. These *Caribbean Dispatches* embrace and reformulate that tradition, creating a dialogue between writers and places from multiple points of view.

There are many obvious gaps and absences, but the idea wasn't to be comprehensive or all-encompassing. In any case, that would be a hopeless task for any book about possibly the most culturally multifarious region in the world. What it reveals is the multiple ways there are of being *of* or *in* the Caribbean: 'belongers' and 'non-belongers,' residents and ex-pats, locals and 'indigenes,' immigrants and returnees, 'visitors' and tourists, creoles, coolies and douglas, red-legs and high-browns. You can be at home in one place and a foreigner in another, plantocracy or illegal migrant worker, pentecostalist, Hindu, Moslem, Church of England, Vodou or Santeria worshipper. The writers who have contributed to this collection are also part of this multiplicity: inhabitants of one island observing and commenting on their own or another; people of Caribbean origin living abroad but maintaining family links; returnees who have come back after many years away; people from elsewhere who have lived here a long time; long-term frequent visitors. Among them are novelists, poets, artists, academics, journalists and broadcasters. The one thing that was required of them all was to write from a 'personal' viewpoint, not necessarily *about* themselves, but providing a perspective uniquely theirs. How these particular individuals have come together as a group is the result, inevitably, of the editor's personal networks and preoccupations.

Living in the region, we are constantly aware of our differences – whether we speak French, Spanish, Dutch, English, Papiamentu, Creole or 'dialeck'; whether we're an independent state or still ruled from elsewhere; sea-surrounded or continental; of African, East Indian, European, Lebanese, Chinese, Carib or Arawak origin. To represent all these would have necessitated a rigorous selection process, probably doomed to failure, and this book did not attempt it. Rather, it took good writing as its primary pre-requisite, whether this took the form of poetry, fiction, commentary, memoir, dramatic vignette or journalistic account. In the event, the writers are, broadly speaking, 'from' the Anglophone Caribbean, though they may be writing about Cuba, Haiti or Puerto Rico. Some places – Trinidad, Jamaica, Barbados – are over-represented, while others – Tobago, Carriacou, Montserrat – only get a look in. Important parts of the region – Martinique and Guadeloupe, Curaçao and Aruba, Santo Domingo and Belize – are missing altogether. But that too is part of Caribbean reality, where some of us make more noise than others, and the sound of one language can drown out all the rest.

What emerges from the spectrum of viewpoints that makes up the collection is a certain preoccupation with change. It's a truism that society in the Caribbean has been in flux since it was first 'settled' some 500 years ago. Transportation, migration and inter-territorial movements, by which large numbers of people have been historically, and are still, caught up in a never-ending flow from place to place, make this region as restless as any in the world. Movement and change are a quintessential part of living in, or being from, the Caribbean, as these pieces demonstrate. Reading the book from end to end, I'm struck by the extent to which each writer is in negotiation with her or his subject, while simultaneously being in dialogue with all the other writers. Themes recur: the relationship between the present and the past; between the anonymity and chaos of cities (traffic in Kingston, urban encroachment in Port of Spain, partying in Havana) and the peace of nature (sunset on the Essequibo, rain falling on a Dominican garden); or the destructive power of nature (a volcano eruption in St Vincent, a hurricane in Grenada) and its orderly containment (walking the Sea Wall in Georgetown, Guyana, or the sea-side in Barbados); or the question of 'home' and finding a place to stand, given a different spin by Hazel Simmons-Mcdonald, Jeremy Taylor and Marina Salandy-Brown.

Then again, there's the range of social attitudes, like the contrast between the unembarrassed incorrectness of conventional attitudes to 'madness' ('Signing for a Madman') and the celebration of 'the kind of human eccentricities that make small island life tolerable' ('Vroom Vroom'). And of experiences, from the young Italian woman's introduction to cricket in a London drawing room by her West Indian father-in-law ('Spirits before my face'), to the hard-core Windies supporter keeping his head in 'Oval Lime'; or the nervous Oxfrod graduate venturing to do his research in Haiti, as against the full-blooded embrace of Vodou ritual by another Haiti visitor. Tribute is paid to parents, and childhood poignantly evoked, by several of the writers. Lastly, the writing itself ranges from formal, 'speaky-spokey' English to broad creolisation, from cool observation to hot participation, from lyricism to cynicism, while every so often, the orality which constantly presses at the margins of all Caribbean discourse explodes triumphantly onto the page.

When it came to organising the pieces, the categories they themselves suggested – Landscapes, Encounters, Personalities, Performances, Retrospectives – seemed to me a far better way of letting them speak to each other than the tired old division along national lines. National categories are altogether too small, too limiting, too divisive and too artificial to represent the diversity of Caribbean life and of the accounts collected here. After all, as one of the writers says: 'The longer you stay, the more complex things become.' Or, to put it another way, 'it all one big commess, so wha' fe do? '

Jane Bryce, Barbados, 2006

LANDSCAPES

Rejected Text for a Tourist Brochure

Olive Senior

*'I saw my land in the morning
and O but she was fair.'*
M.G. Smith, 'Jamaica' (1938)

Come see my land

1

Come see my land
before the particles of busy fires ascend;
before the rivers descend underground;
before coffee plantations
grind the mountains into dust; before
the coral dies; before the beaches
disappear

Come see my land
Come see my land
And know
That she was fair.

2

Up here, the mountains are still clear.
After three weeks, I heard a solitaire.
Down there, the mountains are clear-cut
marl pits. Truckers steal sand from beaches,
from riverbeds, to build another ganja palace,
another shopping centre, another hotel
(My shares in cement are soaring). The rivers, angry,
are sliding underground, leaving pure rockstone
and hungry belly.

3

No Problem, Mon. Come.
Will be one hell of a beach party.
No rain. No cover. No need to bring
your bathing suit, your umbrella.
Come walk with me in the latest stylee:
rockstone and dry gully. Come for the Final
Closing Down Sale. Take for a song
the Last Black Coral; the Last Green Turtle;
the Last Blue Swallow-tail (preserved behind glass).
Come walk the last mile to see the Last Manatee
the Last Coney, the Last Alligator, the Last Iguana Smile.

Oh, them gone already? No Problem, Mon.
Come. Look the film here.
Reggae soundtrack and all. Come see
my land. Come see my land and know, A-oh,
that she was fair.

A Different Sort of Time

Ian McDonald

Every so often I go with my family up the Essequibo for an unforgettable, life-enhancing, few days. We stay in a small and lovely house, whose ownership we share with friends, embowered in the green forest set on a niche of bright sand on the edge of the great river. The peace and beauty of this perfect place cannot be imagined, it can only be experienced. Friends, seasoned travellers around this multi-marvelled earth, who have been there with us have said they know of nowhere which excels, and very few which equal, this place in its unique, uncorrupted loveliness.

There are boating and swimming and wave-running and expeditions near and far and forest ventures and parties in other river-homes. But I care these days simply to spend the time sitting and reading, watching the river change and the sky grow light, then luminous, then dark again and then watch the astonishing splendour of the stars at night. Storms come and go and they toss the river as if it were the sea. I love the storms. And, by now, I have seen scores upon scores of dawns and dusks and not one is the same in how they colour the sky and the river that is more like a sea, where that bright beach and green forest curve. I have seen more colours there than scientists say exist. I remember once, on two successive days, there was a dawn so explosively red it seemed a volcano had burst, followed by one whose sky was silver-pale and veined with lightest blue. One evening, on a recent visit, huge, leaden-coloured, ominous clouds hung over the house. I had just read a poem which described a sky 'the colour of the desperation of wolves' and, as I looked up at those clouds about to fall on us, I knew what the poet meant.

I find there long hours of slow-moving time to read. Is there anything better, more soul-satisfying, at my age anyway, than an amplitude of time, with no commitments in prospect, no business to transact, to read books you have looked forward to reading, saved up for the right interval of unoccupied hours, treasuring the thought? This is not a mere reading of books, it is the long-drawn-out savouring of one of the great pleasures of life. I find a place in the shade of a tree by the river-rocks on the beach and set down a comfortable chair and ahead of me stretch as many hours as I like for the enjoyment of books and the pleasures of reflection.

I read the pages more slowly than usual, often turning back to re-read passages because their beauty or relevance registers with special impact in retrospect as the book progresses, or simply because some expression of an insight is so remarkable that I want to remind myself more than once of how it has been written. Often also my eyes lift off the page, simply to look at the great river and the immense sky which arches over it, to see with ever-renewed wonder how their moods and patterns everlastingly change and I think how each moment is unique and eternal. Sudden shifts of wind or cloud-shadow change the texture of the water from brocade to silk to satin to rough cotton. Progress with my book is slow. But why should I worry about that? There is no need to hurry. There are no deadlines. As it gets too dark to read, I set aside my book and look up at the stars.

Night after night I have sat beneath the stars on the bank of the great Essequibo and have been for hours wrapped in wonder. Here at night the stars are as big as in Van Gogh's mad skies. They burn with a wild freedom you do not see in town. Gradually, a feeling of exultation and an expansion of the mind takes hold which is hard to explain. There is an essay by the 18th century Englishman, Joseph Addison, entitled 'On the Pleasures of the Imagination,' which has a passage which comes near what I have felt many nights up the Essequibo:

> 'We are filled with a pleasing astonishment, to see so many worlds, hanging one above another, and sliding round their axles in such an amazing pomp and solemnity. If, after this, we contemplate those wild fields of ether, that reach in height as far

as from Saturn to the fixed stars, and run abroad almost to an infinitude, our imagination finds its capacity filled with so immense a prospect, and puts itself upon the stretch to comprehend it. But if we rise yet higher, and consider the fixed stars as so many vast oceans of flame, that are each of them attended with a different set of planets, and still discover new firmaments and new lights that are sunk further into those unfathomable depths of ether, so as not to be seen by the strongest of our telescopes, we are lost in such a labyrinth of suns and worlds, and confounded with the immensity and magnificence of nature.'

Up the Essequibo I have wished so often that I possessed the art of a great painter or a great photographer to do justice to the infinite beauty of the changing sky and river scenes and forest in the wind. Horace in his treatise *Ars Poetica* wrote that poetry should reproduce the qualities of painting. Here, more than anywhere I have tried to write poetry, for it is by the Essequibo I have felt the truth that all art is one and takes at such times a powerful cue from nature.

There are days on the Essequibo of brooding clouds, filled with thunder, and brewing squalls and lashing rain-storms marching up the immense reaches of the river, followed by a serene calmness in the air, when I have often deeply felt what soul-satisfaction it would give to be able to paint the wind. If ever there was wind that deserved to be painted it is Essequibo wind – how it moves the caravans of clouds; how it roughs up the shining coat of the evening-water; how it makes a green tumult in the crowns of the forest trees; how the birds ride the heavens on it. Please God, if I am born again with the powers of an artist, let me go again to the Essequibo and read the books I love and, this time, paint the wind.

On the Road

Kim Robinson

5.30 a.m. The alarm clock goes off. It is the third alarm – the first went off at 5.15, the second at 5.25. I am not naturally an early riser, so this wake-up time is not easy for me. I close my eyes, saying, 'Five more minutes ...'

Then I remember that yesterday my daughter was late for school. If I stay in bed another five minutes, she may be late again. I drag myself out of bed.

This is one of the consequences of moving to Red Hills, one of the hills forming a semi-circle of suburbs around Kingston. As all my friends told me, their eyes open wide at the madness of my decision to relocate, the traffic on that west side of the city is horrific. Where I lived before, in Russell Heights, another much more central suburban area, I could stay in bed another 45 minutes and still get my daughter to school by 7.45 a.m.

But then, Russell Heights did not have this view.

As I stagger towards the kitchen to fix my essential super-strong brew of coffee, I do what I do every morning – stop to look at the view of Kingston from my living room window. And, as happens every morning, I am momentarily awestruck. The lights of the city glint gold, white, red and blue like jewels on the jet-black plain. The sky is an expanse of navy blue/purple. There is a faint, very faint, hint of mauve appearing behind the range of the Wareika Hills to the east. Ahead of me, due south, the string of street lights on the Palisadoes strip bordering the Kingston harbour ends in the dimly flickering lights of the village of Port Royal. To the west, the Caymanas estate is black; behind it, another string of lights on the causeway crosses the water to the glittering satellite city of Portmore. As happens every morning, I feel a flood of joy, a surge of optimism after this injection of beauty. I am happy to be alive. I am even happy to be up this early.

That optimism has waned slightly by the time my son, my daughter and I are ready to get in the car – because somehow, despite my disciplined rise from bed, we have lost five minutes this morning, and five minutes are critical. Once, a few days after we first moved here, we left home at this same time and it took us one hour and fifty minutes to get to our first stop, my daughter's school. However, (and the optimism returns) there have been mornings when the school run (which, incidentally, would be a 15-minute drive without traffic) has taken 45 minutes. If it takes even an hour this morning, we will make it.

At 6.35 a.m. we exit our driveway. It is a clean, clear morning: the sun has risen over the pinky Blue Mountains in the distance to our left; my daughter points out a layer of white mist in the valleys.

The drive off the hill is the first test. Sometimes, the traffic is backed up halfway up the hill, and it may take 20 minutes to get to the bottom – possibly, I suspect, because commuters coming in to Kingston from the interior of the island or the north coast early in the morning sometimes prefer to take the steep climb through Sligoville-Rock Hall – Red Hills in order to avoid the frustration of the bumper-to-bumper traffic on the Spanish Town Bypass. (People often bypass the bypass by driving through Spanish Town itself in order to avoid the traffic snarl on the super highway.) Or it may be an entirely arbitrary phenomenon – I have long since given up on trying to understand the prevarications of Kingston traffic. The only thing I understand is that in the last decade, ever since the government allowed the importation of inexpensive deportees (second-hand vehicles from Japan), thereby enabling every Errol, Mikey and Junior to own a car, the traffic problem in the city has become severe.

This morning, however, we reach the foot of the hill in five minutes, zooming past the numerous huge hotel-like mansions which have sprung up on the hillside in the last 20 years (with such ostentatious displays of new wealth causing certain old-money upturned noses to sniff suspiciously, so that the area has been labelled a drug don's neighbourhood – although there are probably more drug dons in respectable old-money Cherry Gardens and Norbrook). My optimism increases.

At the foot of the hill I have a choice of going in any of four directions. The most direct route is straight ahead, along Red Hills Road which will take me directly to Half Way Tree where my daughter's school is located – a seemingly obvious choice for someone trying to get there in a hurry. However, the Red Hills Road has a number of problems. When the traffic is slow on that road, it is very, very slow. Which is tricky because of another problem: Red Hills Road, which runs along the edge of a few volatile communities such as 100 Lane and Whitehall, has had some unpleasant outbreaks of violence in recent years. A friend of mine got stuck once on Red Hills Road a few years ago, in bumper-to-bumper rush hour traffic when various parts of the city were exploding in the gas riots. People were angry, side roads were being blocked by burning tyres, here and there one or two cars were being overturned. He could move neither forward nor backward, could turn neither right nor left. Although the riots were some five years ago, although nobody got hurt, although he still lives in Red Hills, he no longer uses that road.

However, there have been no problems in recent years. And time, as usual, is tight. So, as usual, I take the Red Hills road route.

Within a few minutes the traffic has slowed to a crawl. We inch along past a newspaper vendor – the *Gleaner* headline screams that an economic crisis is looming ('ANOTHER FACTORY CLOSES, Unemployment Soars,' 'TEACHERS THREATEN STRIKE Unless Granted Pay Increase'); the *Observer* headline quotes the government in vigorous denial ('3% GROWTH THIS YEAR says Minister of Finance'). Nothing new. 'Everyone want more,' a passing pedestrian proclaims to the vendor. 'Doctor want more, teacher want more, police want more.' I am not sure whether he approves or disapproves of this trend. We inch past a pan chicken vendor; past a higgler selling green bananas, pumpkin, yam, tomatoes, thyme; past another selling ripe bananas, American apples and otaheite apples to passing school-children. There is a basic school near the foot of the hill: tiny tots, aged four to five, hold hands as they walk along the roadside in their crisp blue and yellow uniforms. Further along there is a primary school. An emaciated man, with wild eyes and uncombed hair whom we have come to look forward to seeing every morning, is responsible for the pedestrian crossing in front of the school and takes his job seriously, threatening cars who threaten to disregard his instructions to halt with a flinging of the arm and a scowl. The schoolchildren are clearly fond of him.

A high school boy saunters along jauntily, green tie loose, khaki shirt out of his low-slung khaki pants, past a few nonchalant cows, a foraging pig and a family of goats, swinging his Digicel bag (the company had a promotion a few months ago where complimentary bags were given out with each new mobile phone purchased) and talking on what is presumably his Digicel phone. Between Digicel and its main competitor, Cable and Wireless, most Jamaicans of all income levels, from executives to gardeners, now have cell phones – we may have 20 per cent illiteracy, but communication is alive and well! How can he be going to school like that? I ask. My teenage son, rolling his eyes at my naivete, points out in exasperation that the boy will, of course, fix the tie, tuck in the shirt, pull up the pants and conceal the phone when he reaches his school gate, which is about a mile further down the Red Hills Road. We place bets as to who will reach his gate first – him or us. There have been many mornings when schoolboy pedestrians whom we have passed at the foot of the hill have reached their school at the end of this two-mile stretch at the same time as us.

We crawl past the burnt-out shell of what was a two-storey building of shops, one of the casualties of the gas riots. Business has been back to normal for many years on this road, but clearly the owners of this building decided they couldn't, or couldn't be bothered, to restore it. Generally, this is a ramshackle stretch. Yet the recently opened swanky PriceSmart membership-shopping centre close by has been doing a thriving business with its upper St Andrew, SUV-driving customers, as are the half dozen or so other shopping centres along this one-mile strip. A little way down the road, Juici Patties' breakfast offerings of hominy, plantain or peanut porridge laden with condensed milk, nutmeg and cinnamon, of ackee and saltfish, liver, salt mackerel or stew chicken with green banana, yam, boiled and fried dumplings have enticed a long queue of white- and blue-collar workers to leave the line of traffic and join the breakfast order line instead.

'Mummy, look! There's the madwoman again.' My daughter has become quite attached to a woman we see every morning, ever since she spotted her standing on top of a wall flapping her arms and crowing like a rooster. She lives in a shack beside the gully running parallel to the road. Most mornings we see her returning to her home with a bucket of what I guess is water on her head, which she must have collected from a nearby standpipe. She always wears pink or red.

The traffic suddenly and inexplicably eases up and we are able to sail along for a minute or two … until we get stuck behind a bus, which stops long at every bus stop to allow its passengers, rammed into every available inch of space, to squeeze on or off. This is not good – but I cannot overtake because the traffic in the other direction is nearly as heavy. In any case, I soon realise, there is no point, because the traffic ahead of the bus is not moving. We stay immobile, and the minutes tick away. My neck muscles start to tighten.

There is a certain powerlessness that one feels when one is stuck in bumper-to-bumper traffic, especially when one has a daughter who hates being late. The frustration threatens to swamp me. In an effort to fight it, I reach for my map of Kingston, and for the umpteenth time scan the Red Hills Road section for the shortcut that *must* exist. Surely there must be a set of back roads somewhere that would allow me to avoid this torture? I am usually good at finding back roads … Apparently not this time!

Well, at least the stops enable the children to finish their homework and start their packed breakfast (both normal en-route-to-school activities in this car) and allow me to skim the front page of the *Gleaner* which I carried from home. Other than the usual doom and gloom about the economy, there is also doom and gloom about corruption and ghetto violence. I flick to the entertainment section and find the horoscope. It tells me to reconnect to my inner resources of patience and resilience. All-righty!

My son turns on the car radio – too loud, as usual. Politely, I ask him to turn it down. Sulkily, he complies. A popular dancehall DJ is suggesting that in return for the fridge, stove, video, DVD etc. etc. that he has been persuaded to give his gal she should 'tek de buddy.' Any righteous indignation on my part is cut short by the female dancehall singer who, a few songs later, extols her spiritual values: 'The Prado and the Gucci and the Fendi dem a fe me.' My 11-year-old daughter sings along. 'Oh, for goodness' sake'! I say. 'What's your problem?' asks my son irritably. He is still annoyed that he has been forced to listen to his music at a volume which will not entertain the entire Red Hills Road. But the next song, where another popular local singer stirringly bemoans the little white lie she has had to tell her husband about the identity of her baby's father, evidently offends him: 'That jacket song again,' he mutters in disgust, and surfs the radio stations for an acceptable alternative. News, news, a talk show, another talk show, yet another talk show … He finds a station that is playing rap music. The artiste refers to 'hors d'oeuvre' with an aspirated 'h.' I take this opportunity to educate my offspring about correct French pronunciation. 'Mummy,' my son says patiently, 'he's saying *whore* d'oeuvre.' Okay, then.

The traffic eases up again for a few seconds, until we reach the gate of the high school where there is, as always, another hold-up. My son nudges me, triumphantly: there is the young man I spotted earlier, entering the compound with hordes of other boys, his Digicel bag swinging, shirt tucked in, pants pulled up, tie tied and phone concealed.

It takes forever to get past this school gate thanks to a stream of cars forcing their way onto the main road; but then, finally, the traffic flows freely again; and soon we have reached the point where Red Hills Road feeds into Constant Spring Road. I brace myself – this is the stressful part of the trip. On this stretch, you have to be sharp, you have to be on the ball, you have to be aggressive, you have to be *hard*.

This part of Constant Spring Road, the main shopping centre strip in the city with some nine or ten shopping plazas side by side aligning it, has four lanes of traffic heading down to Half Way Tree, with cars, buses, minibuses, legal and illegal taxis manoeuvring and cutting across lanes in a manner that suggests survival of the fittest. The fittest are the illegal taxis, which are easily identified. Look for a white or grey Nissan or Toyota deportee, packed with passengers; the driver, often sporting metallic teeth, steers with his left hand while his right arm, bling-bling bedecked, dangles outside the vehicle. Someone told me once that the dangling arm allows the driver to position his head outside the vehicle more easily to get a better view of what's ahead or around the corner whenever he wishes to overtake – which is often – or whenever he wishes to see if any policemen are lurking down the road waiting to entrap him – which is not often enough.

These illegal taxis are usually found hurtling down the bus-only lane in between the hurtling buses. This lane is the fastest, until it inexplicably converges with the second lane, at which point the traffic flow grinds to a near-halt. Here, inevitably (except for the rare occasions that the traffic police are on duty at this part of Constant Spring Road – and I have seen them only once in the six months that I have been taking this route in the mornings) taxis can be seen resolutely forcing their way diagonally, horns blaring, from the bus lane across the second and third lanes to get into the fourth lane, which is the second fastest. Unfortunately, I am not brave or brazen enough to do likewise – if I were, I am sure I would save a good 15 minutes on this part of the trip. Instead I can summon up enough aggressiveness only to switch back and forth between lanes two and three as I gauge which one is going faster at any particular moment then cut into it with precision timing, ignoring any dirty looks from drivers who may have to brake suddenly, and making sure to look out for racing bus and mad taxi drivers.

There are many close calls and near misses. Ahead of us, a car runs into the back of another. But it is rush hour, and everyone is rushing – so the drivers get out, make a quick assessment as to damage, decide it's not worth a hassle, and jump back into their cars. A taxi driver tries to switch lanes by pushing his white Nissan Sunny sedan in front of a bus. 'He's brave,' comments my son. 'Go through, star'! pipes up my daughter unexpectedly from the back seat, her head raised from her social studies textbook. The bus is one of those three-carriage articulated monsters and towers over the Nissan. However, the taxi driver is younger and more fearless than the bus driver. He is victorious. The bus driver sticks his head out of the window and informs the taxi driver about his bumbo raas claat. In response, the taxi driver advises the bus driver in minute detail what he should do to his mother. We wait with bated breath for the next stage of this exchange. Such advice regarding one's mother is not usually treated with indifference. Surprisingly, both drivers continue calmly, rather than stopping their vehicles and jumping out to continue the discussion physically on the road – as has happened in the past. 'If any one of them said "batty bwoy," gunshot woulda pop,' observes my son. True.

In the midst of all this, a vendor wanders unperturbed between lanes shouting 'Arinj!' and displaying his bag of large, peeled oranges – another offering in the breakfast-for-commuters trade.

Some progress is eventually made. We round the last bend before the final stretch to Half Way Tree, so named because there used to be a tree here which marked the halfway point between Constant Spring and downtown Kingston. The Half Way Tree clock is in sight. Built in 1913, it hasn't worked for most of the last couple of decades, but it is always a reassuring sight. Once we pass the clock it should take only five minutes to get to my daughter's school. Surprisingly, the clock is working this morning, and proclaims that it is now 7.40 a.m. We might barely make it.

Half Way Tree is its usual bustling self. Four major roads meet here, coming from the north, south, east and west of the city. Bus stops and shops abound. In another hour or two, dancehall music will be blaring from music stores. The police, making up for their absence up the road, are very much present here. As a result, the traffic is extremely well mannered. No one drives through red or amber lights. Cars courteously allow pedestrians to cross, and vehicles from side roads to feed into the main.

We make it to my daughter's school barely in time. I am exhausted, but this is only the end of the first leg. I still have to take my son to his school, then proceed to my office. Thankfully, this first leg is always the worst. I should make it to my office in another half an hour or so. So I will only have been on the road for one and three quarter hours on this morning's run. At lunchtime I will, of course, have to pick up the children – not a pleasant prospect because it is Friday, which means the traffic will be backed up in the city from 2.00 p.m. for the rest of the afternoon, right into the evening rush hour ... And that Friday evening rush hour will mean that my trip home (which without traffic would take 20 minutes) will take another hour and a half – unless I take a number of seemingly convoluted but, trust me, time-saving shortcuts, like going up over Jacks Hill, down through Cherry Gardens, up again through the back of Norbrook, down through Manor Park, across Cassava Piece, and through the back of Havendale – in which case the journey will take merely an hour.

But then, I will have my view to look forward to. (A few weeks ago, we were early enough to see a huge, blazing flamingo-red ball setting behind the green-black Hellshire Hills. Even my son acknowledged that it was spectacular.)

We Kingstonians spend a lot of time on the road. It has its uses, though. If, for example, one needs to be away from one's desk for many hours without any questions being asked, all one has to do is casually declare, while stepping through the door, 'I'm gone on the road,' or simply, 'On the road.' Nuff said. Reappear four hours later looking slightly frazzled, perhaps muttering the curseword 'traffic' under your breath for added effect, and no further explanation will be necessary.

That's one of the perks of living in Kingston.

Loving Guyana's Rivers

Mark McWatt

My earliest memories are of crossing the major rivers of Guyana – the Demerara, Berbice and Essequibo – in colonial days, on proper ferries: large white vessels, probably made on the Clyde, that always worked and were on time and that had three different classes for passengers and (in those days) could carry only a few vehicles. I suppose it was those early crossings, when I was held at all times and sat on the knees of mother or father on polished wooden benches, that first formed my concept of 'river' and the association that it has since had in my mind with 'excitement' and 'adventure.' It was in Guyana's North-West District, however, that I first became 'intimate' with rivers – the names of which I still love to pronounce, to have them cast their spell again, arousing memories of a total surrender to the seduction of sun and living water: swimming in them, travelling upon them – experiences that for me are still charged with a real physical – in fact sexual – pleasure.

From the morning I first arrived at Morawhanna on the Barima River at age seven I knew I would always be hopelessly in love with rivers. The overnight coastal steamer (at that time the SS *Tarpon*) arrived and tied up at Morawhanna stelling shortly after dawn. The air was a little chill and I watched the sun burn off the morning mist on the river, and felt it leap into my eyes, reflected from the surface of that wonderful stretch of living, black water. It also, I was to discover, had a special smell, a strong musk that I found thrilling. We had to get into a small boat with an outboard engine (an *Archimedes* 10/12) to cross the river to Barima Landing in order to travel by road to Mabaruma, where my father was beginning a tour of duty as a Government District Officer. The bow of the little open boat pushed up high mounds of water on either side as it sped across the river and left a creamy wake behind. The vibration from the wooden seat and the smell of the river mingled with gasoline and oil from the bilge conspired to create a heady sensual experience for a seven-year-old, and this combination of smells can still summon today every lucid detail of that first trip and others that followed.

I learnt to swim in the rivers of the North West. When I could just about manage to stay afloat, my brothers and I (mostly I) used to pester my father on Saturday afternoons after work to take us to the river to swim. We would fool around in the muddy shallows at Barima Landing and he would stand at the end of the jetty and look out on the big river. One Saturday, I went out on the jetty to ask him something and, without answering, he picked me up and threw me into the deep river. I was astonished and broke the surface spluttering and apprehensive. I looked up at him and gasped: 'What to do now, Dad?' and he replied: 'Swim, dammit! You always ask to come here to swim and all you do is splash around in the mud like a crab.' So he directed me: 'Hold on to that pile ... now push off and swim to this one ... now swim out into the river a little way and when I shout, turn back ...' From then on I would joyfully jump off jetties and wharves all over the country and enjoy the embrace of the river-water and the tug of tide or current ... and that wonderful smell of the secret life of the river.

I got to know more of the rivers of the North West because my father sometimes had to serve as travelling magistrate and hold court at various small towns and locations on the rivers, and if any of this travel was during the school holidays he would take me with him. We would travel in the District Commissioner's launch (the *Arawak),* which was an enclosed vessel powered by a Lister Blackstone marine diesel (another combination of sound, vibration and smell that has become for me a part of my hallowed experience of rivers). I remember vividly one trip to Arakaka on the upper Barima river. It took three days to get there, overnighting at Red Hill, opposite the ruins of Mt Everard, and at Koriabo. At first I hadn't wanted to go because I was 10 years old by then and attending school in Georgetown, where I had recently acquired a passion for cricket. It was the summer of 1957 and the West Indies were playing in England and I dreaded not being able to listen to the matches. My father surprised me with a special wooden box built to contain a large green radio that worked off huge batteries, stored in separate compartments of the box. The box would be lifted onto the roof (the 'tent' we called it) of the launch and we would sit up there listening to the commentary, which was punctuated by the beat of the diesel engine which the radio somehow picked up – perhaps through the long wire strung as antenna from bow to stern. In the evenings, I would bathe in the river and we would sleep in would-be hammocks slung in school-rooms, draped with very fine nets to keep out mosquitoes and sand flies. On that trip, I saw one evening, for the first time, a family of capybara – the world's largest rodent – bathing in the river shallows near the far bank.

When we reached Arakaka I was supposed to amuse myself while Dad was in court hearing the accumulated cases prosecuted by Sergeant Elcock, who had also travelled from Mabaruma. I realised later that Arakaka in those days was like a wild-west frontier town, because of the influx of (mostly male) workers for the manganese mining that had begun in nearby Matthew's Ridge. I spent lots of time on the river, swimming or in corrials, but I also had cricket on the radio and lots to read. One day, in quest of a new experience, I wandered into a building and found myself in an adjoining room to the one where court was in session. I heard my father's voice and found a gap in the planked wall through which I could peep at the proceedings. Dad was sitting on a dais surrounded by tables and chairs, and a loud, strapping woman being charged, apparently, with 'disturbing the peace' because she had started a fight – she had pulled out a knife and threatened a young man. She was one of the town prostitutes doing a thriving business with the mine-workers. I remember my shock when I heard her assert loudly: 'I don' mind him calling me a whore, but he call me a **fucking** whore, and I can't put up with that kind of disrespect … I sorry I ent ketch him with the knife and cut him up good.'

Far greater, however, was my shock at what happened next. I saw a completely new and astonishing side to my father and I squinted at the scene in wonder as I heard him say,

'I don't know about you, Sergeant, but I'm having some difficulty with this argument: she doesn't mind being called a whore, but objects to being called a fucking whore. Now I have always understood that it is the business of a whore to fuck. Isn't that so, Sergeant?'

'Yes Sir.'

'And in fact a whore who does not fuck – apart from being unable to make a living – would be a contradiction in terms?'

I thought I could see Sergeant Elcock's moustache quiver briefly before he put on the most serious of faces and said 'Yes indeed, Sir.'

In the end, the woman was fined US$40, but you can imagine the state I was in – it had never occurred to me that my father **knew** those words, let alone that he would utter them in public!

That very evening, when I went down to the river to bathe, I was a little frightened to find that the woman and her cronies were, themselves, in the water bathing. I didn't want to turn back, as they were looking at me, so I slowly eased myself in and heard one say: 'Is Mr McWatt li'l boy; look, he goin' be handsome like he father,' and the woman responded, 'I suppose the father handsome, but he mout' nasty!' I felt a strange excitement then, as if the river contained and reconciled everything, my unease dissipated and I treasured these little snippets of adult conversation and experience that I sensed would come my way from now on.

On the way back to Mabaruma I listened in agony as the West Indies collapsed in the final test at the Oval and lost the series. Not even Sobers nor Colly Smith could stand up and make runs. I remember, distinctly, Laker bowling to Colly Smith and the commentator saying '… and he pops that one up into the air and is caught by May at mid-on,' at which point I retreated into the noisy interior of the launch and consoled myself with the thought that England might take away my pride in West Indies cricket, but nobody could ever take from me the constantly unfolding wonder of the Barima river as we rounded each bend, every new reach presenting something fresh and awesome. I affirmed then with a 10 year-old's ferocity born of disappointment, my undying devotion to these rivers and forests and told myself that they would always, always, always belong to me.

There was another such memorable trip, this time on the Waini river, near the mouth of which, on the first morning, my father shot three wississi ducks as they flew up from a patch of reeds and we had curried duck for days. In the lower reaches of the Waini river there are wide lagoons and I always felt that this was a more 'serious' river, whereas the Barima was friendlier and with a great meandering sense of humour. I loved the rest house at Baramanni and every time we spent a night there I would look through the big guest book at all the names of land and forestry officers and the other government officials and visitors who had passed through, spending the night in the middle of nowhere. Many of my published poems are about these rivers and the experiences associated with them. Further up the Waini there was the sawmill and the little settlement at Barama Mouth, where I first met Comrade Morgan (I forget his first name) a forestry officer, prodigious rum-drinker and rabid communist who thought that I was good material (at 12 years old) for conversion to the cause – if not to the lifestyle (my father forbade me to have a drink with him). It was from him that I first heard about the 'bourgeoisie' and 'surplus value.'

One more memory about the Waini river about three years later: by then my father had been transferred to Bartica on the Essequibo, but I refused to break up my relationship with the North West and its rivers just because of that. I was a scout in my Georgetown high school troop and I used to organise camps to Hosororo, on the Aruka river: groups of 10 to 15 of us would 'camp' in the school or in tents in the school-yard and spend our time swimming in the river, hiking to Kumaka or Mabaruma, raiding the fruit trees and bathing in Hosororo falls in the evening.

We heard, this one time, that a boat-load of young people from Hosororo were going to catch crabs at Waini mouth, and some of us managed to get ourselves invited on the trip. Apart from my well-known love for the rivers, there were two important features of this trip: the first was that we all loved to eat crabs, especially the big blue 'bundaree' crabs we were going to look for; and the other was that there was a very lovely half-Amerindian girl whom I adored from afar, who was also going on the trip. For me it was heavenly. I actually sat next to Linda and spoke to her for most of the way as the outboard engine droned on and we made our way down the Aruka, down the Barima, through the Mora Passage and along the left (southern) bank of the Waini towards Punta Playa, the northernmost point of Guyana. The estuary of the Waini is vast and empty and magical and as we made our way towards the mangroves on the river bank, the boat ground to a halt about three hundred yards away for the tide was out and there was this vast mud-flat all around us, covered by scarcely an inch of brackish water. We got out and tried walking towards the trees, but with each step we sank up to the knees into the softest, warmest and purest mud you can imagine. It was slow progress and hard work – until we saw one of the Amerindian boys lie on his belly, push off with his feet and skate twenty yards in a few seconds. All the boys soon followed suit. Try it if you ever get the chance – it's best on your bare chest and stomach (probably best of all completely naked) – you just lie on the mud and push off with your feet. The mud is almost frictionless and you speed over it with ease. I can also report that, as a teenager with frenzied hormones who had just sat for hours beside a beautiful girl he longed to touch, it was a very 'arousing' experience as well – lying on the warm slippery mud was what I imagined lying on a warm slippery body would be like, and I was at just the right age to make the most of that. In the end, the crabs (of which we caught several quakes, for August is crab season), the trip on the river and even Linda herself, take second place in my memory to that wonderful sensation of skating, almost naked, over the warm mud, making sweet love to a river and a continent ...

There is also the mystery of creeks, like Wauna and Warapoka. To the uninitiated, their entrances are invisible along the seamless vegetation on the river banks, until the experienced steersman suddenly points the bow towards the trees and, at the last moment, you see the narrowest inlet at an acute angle to the river. When the boat enters, it opens up into a green world of towering trees, diminished light, darting birds and large blue morpho butterflies fluttering ahead of the boat. You have to travel slowly in creeks because of the narrowness and the sharp bends. In larger boats the bow-man has to pull the bow around the sharper bends with a giant paddle and to signal to the captain to slow or cut the engine – when, for example, there is a corrial full of children on their way to school, or when a large tree has fallen across the waterway. Often the creek widens at villages into a large and pleasant pool of dark water with a sandy bottom, people bathing and corrials pulled half out of the water. Amerindian corrials (hollowed out forest trees cured and shaped in fire) are the best craft in which to travel the creeks and smaller rivers of Guyana. There are only inches of freeboard and in them you feel very close to the river and to its intimate sighs and whispers, which you can never hear above the noise of engines. Graceful, sturdy and easy to paddle and steer (once you have learned to balance in it), the corrial is a timeless craft, a link to the inscrutable past of these rivers, a guardian of secret creeks and inlets and a comfort for the future, in that, whenever all the engines stop and turn to rust, the corrial's magical presence and movement means that the rivers and their remote settlements will still live.

I remember steering a corrial with four of us campers one moonless night from Kumaka stelling to Hosororo. The darkness was profound, except directly above the river, where I knew that the lesser darkness was the sky, my only point of reference. The sounds of the paddle strokes, the little gurglings of the river among the stilted roots of the riverside vegetation and the cries of night-birds and other creatures seemed strangely amplified and not without an edge of fearfulness. None of us spoke much until the lights of the houses and sawmill of Hosororo came into view as we rounded a bend. Then we all spoke loudly with relief, but what **I** felt was an extraordinary closeness to the river itself, as though I had rested my head on its soft, cool belly and listened to all the intestinal noises while it breathed on my neck like a lover. Much as I was excited by engines (the outboards common in those days like Archimedes and Seagull and the flashier Johnsons and Evinrudes, and also the Lister, Kelvin and Volvo Penta marine diesels that powered the launches and speed-boats of my youth) nothing can match the special feeling I have for the ageless corrial.

Since those North West days, I have come to know many other of Guyana's rivers – the mighty Essequibo, the Mazaruni, the Potaro, the Ireng. None has disappointed in its power to thrill my senses and produce new wonders: great waterfalls and smaller cataracts and rapids, ruins of ancient Dutch forts, large islands, paradisal beaches like Saxacali and even man-made wonders like the suspension bridge over Garraway stream. Things have changed over time. Today, on most of the rivers of Guyana it seems that all of the smaller boats are powered by the giant Yamaha engines, from 80 to over 200 horsepower which turn the river and the riverbank scenery into a dancing blur and you focus simply on time and destination. These days, there are also 'jet boats,' which travel at over 50 miles per hour, and the major rivers are crossed by large Government car ferries and pontoons (when these are actually working!). It is not the same and yet it is exactly the same: the romance of the rivers endures. If you still have a spirit of adventure and wonder and you get close enough to one of the rivers, then its colour and taste and touch and smell cannot fail to tug at your heart. And if you board a Bartica-bound speedboat at Parika with your partner and it begins to rain, you can touch intimately and unnoticed beneath the plastic or leatherette sheets provided for shelter – an experience that will demonstrate what I have always known: that the rivers of Guyana are really for – and about – love.

Walking in Paradise

Jane Bryce

For Colin Hudson, 1938–2004

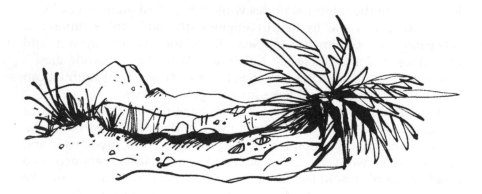

When I came to live in Barbados, a friend said to me, 'But you're going to live in Paradise.' Sure enough, when I arrived I *was* in Paradise. I was staying in a hotel on Paradise Beach, a postcard perfect strip of white sand lapped by pellucid blue water. This is the experience the tourist board sells by way of the slogan, 'Just beyond your imagination' – a tantalising promise of indefinable pleasure endlessly renewed. Nowhere, of course, is Paradise when you actually live there. No doubt the tourists in the lavish West Coast hotels can ignore the traffic that clogs the roads in rush hour as a quarter of a million people converge on school and work-place. Bumbling through the cane-fields in an amusing little open-sided vehicle, they remark only upon the quaintness of wooden chattel houses and the friendliness of people slapping dominoes under the tamarind tree.

Yet, in this island 21 miles long by 14 miles wide, there are now almost as many cars as people, and it seems honour won't be satisfied till the whole surface of it is covered in concrete. Multi-million dollar condos are nudging the chattel houses off the street. American-style hypermarkets and shopping malls glisten in a riot of tinted glass and vaulted archways. Village and cricket field, variety store and church, rumshop and fish market are all still to be found, but you have to look harder every day. And the natural environment, which is the island's greatest legacy, is increasingly under threat from construction and roads to carry all those cars. Conservationists, few in number and low in public estimation, tilt quixotically against the windmills of development.

But conservationists there are, and they have their weekly rituals like any other believers. Twice every Sunday, at dawn and again in the afternoon, you can join them in a National Trust Walk, led by Hudson, an eccentric and embattled eco-warrior. Hudson is one of those people whose existence proves the development pundits wrong. You find them in all the islands – individuals who have chosen their own way of life, aside from the world of corporate profiteering, tourism expansion and globalisation. The alternatives they pursue are part of a tradition intrinsic to the Caribbean, from the maroon villages of slavery, to Rasta communities in Jamaica, the Black Caribs in Belize and the rag-pickers on the dumps outside of Port of Spain. Hudson, who adopted Barbados as his home 40 odd years ago, has devoted his life to making people *see*. For him, the symbiosis of landscape, history, society, nature and the future is self-evident. When you go on one of his walks, you become one of a straggling column led by an Old Testament prophet striding towards the Promised Land. You visit parts of the island you never knew existed, and see things that only he knows how to reveal, a secret world at the end of plantation driveways, in gullies, at the edges of cane-fields, along coastal stretches.

One full moon, the meeting place is a solitary hotel on a remote beach on the south-eastern side of the island. We drive along the highway, past the airport where another jet load of visitors roars towards the runway, through sprawling housing developments, till we meet the gaggle of walkers already setting off. We walk for the first hour on tarmac. Hudson explains that the original pattern of development around defined centres has died, as roads and houses have simply accrued to existing roads and houses in a seemingly endless sprawl. He stops at a crossroads with a church named for St Christopher and we all gather around him to listen. There was a man, he says – as if it only happened yesterday and he was just passing on the news – who ferried people across a river on his back. One day, he found himself carrying a child who grew so heavy he had to struggle to reach the far bank. When at last he deposited the child on dry land, he realised he had been carrying the son of God. As he talks, the ferryman who kept faith with his calling is there in front of us, whip-thin and slightly stooped under his burden, in a battered hat and walking boots.

At dusk we find ourselves clear of housing, on a rocky beach where spume spurts up through blow-holes with every restless forward motion of the sea, and a warm wind soughs in the casuarinas. A tropical storm is brewing, and Hudson throws back his head to read the sky, explaining the cloud formations in terms of wind patterns. There, he points, is the evening star, which might be all the light we'll get tonight. We walk single file along the coastal path, the great Atlantic moaning softly on our right, single houses dotting the landscape on our left. As we pass a clearing, Hudson tells us the landowner bought this plot expressly to prevent it being built on, so the unique vegetation of the area could thrive. It's grown dark and flashlights come out to guide us single-file through the rocks, all our concentration at our feet. As we clear the rocky path, we congregate again around Hudson, silhouetted against the night sky, holding up things he's picked up along the way: a sea-fan plucked from the ocean bed by the tide, a sponge garnered from the sand. We stand, quiet and respectful, while Hudson, taking nature as his text for the day's lesson, muses aloud on the intelligent adaptability of cells.

Towards the end of the walk we come to a marshy area, site of one of the Arawak settlements which preceded the Portuguese 'discoverers' of the island. To the uninitiated, nothing really marks such sites, though sometimes people who've innocently blundered into them report a special atmosphere, a sense of presence. To identify them, you have to know the landscape and what you're looking for. Hudson stoops and picks up two pieces of carved shell – decorations, he says, from an Arawak initiation necklace. He speaks about the Arawaks with the intimacy of someone who knew them personally, even as he tells us they were all wiped out by disease 500 years ago. Leaping the centuries, he reminds us it's 40 years to the day since Janet, the last hurricane to hit the island full force. As tension gathering in the air around us warns of weather to come, Hudson indicates something at our feet. A palm-tree growing horizontal at ground level, like a fat striated creeper. He traces its trunk in the undergrowth from root to fronded top. Knocked down by Janet, it's survived all these years, creeping sidelong along the sand. Stepping over the recumbent palm tree, we feel the power of nature's instinct to survival in this spot whose human inhabitants succumbed centuries before. As we turn away from the sea and head for the end of the walk, the first rain spatters our faces, and we run for the cars parked close to the hotel. During the next two days, Tropical Storm Lily sweeps over us, sending us scrabbling for emergency supplies, closing down the island and its airport. But we're just a rehearsal: by the time she hits Cuba, Jamaica, the southern US, Lily is a hurricane, and we are safely left behind.

Gardening in Dominica

Polly Pattullo

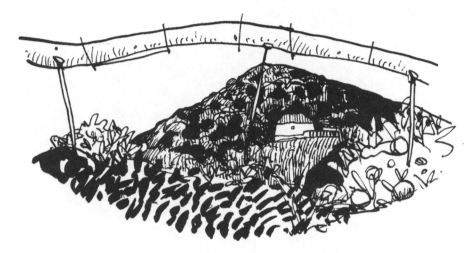

'Rain come.' I look towards the head of the valley that looms over my little house, above the swirls of forest that rise up to the junction of mountain and sky where the clouds are scudding east to west. I am in the lee of Dominica's great mountain spine, where the rain gods are always *en fête*. Not far away are the Trafalgar Falls – twin waterfalls which propel their load into a rock-strewn basin and then into the river which borders my land, sometimes trickling like a Scottish trout stream, at other times – when it is 'down' – pounding in a terrifying force of brown tumbleweed.

Rain here deserves a wider vocabulary. Drizzle, shower, downpour, tropical wave, depression, storm, hurricane are inadequate to describe the moods of the rain. At night, its pattering and clattering on the tin roof is like a protective blanket. By day, I sometimes hear it before I see it – as it hisses on to the leaves of the forest above me before, once again, falling on my water-washed garden.

Water is everywhere. The water tank is always full, fed by up to two hundred and fifty inches of rain a year. A three-foot diameter cast-iron pipe edges my land: it carries water from the Freshwater Lake, high above in the montane forest, in the old volcanic crater of Morne Micotrin, down to Roseau, the island's capital.

From the road, I duck 'under the pipe,' skirt around my 'new flower bed' of dwarf Cavendish banana plants and on to the side porch of my tiny, one-roomed house. There, I become the audience in a tropical amphitheatre: below is a meadow dotted with guava trees and rock, beyond is the river, glistening through the ferns and trees whose foliage often masks the sight but never the sounds of the river. Beyond is dense, undisturbed forest which reaches up so far you have to crane your head to see the sky.

When I first became the owner of Under the Pipe, I wrote: 'I have a garden in Dominica, an island which is all garden.' For this is a place where farmers put their children through university on a couple of acres of land – at least they did until the banana market came under threat from America's free-trade overlords. Dominica is a melting pot, not just of people but also of plant life. The first arrivals – pineapples, guava, cassava – came with the Amerindians, from south America. European empire-builders, who pillaged the world for its bounty, also brought plants to the Caribbean – from Africa, in slave ships; from Asia, from the Mediterranean.

Breadfruit, mango, yam, banana, coffee, grapefruit were all, once, new arrivals. Now these crops are all around me at Under the Pipe. They are my precious inheritance. Although it is surrounded by some of the best surviving rainforest in the Caribbean (the biodiversity of Dominica is remarkable and irreplaceable), my one-acre patch, which might be called disturbed tertiary rainforest, reflects generations of human activity. Since just after slavery, the land was part of the island's peasant economy: not long ago it was home to a farmer with a cow, who grew dasheen in the moist pasture, picked guavas and harvested from the gnarled grapefruit trees.

But I am not a Caribbean peasant farmer. I have no cow, I do not live there all the year, I do not plant when the moon 'coming up,' I do not need to sell my crops to live. I am an English journalist, who, unexceptionally, loves gardening. I have a different relationship to the land from my predecessor. Indeed, I have to admit that part of my response to the extraordinary drama of the Dominican environment is not unlike that of visiting Europeans such as Coleridge, Trollope, Leigh Fermor. All paid their respects – in wonder and passion – to the landscape of Dominica.

Others, such as the estate-owners, had a slightly different gaze, in a sense more like the contemporary peasant farmer. The tropical environment had to be tamed: the driving force was to create order – and productivity – out of anarchy. The bush, the wilderness, the 'demented vegetation' had to be controlled and contained.

The Dominican writer Jean Rhys, in her novel *Wide Sargasso Sea*, shows Mr Rochester, the Englishman, responding to what he perceives as the hostile power of the landscape – too red, too green, too blue. The consequence of such mental anxiety was the creation of gardens that hark back to Europe, a manicured oasis of calm amid the 'primitive,' re-creating memories of temperate gardens strewn with roses.

There are echoes of this in Rhys' description of her grandparents' garden at Geneva, perhaps 15 miles from the Roseau valley, although she reveals, too, her Creole sensibility. In *Smile Please*, her partly written autobiography, she remembered:

> The steps down to the lawn. The iron railings covered with jasmine and stephanotis. In the sunniest part of the garden grew the roses and the 'English flowers.' But in the shadow the Sensitive Plant which shuts its leaves and pretends to die when you touch it, only opening again when you were well away. The gold ferns and the silver, not tall like tree ferns but small and familiar. Gold ferns green and cool on the outside but with gold underneath which left an imprint if you slapped a frond on your hand.

Here, the temperate and tropical mingle. It is the tropical which she associates with 'the shadow.' For Rhys, however, her embrace of the Creole was part of her own identity.

That Creole relationship with the environment is echoed in Phyllis Shand Allfrey's book *The Orchid House*, about three white sisters who return to their Caribbean island home. One of them, Stella, the sensuous one, 'put her arms round the trunk of a laurier cypre and rubbed her cheek softly against the bark. I've come back, she said to the tree … as if she would strangle it for joy.'

One of the first tropical landscape architects to embrace this love of the natural environment was Roberto Burle Marx of Brazil. Marx, who was also a conservationist, rejected the idea of tropical nature as symbolic of the useless and the primitive; instead, he used those native plants in his designs and so made a public statement of their importance.

This, indeed, is the philosophy of my Dominican neighbour and gardening mentor Anne Jno Baptiste. At Papillote Wilderness Retreat she has created one of the best gardens in the Caribbean. Carved out of the steep hillside, it nestles under a canopy of breadfruit and tree fern. Home to remarkable plant collections, it is a sanctuary of conservation and sustainability.

'Under the Pipe,' I hope, might one day also reflect part of such a tradition. But, first, I have to learn to understand the heartbeat of my little patch of land.

I must learn how to stop the erosion with terracing for, if unchecked, the rain takes the thin soil ever onwards down the valley. I have to know, when 'cleaning' the bush, what to keep and what to cut. I can take the cutlass to the mal estomac, a ubiquitous, straggling shrub; I can take out the wild dasheen which peppers the meadow; I can 'weed out' the 'zeb gwa.' I must watch the light, to see when the sun – which appears late and disappears early – reaches the shade-loving anthurium tucked into the slope. I must learn to recognise the flowers that attract the hummingbirds and the butterflies, and, above all, not to cut a heart-shaped leaved vine, the food of the iguanas which I hope still live in a pois doux tree across the stream not far from the house.

Gardening in Dominica exposes my ignorance. I know about English gardens – about the quirks and fancies of pansies and hollyhocks, their qualities and needs. Tropical plants overwhelm me. Heliconias, for example, are one of those great tropical plant families, their swaying banana-style leaves protect magnificent coloured bracts. They love it in the cool of the higher reaches of the Roseau Valley. I planted a line of *Heliconia wagneriana* below the house. Within months, a towering forest had evolved. 'Too much in your face,' said Anne. So they were moved to a better home by the edge of the river close to where the fabulous pink torch gingers – 20 foot high or more – cling to the bank.

On all sides are walls of dazzling greenery. Any other colour is somehow a shock. Bright colours need to be carefully handled. Sometimes I want my garden to look like the village gardens – a great clashing encounter of purple, yellow, magenta and orange. But those brash crotons, cordylines, gingers need to be rationed in my natural forest haven. So does the perky bizzie-lizzie, a recent immigrant to Dominica. Anne has taught me to weed it out and reluctantly I do – their pink and red flowers threaten the hegemony of green.

Now, three years on, I have, I hope, begun to make a garden that reflects the spirit of the land. I have broken my reluctance to cut down trees and some of the straggly examples on the river edge have been removed. From the verandah I can now see the river rushing over the rocks and beyond to the other bank, decked in tree ferns. I like looking at the other bank, which is, bizarrely called Poland (it is not even the east bank).

Bojo, a young man from the village, likes chopping: his cutlass, finely sharpened and cared for as if a baby, does a merciless job, slashing at everything from the wispiest blade of grass to the chunkiest tree trunk.

Other villagers, who come and admire my amphitheatre and pronounce the view '100 per cent natural,' urge me to grow fruit and vegetables. The watery meadow would, for instance, be ideal for dasheen – that almost iconic root vegetable, grown since slavery as a staple crop. If I cut down the lofty tree, which probably holds up half a hillside, I would get more light, more sun – and bananas and guava would flourish.

Bojo would also, I am sure, do something different to this land if it were his – he grows cucumbers and lettuces, plantain and dasheen on his land further down the valley. But he rarely questions my instructions, amiably moving towering plants from one place to another, carefully nursing each specimen and using his cutlass as hoe, spade, trowel (spoon shovel, he calls it) and axe.

I have had lessons on how to care for my bananas and seen some lost in summer storms. A banana, it is said, takes nine months ('just like a baby'), but my bananas seemed to take longer. Would Geest buy my bananas? No, I was told, you did not deflower the end of each tiny banana before it developed. As a result, latex drips from the tips and makes those marks on the banana so hated, it is said, by the western consumer. Who cares? I have eaten my own bananas, my luscious grapefruit, and, best of all, the red seasoning peppers that were given to me as seedlings and, now shrub-sized, are sturdy and prolific.

I am learning to see each corner of the garden as a 'room' with its own characteristics and possibilities. I am now planning to create a 'design' for the garden. On my fantasy plan, I have a jacuzzi in the warm-water stream, a tree-house – to watch the herons from – on stilts on the flat little island in the middle of the river, African sculptures made of the trunk of the fougere adorning the septic tank, brightly-painted oil drums as plant pots, a bamboo walk and a raised bed for herbs. I am learning to develop a designer's eye – looking at form, function – to this piece of land. I am daring to bring an outsider's gaze to the forest – a baggage of my memories and desires, just like Dominica's other settlers.

It will be, I hope, more than a form of post-colonial re-occupation. The historian Simon Schama says in *Landscape and Memory*: 'Even landscapes that we suppose to be most free of our culture may turn out, on closer inspection, to be its product.' That will be true of 'Under the Pipe,' too. It will reflect who I am but also, I hope, incorporate the legacy of knowledge of all Dominica's gardeners.

I will experiment with different ways of re-presenting the tropical world and I hope my 'Under the Pipe' will be true to itself. But, in the end, Dominica will reclaim it. After all, I had only dared borrow it.

Before Columbus: Travels with the *Gli Gli*

Simon Lee

A square sail slices the channel between the island of St Vincent and its smaller sister, Bequia. It belongs to neither yacht nor catamaran but a craft not seen in these waters for more than 500 years. From the deck of the 120 foot Dominican schooner, *Carmella*, I follow the speeding sail of the 35 foot Carib canoe, *Gli Gli*. It dips below the waveline, rearing up moments later to plunge onward before disappearing round the headland into Bequia's Admiralty Bay.

Built in the Carib Territory in Dominica, the *Gli Gli* is living up to its name: a small aggressive hawk revered by ancient Carib warriors as a symbol of bravery. Under sail, the *Gli Gli* is swift, easily outstripping the schooner and matching pace with modern yachts. This modern 700-mile voyage of rediscovery will take the 11 man Carib crew, in their uncovered dug-out, from Dominica, down the southern chain of islands, through the treacherous Dragon's Mouth between Trinidad and Venezuela and the equally dangerous passage through the Serpent's Mouth, into the great Orinoco delta, and, finally, along the Atlantic coast and into the river system of north west Guyana, before they arrive at the Carib tribal homelands at St Monica and Kabakaburi on the Pomeroon River.

This 20th century Caribbean adventure, linking the Amerindian past with the future of the region's indigenous people, began in 1994 when two men met by chance on a bus. One was a Carib, Jacob Frederick, the other, Aragorn Dick-Read from Tortola. Jacob was born and bred in the Carib Territory on Dominica's rugged north west coast, the only such reservation left in the Caribbean. Here some 3,500 Kalinago subsist on farming, fishing and the traditional crafts of canoe building and basket making. The inroads made by Creole society and, more recently, televised American culture, have threatened traditional Kalinago culture and lifestyle. Despite repeated promises by Dominican politicians to finance the building of a model village on the territory depicting Carib lifestyle 500 years ago, so as to provide vital employment for craft workers, youths, farmers and fishermen, the project remains on hold.

Carib identity had always inspired Jacob's paintings and sculpture. Growing up, he'd long been aware, 'We're the last of our race. Our identity is disappearing so fast that we can't afford to waste a single moment.' Since he was a boy he had dreamed of building a traditional dug-out canoe and retracing the voyage his ancestors made from the South American mainland, searching out surviving tribe members down the islands and re-establishing ties with the Guyanese Caribs.

Aragorn, who had studied tribal and 20th century art in the UK, is an experienced sailor and, together, the two artists conceived their multi-faceted project. The journey would be an affirmation of the survival of canoe building and Carib navigational skills and an opportunity to exchange and research craft techniques, culture, food, drink and traditional medicine preparations. Most importantly, it would expose the Dominican Caribs to their ancestral language, still spoken by the Guyanese Caribs but now largely forgotten in the islands. By December 1995, a gommier tree had been selected high in the Carib Territory at Morne Lasouce, two and a half miles above the nearest village of Concorde. Once felled using chainsaws, it took 20 men three weeks to hollow out the belly using axes and the ancient ti-ame, or hand adze. The work was done almost completely by eye; a palm leaf used to trace the shape of the bow and stern and the only measurement taken was for length.

Jacob chose master canoe builder, Etienne 'Chalo' Charles, to direct operations, simply because, 'He's the best, he takes his time and likes to see a thing of beauty. Whether he's building for himself or someone else, you're confident it'll be a work of art.' When the carving was complete, 40 men struggled for two days hauling the 35 foot shell down to Salybia. Here the hull was opened, literally spread from two to six feet at its widest point by filling it with stones and water and lighting a fire underneath. Gommier sideboards and cedar ribs were added; seats, rudder, oars and mast were built. Although not as long as the 80-footers which carried 50 to 60 men, women and children on the original voyages, the canoe was constructed with double ends, following the ancient pattern that allowed for speed, versatility and quick getaways.

By early 1997, the *Gli Gli* was ready to sail, its blue hull painted with a yellow and roucou design Jacob had based on a Ciboney motif from Puerto Rico. A scaled up version of a traditional Carib square sail emblazoned with the black Gli Gli hawk logo was the final touch. By May 13, *Gli Gli* was skimming the waves towards Martinique.

While the *Carmella* catches up with the *Gli Gli* at her berth in Bequia's Port Elizabeth, I get a chance to meet some of the expedition's multinational support team: the taciturn Dominican captain of the classic two masted schooner, Anthony Agar, his son Maurice and mate Sammy from Carriacou, a Brazilian photographer and his svelte Russian girlfriend, and two Brits – G, ship's medical advisor-cum-bush doctor and his lanky friend Lou, who's never without his gold embroidered black Turkish waistcoat, even when he's doing Tai Chi exercises on deck at dawn. Technical advisor is the diminutive Clay from Tortola, who astonishes me one morning with the deck chair he's built from a wooden crate.

Dropping anchor in Port Elizabeth, we join the lively reception already underway outside the Frangipani Hotel, only yards from where *Gli Gli* is beached. An impromptu choir of local Black Caribs (descendants of escaped slaves who intermarried with Caribs) led by a delighted Bernice Baptiste launches into 'Bring Back My Bonny to Me.' Soon Hamlet Prince, one of the older Dominican Caribs, is dancing with her, peering happily down his nose with his permanent squint. 'I feel so happy to see my people,' beams Bernice, misty eyed.

This is one of the many scenes of spontaneous recognition and celebration which will recur throughout the voyage, as the Kalinago of Dominica reunite with other island and mainland members of the Carib tribe. I greet the other members of the crew, who I left a few months before relaxing in a rumshop in the Dominican fishing village of Marigot after a day of sea trials and emergency procedures. It was after volunteering my services as a 'man overboard' that I was invited to join the expedition. Master canoe builder Chalo hails me like a long lost son, 'Yes Papa!' It was Chalo, Hamlet and Mullin Stoute who supplied the canoe building skills necessary to create the longest dugout in living memory in the Carib Territory.

The stopover in Bequia allows me to adjust to sleeping amid the creaking timbers of the *Carmella*, Chalo insisting I take his hammock in the hold. The Caribs rise at dawn and I join them, clambering up on deck for strong coffee in the semi-darkness. We set sail for Canouan, another island in the Grenadines, at noon and I'm silently grateful for the overcast sky as I'm in the open *Gli Gli*. Aragorn's farewell, blown on a conch shell, moans across the still water. Soon we've passed the guano stained cliffs of the penultimate islet, with its incongruous concrete minareted shoreline structure, and are bouncing out to the open sea. The wind carries us smoothly enough to enjoy a lunch of fresh Dominican grapefruits and fish broth. In the semi-siesta which follows, Pan, the expedition's American sailing advisor, settles in the bow to play his wooden flute.

Around 4 p.m. the clouds open and *Gli Gli* rolls in choppy seas. To balance her it's necessary for the crew to shift from side to side, leaning as far out over the hull as possible without toppling overboard. This is where the safety harnesses come in. Our only company is a lone seagull and the occasional plane passing overhead. With dusk spreading across the water, we're tossed by strong gusts coming into Canouan and reach land below the Tamarind Beach Hotel, cold, wet and tired.

On Canouan, the old village of Carenage has virtually disappeared, its stone church now a storehouse for construction materials for a major tourism development. The graveyard, tombs and headstones were unceremoniously removed to the other side of the hill, before being returned to a communal unmarked grave. Over the hill we find the remains of our guide, Cynthia Sarjeant's father's tomb, its black cross smashed in half, tilting tragically over white tiles. Sliding out from Canouan, *Gli Gli* is momentarily dwarfed by the huge container ship which has just delivered another consignment of heavy construction equipment.

We flee down the Grenadines to the tranquility of the uninhabited, unspoilt Tobago Cays. When I wake on *Carmella*, I see the dinghy has already left for shore. No problem, the white beach beckons a few hundred yards over the inviting turquoise water and I dive in. At night we feast on a beach cook-up of freshly caught cowfish, snapper, redfish and jacks, washed down with Italian wine and Mt Gay rum. Under the starlight, Mullin Stoute sits in the sand singing an old Martinican song, accompanying himself on a drum.

The idyll of the Cays ends with a short run to Union Island, where we have to clear Immigration and Customs before leaving the

Grenadines for Grenada waters. We miss the calypso show, but spend a night carousing onshore. Next morning Chalo wakes me gently in the hammock. 'You was a lickle tired larse night?' he enquires, grinning.

The crossing to Carriacou is rough. The bunk I'm asleep on below deck on *Carmella* shoots across the cabin. We're rolling on a heavy swell. When we arrive, I stroll through Hillsborough and spot posters advertising Lady Salsa, a 12-strong, all-female salsa group from Havana, Cuba. Onshore I meet Nick, a cockney stand-up comic and magician who's managed to travel the English-speaking Caribbean for less than US$80 by hopping cargo boats.

Today's fishing has produced a wonderful kinetic dish of barracuda and pink, turquoise and dayglo orange parrot fish. By midnight, suitably fortified, all able-bodied members of the *Gli Gli* expedition are ready for Salsa at the 'After Hours' nightclub. Lady Salsa hit the stage scorching, in black fringed hot pants and tops. Technical advisor Clay solemnly declares this the highpoint of the voyage. When the tempo reaches boiling point, one of the three vocalists calls me onstage for a wining competition. Have I been living in Trinidad 10 years for nothing? In the interest of pan-Caribbean relations I rediscover the joys of syncopated pelvic rotation.

My time with *Gli Gli* is coming to an end. I'm going to miss watching sunrise at sea and early morning old-talks with my Carib partners, cocoa tea with arrowroot, fresh fish daily, the stars and swinging in Chalo's hammock. On my last day, I pay a visit with Jacob to Carriacou's renowned naive artist, octogenarian Canute Caliste. He entertains us in his one-room wooden studio, its walls hung with his paintings which chronicle the life and dreams of his island. Canute is also a self-taught multi-instrumentalist whose gifts were given to him by a mermaid he met on the beach when he was seven. He produces his violin and plays his way through the sets of the Quadrille dance. His daughter Clemencia and granddaughter Cleddie overcome their shyness to dance a waltz for us to Canute's accompaniment. 'My feelings get so wild,' grins Canute 'sometimes I cyan unnerstan dem. I put me violin behine me neck or unner me leg den.'

I rejoin the expedition as it sets sail from Prickly Bay at the southern tip of Grenada bound on its overnight crossing to Trinidad. Only experienced sailors will be onboard *Gli Gli* during the night, but I'm hoping to join the relief crew when the sun comes up. For now I'm at the bridge of *Make It So*, a three quarter million US$ luxury yacht owned by an Arizona brain surgeon and captained by an irascible Frenchman with a German accent.

It's a long night of rough seas and, for all its state of the art equipment, the yacht loses radio contact for several anxious hours with *Gli Gli*. When we do sight her at dawn, we realise the combination of adverse current and cross wind has blown her off course and she's heading straight for Venezuela. Aragorn and Jacob take the decision to accept a tow back on course and through the Bocas to Trinidad. A couple of miles offshore we're met by a coastguard launch and a welcoming committee of dancing dolphins. When I get on dry land at Chaguaramas my sea legs rebel and I can't stop rolling.

Nearly two weeks are spent in Trinidad while *Gli Gli* is repaired. The Caribs spend a weekend with their Santa Rosa cousins at the Carib Community Centre in Arima where I live, and I have the pleasure of introducing Chalo and crew to the delights of Trini rumshops. Then they set sail again for Guyana, where they receive a full state welcome from the defence force entering territorial waters. When I try to catch up with them later, I find the *Gli Gli* left the previous morning and the only way to catch her is by helicopter.

Weather Reports: Grenada

Philip Nanton

I

... like a sheet left out by a forgetful washer woman
a rectangle of blue galvanised roofing, creased in the middle,
momentarily hangs high on the electricity poles' connecting wire.
Another is kitchen foil wrapping itself around a concrete bollard ...

... are we off- air? ... It's like a mad-arse intruder is beating on
my roof ... he can't find the door ... determined to enter
ceiling's cracking ... pissing rain down the inside walls ... signal's breaking
up ... I'm out of here ...

> The ordinary in the extraordinary. Oxymorons collide.
> The brain lurches, searches for a peg, a paradigm
> to frame Hurucan the angry god, Leviathan the leveler,
> tireless Father Time, who keeps tapping. Oh God,
> how swift the wind, how fast the journey of prayer?

... September. The sea's a steely sheet, the sky a shitty smudge ... trees left
standing are limp, without foliage ... air conditioning units rest on the roadside
... the postcard pink beach resembles an airplane crash site, mangled metal
protruding from the sand ... no black box to explain its descent ...

meteorologists ... coriolis force ... moist warm air rises ... makes the whole
mass whirl ... your reporter ... moist warm air.

    And when you lift your head, there above you, the hillside,
carpeted with debris, suggests some madness had overtaken
the householders; made them unhinge doors, smash windows,
kick out walls, slam mattresses onto rain sodden ground,
send roofs spinning in the wind and, finally overcome, straight
jacketed by weariness, helplessly watch the erosion of their
worlds.

II

>hi, lighten up guys. i'm rosie-leigh, black folk
>dance and sing through all kinds of tragedy
>kept the spirit down those dark days of slavery
>i'm at u c... doing a cultural studies degree
>for this research with my buddy joe
>i really, really want to know
>does anyone have a good calypso
>about high winds that blow?

>way to go sis, way to go
>check the clever lines below
>in the consternation
>you can *feel* the preparation

>bar off de door
>board up de window
>pung in de nail
>doan pung yuh finga

... gunshots ring out the next morning
... broadcast their intended warning ...

... fellow citizens of this now sad fair land
the nation grants itself one thousand grand

'... express our gratitude to our friends around the region and
internationally. (If we have a hurricane a week, by Christmas the Caribbean could be
united – English speaking of course.) ... We know that in any country one or

two people will do foolish things ... this is absolutely out of bounds ...
my government won't allow a few to behave so selfishly in a time of
national tragedy ...'

>dear melanie, tom and I can't leave the house for long,
>a mother who went out to help others ... came back to nothing
>they carry machetes

a standpipe in church street
has become our community oasis

                                        each day i fill four buckets

yesterday i shared
a coconut from a fallen tree
a bottle of drinking water
donated to my son and me

        once again, small kindnesses are valued.

ENCOUNTERS

Whales

Stewart Brown

Each Christmas they come
White and blubbery from the frozen North,
Strange bloated creatures pale as snow
Cruising in vast, unnatural shoals.

Whales: the great white whales of myth
And history in all their arrogant splendour.
Flopped ungainly along the sea's edge
Or hiding, blistered, under a shadowed palm,

Incredibly ugly, somehow, in their difference.
Designated a protected species
They are chauffeured around, pampered like babes
And generally kept in the shade.

Few stay long or leave anything behind
Except litter and small hostilities.
'Peace and Love' we tell them –
the government says we must show respect –

so we smile, sing, play Sambo:
secretly long for a black Ahab.

Peace an' Love

Stewart Brown

Imagine a conversation between a tourist and a rather cynical resident of – let's say, Jamaica – in which the tourist gushes about the abundance of exciting, exotic sights he's seen in his week's stay, to which the resident responds that if he stayed a little longer he'd soon be complaining that there was nothing in the place *to* see... The traveller who stays, who settles and, after a significant length of time, identifies himself with a place, is distinguished from the tourist in that he gradually does comes to see that place in a different way, and so – if he is a writer – writes about it in a different way. Gradually, he sees beyond the glittering 'otherness' to understand – to some extent at least – the contexts of what he's seeing, noticing the shit and the rubbish and the aggravation that's left behind after the colourful parade has gone by. The picturesque becomes *ordinary* and so the writer's imagination has to engage with it in more complicated ways to re-make it *strange*. The settler, a kind of convert to the place, becomes sometimes and in some ways 'more native than the natives,' feeling himself entitled to make public statements that local people might not – for various social, political or cultural reasons – feel able to make. The settler is both of the place and yet not really bound to accept the consequences of what he might say in terms of whoever he might offend. If push really comes to shove he can (almost) always go home.

But the insights that he gains from staying allow him a kind of licence and give what he says is a measure of authority

The poem 'Whales' draws on that privileged experience, that trouble-making licence – it certainly stirred up a deal of trouble when it was first published in 1974. The poem dates back to the years I spent teaching in Jamaica in the Seventies. The tourist season in the Caribbean is around Christmas time and the tourists will come down, usually from the US and Canada, to flop about on those beautiful brochure beaches which are consequently effectively closed to the local people except in their capacity as waiters or servants of various kinds in the hotels. I was teaching in a junior secondary school, a kind of comprehensive school, in St Anne's Bay on the north coast, the main tourism area of Jamaica. It's difficult enough to motivate secondary school kids anywhere, in my experience, but when the best prospects of a fulfilling career you can hold out to those who 'behave' is that they can become latter-day house slaves for fat, rich and usually rude white folks, it is difficult to generate much enthusiasm oneself, as a teacher, let alone inspire it in the kids. So, anyway, as a VSO teacher on a local salary I quickly began to identify much more with the people I taught and lived among than with the people who looked more like me – strangers, tourists. In those days I looked less like the kind of blubber-bound 'whale' that inspired the poem than I do now – and, indeed, one of the ironies of the poem now is that my only return to the island is as a sort of 'whale'…

'Whales' looks at tourism in the mid Seventies and the trouble-maker part of it stems from the response it generated when it was first published in the *Jamaica Sunday Gleaner* – the national newspaper which has a regular literary page and always publishes a poem or two. The poem was published just as I was about to leave Jamaica, at the end of my VSO stint, and I got back to Britain a couple of months later to find a telegram from the literary editor of the *Gleaner* saying that an international incident had ensued from the publication of the poem! Apparently it had been noticed by some Canadian tourists in the island and sent back to a newspaper in Toronto which had re-printed the poem under the headline 'Anti-White Racism in Jamaica' and presented it as the work of some black radical who was inciting his people to murder and revolt. Then, apparently, the government of Jamaica had issued a disclaimer to say that this Brown person wasn't a Jamaican at all, that his views were eccentric and nothing to do with them and that, basically, he'd better not try to come back …! I felt quite proud of this really. I received hate letters sent on to me from disgruntled Canadian tourists saying, 'You have spoilt our holiday memories forever; I always took the happy smiling faces that greeted me to be of genuine friendship, but now, thanks to your disgusting poem, I know that those people really always resented me ...' I felt quite proud of that too! I had become a 'trouble-maker'.

The Bull Whisperer

Ian Craig

I'm liming with two young *habaneros* on a busy street corner in Havana. Over their shoulders, I see a young woman step off the pavement and faint in the road. She lies open-mouthed, dress riding up over white underwear, palms skyward as if meditating. In the capital of the classless republic of socialist solidarity, nobody lifts a finger. A nearby taxi sputters into life, briefly intensifying the pervasive stench of diesel emissions, then lurches forward, perhaps to put her out of her misery, but eventually slows and negotiates the inert form gingerly, as if to avoid soiling the tyres. I suggest we at least move her onto the pavement. A man jabs his finger and gestures disgustedly that she is drunk. The first words she utters on regaining consciousness are 'I'm pregnant.' A crowd now gathers quickly and she is borne away.

What is wrong with the integrated revolutionary society? Our young *habaneros* suggest people were afraid to intervene. Was this because they suspected malign supernatural forces, or to avoid being embroiled in an encounter with a policeman? The first explanation is as plausible as the second: even those who scornfully claim to have 'advanced beyond' Afro-Cuban religion will avoid an apparently discarded red handkerchief 'just in case,' and Fidel is said to consult with the *babalao* in moments of particularly acute crisis (the norm for Cuba being continuous low-grade to medium crisis). Meanwhile, an encounter with the police often results in protracted detention whilst 'waiting to be questioned' or 'verifying documentation.'

Did both fear of the *orishas* and distrust of the police combine to explain this incident? Contradiction is the essence of the outsider's experience of Cuba – this is the country after all, where an eight-year-girl can be scripted to speak the words 'Down with Yankee Imperialism' at a public meeting outside the American Interests Section, whilst a 20 year-old woman parades down a nearby street in a one-piece lycra body-stocking patterned on the Stars and Stripes.

Only one explanation remains for the woman in the road: maybe Socialism just isn't what it used to be.

* * *

'Socialism just isn't what it used to be' is the punch line of many jokes circulating in today's Cuba. Such a punch line was the last thing said to me by Guillermo before he was arrested. He had approached me as I wandered the centre of his hometown Santiago de Cuba in search of 'authenticity.' I hadn't yet heeded García Márquez's sensible advice to stop suffering a complex about being a tourist. In Havana, for most people you are and always will be a *yuma*, a foreigner, recognisable at a distance as an alien creature to be performed to, plied for donations or cajoled into trade. Going native is not an option.

I was not impressed by Guillermo at first. To start with, one of his front teeth was embossed with the Nike logo. I tried to persuade myself that in Cuba this gesture carried some kind of ironic charge. The problem was one of context. After 10 days of a steady stream of jaunty patter from similarly amiable young men in both Havana and Santiago, insisting they had the cheapest authentic Cohibas in town ('as smoked by former Spanish premiere Felipe González and our very own *Comandante*') or the best-value rum, or the most enticing sister, I was ready to believe Cuba was a nation of hustlers and pimps. In fact, hustling is one of the truly authentic features of contemporary urban Cuba, for many literally a matter of life and death during the 'Special Period' of the early Nineties. Trying to ignore it in search of something 'deeper,' more benign, is to miss the point. With a monthly salary of around US$12, but armed with the knowledge that the tourist has probably spent over $500 just on the flight, who wouldn't hustle?

I thought I had Guillermo's number straight off when he replicated the opening gambit of the Havana hustlers:

'And where are you from, *caballero*?'

'England, but I live in Barbados.'

'Ah, yes of course, Barbados ... *Where?*'

The Cuban tourist-hunter prides himself on being able to tell his new acquaintance something about his own country: 'England, yes of course ... Anthony Blair, how do you find him after Mrs. Thatcher?' (Mr. Major does not figure at all in the Cuban political history of England). Or more recently 'Ah yes, David Beckham ... how are you people holding up now he's gone to Spain?' Mention of Barbados always triggers instant recognition, followed by an initial failure to summon up any concrete information. After a while, though, they lower their voice and say: 'Sí ... el Crimen en Barbados.' This refers to the explosion of a Cubana de Aviación airliner off the west coast of the island in October 1976, which killed 73 people, including the youth fencing team returning victorious from the Central American Games. A monument, visited by Fidel, marks the nearest point on the shoreline.

Once we had gone through the sombre ritual of lamenting the 'crimen,' we headed for a bar. I hoped he would be content with some free food, drink and access to the establishments reserved for tourists and their guests. Merely being granted entrance, however fleetingly, into the other side of the dual economy, where 'dollar' products such as beer are sold, was reward enough for many back then. However, Guillermo steadfastly refused even a sip of the abundant *mojitos* or Mayabe beer on offer. 'I just like meeting people from outside,' he insisted. 'What I want is for here,' he said indicating his head, 'and for here,' he pointed to his heart. 'Not for here' – his mouth – 'nor here' – his belly. 'And least of all for here,' he cupped his genitals, smiling. 'I have those areas covered.'

We took to the streets, talking freely about the under-representation of Afro-Cubans in the power structures, about access to information, about tourism and the limited economic reforms of the nineties, about how you could manage to teach languages whilst avoiding cultural materials that would make everyone want to leave the island, about the clandestine *bancos de video* (video clubs) selling pirated foreign films and even pornography ....

Observing that I had shed my suspicions about his motives, Guillermo decided to tell me the joke. A Cuban manages to get out of the island and heads for Europe. He is penniless but convinced that having survived decades of Caribbean Socialism, nothing is beyond him. He ends up in Spain and sees a poster advertising an all-comers bullfight. Though the bull has already dispatched a series of experienced matadors, our man eagerly signs up, sure he can find a way of subduing the beast and so claim the huge bounty on offer.

Placed fourth on the bill, he observes as his predecessors are sent to the infirmary by the raging creature, now thoroughly unimpressed by the usual trick of waving a cape in front of it. Undeterred, he takes his place in the *rueda*, cape in hand, and waits for the furious animal to be released once more. With a few muttered imprecations to the *orishas*, he stands his ground for the first charge and barely avoids the bull's bucking horns as it thunders past him. Three or four equally inauspicious passes follow and, by now, the arena has the atmosphere of the Coliseum just before thumbs-down. But on the fifth pass, our exile performs a nimble sidestep, confusing the bull momentarily, leans towards its ear and whispers something. The beast immediately crashes to the floor. Dead.

An incredulous hush falls over the arena for a second before the crowd erupts in wild applause as our man is paraded around the ring in glory.

'But, whatever did you say to the bull, *compadre*?' the press demand of him.

'Quite simple,' he replies, 'I just gave him the choice our *Comandante* is always giving us: *Socialismo o muerte!*'

I had barely recovered from this when two policemen materialised from the walls flanking the street and demanded to see our papers. Guillermo instantly started jabbering in Santiago argot. I couldn't understand most of it, but it was evidently not designed to appease: the *agente* in charge told his partner to take Guillermo away and fine him the massive sum of 30 pesos – over one tenth of a normal monthly salary – for 'lack of respect.' I still couldn't tell whether they'd heard the joke, or whether the 'lack of respect' was merely Guillermo's less than compliant response to being stopped. He continued to fulminate sarcastically as he was frogmarched away. That was the last I saw of him.

I now became irritated. Carrying identification is not a requirement in England and hardly ever necessary in Barbados. I didn't have any. Anyway, it seemed so absurd to be persecuted over a piece of comedy. With perhaps one *mojito* too many on board, I was suddenly gripped by the desire to demand of my *agente* whether he had read Milan Kundera's *The Joke*, in which a man spends years in a labour camp for sending a postcard saying 'Optimism is the opium of the people! A healthy atmosphere stinks of stupidity! Long live Trotsky! Ludvik.' Closer scrutiny of his face quickly dissuaded me: the prognathous, faintly Habsburg lower features and beadily suspicious eyes told me I was before a species known to me from other climes. For all its uniqueness in other ways, it was clear that Cuba shared the universal failure to dissuade the least gifted and discerning of its populace from joining the police force. I shut up. After a brief lecture about respecting the local laws, he sent me on my way. I trudged back to my rented room on the outskirts, reflecting on the iniquity of it all. Not one peddler or panhandler had encountered any impediment to involving us in illegal transactions of various kinds, but this entirely undemanding, curious and intelligent young man was treated like a common criminal, apparently just for telling a joke.

Since then, Cuban friends who have heard this story have insisted that the joke could not have been the motive – or at least the sole motive – for the police intervention. Guillermo must have been 'known to the police' for fraternising inappropriately with foreigners and probably for other misdemeanours. When I point out the irony that he was one of the few that wanted nothing in return, one of them remarks, 'That's the point. It makes his testimony more credible to you and therefore what he says more subversive. This was someone whose only interest was in learning from you and speaking his own truth. And they would know that. Life is not easy for such people.'

* * *

'Bicitaxi, ecological, economical,' chimes a Havana bicycle rickshaw driver as we pass. It must be the 'ecological,' with its appeal to our earnestly anti-exploitative self-image, that persuades us to accept the offer of a ride in one of these ailing Chinese contraptions, but as it turns out this is strictly money for sweat. Our sense of shameful passivity grows, as we perch colonially behind the toiling figure, who perhaps till recently was a medical researcher or a civic architect. In time, the discreet island of perspiration between his shoulder blades spreads to form a vast, overpopulated continent of exertion covering his entire shirt, and his whistling is replaced by rhythmic heavy-breathing. All for a paltry three dollars. As well as feeling guilty, we feel unsafe. Our human mule – it seems that bad now – does his best to avoid the treacherous cracks and chasms of the Calle Obispo, but, in doing so, barely takes notice of the rattling succession of Chevrolets and other improbable vehicles that threaten to turn our folly into tragedy. At the same time, the supposed ecological advantages of his own vehicle seem supremely irrelevant as renewed clouds of diesel engulf us. Maybe he doesn't really care. As we swing inland away from the breakers pounding the Malecón towards the Hotel Vedado, openly panting now, he half turns and nods towards a shop-front selling outboard motors, and remarks 'I could do with one of those.' I chuckle, supposing he is deadpanning a harmless joke – he needs a motor to propel his punters about less arduously – but his face stays solemn and he jerks his thumb towards the sea behind us: 'To get away from this place.'

* * *

'I can't have a natural conversation with a Cuban woman. Either she thinks I think she's a *jinetera*, and flees, or she *is* one and starts trying to seduce me.' I made this lament in the late Nineties, during the most open period of sexual tourism in Cuba, before the police started to crack down on soliciting in the streets. Incongruous couples abounded, typically comprising beaming, desiccated Euro-septuagenarians got up as if on safari gripping the arms of sassy *mulatas*, barely 20, in skin-tight apparel.

The pair I was addressing were León, a rangy *mulato* with a spectacular mane of dreadlocks who said he was 'in the music business,' and Chucho, a squat fireplug of a man who claimed, convincingly, to be a professional judo instructor. Both were unemployed, officially very rare in Cuba, but in reality rather common. They nodded understandingly and were quick to offer advice: 'Forget all that, *mi hermano*, we can introduce you to some real Cuban girls. Our homeys don't hustle and won't try to marry you. They're cool. We can all just go out together, hang, and maybe if one of them likes you, she'll want to get it on with you. They just like a good time.'

I instantly took to Mikaela. She was a little demure, a welcome characteristic after the imperious exhibitionists who had intimidated me in Havana. A light-skinned *mulata*, she grew her hair long to show off how 'good' it was, wore an unforced smile and moved well. She seemed to like me. We had dinner and drank a lot. León and Chucho were right; their homeys were cool.

As midnight approached, I became aware that I had spent a great deal of money. This didn't matter too much, as I felt buoyant, *authentic*. As if on cue, Chucho approached and asked if, well, I fancied being alone with my new friend. I assented. 'No problem, boss, I know a place round here where you can get cosy.'

Before I had time to take stock, Chucho was introducing us to a family watching television in their front room. Two early-teenage children nodded guardedly, an old-timer recumbent in a kind of abbreviated hammock raised a stiff hand in greeting. *El señor* addressed us politely whilst *la señora* went off to 'prepare the room.' Where was I from, how long had I been in Cuba, which *barrio* did Mikaela live in? All this urbanity was highly unsettling in the circumstances and I contemplated faking a trip to the bathroom and making a run for it. Fate was against me, however: *la señora* returned, announcing that the room was now ready and that would be US$20, please. The children barely turned away from the weather forecast as I handed over my last bill. We followed her down a dank corridor to our love nest.

The first thing that sprang to mind was Philip Larkin's poem *Mr. Bleaney*, never normally a spur to eroticism. It was all there, the 'Flowered curtains, thin and frayed, fall[ing] to within five inches of the sill,' the 'Bed, upright chair, sixty-watt bulb, no hook / Behind the door, no room for books or bags,' even 'the jabbering set he egged her on to buy,' a small Soviet transistor radio droning out a relentless Socialist transmission. Words like 'sovereignty,' 'inalienable,' 'everlasting' and 'unfalteringly' made brief appearances in my sensory apparatus as *la señora* smoothed a crease in the yellowing sheet. 'I left the radio on because of the animals,' she said before departing. The meaning of this bewildering remark became instantly clear when, at Mikaela's insistence, I switched the radio off. Though we were in the heart of Santiago, it was apparent that the room abutted onto a farmyard. All manner of sounds and odours penetrated our ineffectual cocoon and I found myself distracted by trying to match sounds to species. I made a first attempt at concentrating on the matter in hand.

But it wasn't easy. Flatulent pigs truffled inquisitively beneath the window-ledge. A dog seemed to be in the mix somewhere, on the evidence of a kind of frantic scratching that joined the orchestra now and then, and one part of my consciousness devoted itself to solving the enigma of an oddly squawking bird that clearly wasn't a domestic fowl but didn't sound quite like a parrot either. I again summoned up all my resources, making a Herculean effort to shut out everything extraneous, including most of my own brain functions.

It remains my least edifying sexual memory to date, including the unforgettable sensation of seeming to have my lips sandpapered when kissed by a transvestite cabaret artiste whose stubble required attention. I did the only thing I could to avert the monumental downer that was fast approaching. I fell asleep.

We were awoken by another urgent, scratching noise coming straight through the ceiling, which seemed to be made of thin cardboard. As I rummaged my memory for my current location and the identity of the stranger at my side, a furious hammering on the door began and *la señora*'s aggrieved tones were heard. We had overstayed our welcome by over two hours. We must leave immediately or pay more. We rose, dressed and suddenly found ourselves in the street.

'I'd love to pay for a taxi for you, but like I told you, I'm out of cash now, *cariño*.' I tried to invest my words with genuine regret, but I knew she lived very close by, so was really just being polite. She didn't look impressed. 'Hey, I'm walking home too, and a lot further than you,' I pointed out. 'Look, I'm sorry, lets meet tomorrow in the Parque Céspedes at 8 o'clock.' She pouted, straining not to let it become an outright scowl, but then seemed to soften and kissed me before turning and leaving.

She was on time, but didn't look at all pleased to see me. Something was on her mind. 'Look,' she eventually volunteered, 'I know you said you ran out of cash yesterday, but I really could've done with that taxi money. I have a child to support, you know, and I'm out of work at the moment.' A child? This was news to me. And no job? Didn't anybody work in this town? I now saw why no ride home was so significant. She was taking me for one. I visualised Chucho going to pick up his cut of the room rental, as in a movie flashback of a sting operation.

'Listen,' I began vehemently, 'your friends told me this wouldn't be about money. If you're saying I have to give you a cash handout, you may as well just save your breath and leave now.' I was confident she would accept, if only for some distraction from the monotony of perpetual revolution.

She rose and walked unhurriedly towards a street that began on the other side of the square. She didn't look back.

Fitting In

Jeremy Taylor

Lord, I thought, this is hot. Not as hot as the Arabian desert, true; but still, Trinidad greets you with a blast of hot wet air, like dragon's breath, as you emerge from an air-conditioned aircraft.

People in temperate countries romanticise heat. The Caribbean, they think: beaches, hammocks, rum punches, tans! But they don't have to work in it. I was soon romanticising autumn chills. I would come back sodden and exhausted at the end of a day's teaching and sit in my shorts in my father-in-law's upstairs annexe, under the hot iron roof, while sweat dripped off my nose onto the exercise books I had to mark. There were ventilation spaces at the top of the wooden partitions between the rooms, just in case any breeze should stir.

The school where I taught for my first five years in Trinidad was one of Port of Spain's 'prestige' establishments, a Catholic single-sex boys' school run by Holy Ghost Fathers, some of them Irish. The classrooms were open on both sides; passing priests, their white gowns billowing, patrolled the corridors in search of heresy or disciplinary mayhem. Classes were big, with forty five to fifty adolescents in each; they were bored, restless, streetwise and rebellious, their heads closer to Brooklyn than Benin.

In the crushing afternoon heat, we struggled with TS Eliot and Jane Austen, and the choir learned English folk songs and sea shanties for the English-style music festival. We ventured into Sam Selvon and the early Naipaul stories, until parents complained – Trinidad dialect (now exalted by some academics into a separate language) was simply 'bad English,' and what was this ignoramus doing 'teaching' it? When I announced that our history text would be *The People Who Came*, it took me the rest of the class to restore calm.

My liberal teaching methods went out of the window in the first week. A rather more Dickensian approach was called for here: tight discipline exercised from the podium and backed up with swift and merciless punishments ('penances'). The alternative was rioting. Any ideas about education as an exercise in independent thought went out of the window too, when, one day, the discussion in a senior class turned to contraception. In no time at all, a big burly priest strode angrily into the room and took over the class himself.

The only thing I did that pleased the priests, as far as I remember, was to play the organ in local churches. The trouble was that these Victorian engines, designed for chilly English country churches, were deeply unhappy in a humid tropical climate; their pipes were filled with pigeon droppings, and the Bible's famous 'moth and dust' had long since corrupted the leather and wood of their intestines. This produced a cacophony of squeaks, groans and stuck notes. And people had such odd tastes. Brides would ask for, say, *Moonlight and Roses* followed by *Yesterday All My Troubles Were So Far Away*. One day before a funeral, as I played what I thought was a dignified and eloquent tribute to the unknown departed, an irate relative came scrambling up into the organ loft. 'Stop that music!' he hissed, 'Yuh makin' everybody sad!' I stopped. Since then, the churches have scrapped all their costly organs in favour of little electronic dance-music machines with half-keyboards and built-in drumbeats.

Trinidad and Tobago was nearly 10 years into independence, and I was six years out of college, by the time I got to Port of Spain at the end of 1971. I went there because I had just married a Trinidadian, and because I had had enough of England. I knew virtually nothing about the place apart from hearing The Mighty Sparrow's hymn to oral sex, *Sixty Million Frenchmen Can't Be Wrong*, and the plaintive sound of a steelband one night in Notting Hill. I had already missed the Sixties – I had been teaching in eastern Africa, where the sexual liberation of the west was not a top priority and Jim Reeves still outplayed the Beatles. It took me a while to catch up. But now it was time to travel again. I wanted somewhere new – somewhere young, somewhere black. I wanted a new identity.

But clearly it wasn't going to be as a teacher.

Writing about Trinidad was more fun, and the only other thing I could do. I already had my theme: nationalism and self-determination (I'd been reading people like Julius Nyerere since I was at school).

There was a lot going on in those days. Derek Walcott was regularly staging new plays with his Trinidad Theatre Workshop at the Little Carib Theatre; there were serious modern dance groups, even an opera company. I wrote theatre and music reviews and features for the local papers, and a weekly column about television. There was one TV station with a single part-time channel in black-and-white; I dutifully watched it most nights for nearly ten years, trying to persuade a bemused audience to eschew cheap imported shows and to demand a local TV and film industry instead.

But there were certain realities which I overlooked. Everyone in Trinidad, except me, understood that the arts were not an election winner and were thus destined to remain on the sidelines. The TV station was government-owned and terrified of its own shadow; the last thing it intended to do was let creative or imaginative people loose on screen. An abrasive chairman was in place to hack them down; on one occasion he even tried to get me deported. (Today, television consists of over 60 satellite channels from North America, and indigenous production is minimal.)

The weekly tabloids had their fun at the expense of my missionary zeal. When I suggested integrating Indian and mainstream TV programming, one produced a cartoon of me dressed in a dhoti (it later wittily called me Blackman's Burden, Blackman being the name of the programme director at a radio station I freelanced for). And while artists liked the publicity of regular reviews, they were not keen on being reviewed by a white foreign-born outsider; every word of detraction caused a personal hurt.

So I tried another journalistic tack. There's nothing like a whiff of socialism to excite editors, and in the Caribbean of the Seventies and Eighties the odour was strong. The leading anglophone countries had diplomatic relations with Cuba; Forbes Burnham was busy wrecking Guyana; Michael Manley was striding Jamaica waving his rod of correction; there were rumblings in St Lucia and Dominica; and in 1979 Maurice Bishop overthrew the crazed Eric Gairy in Grenada and established an alliance with the Cubans.

All this was good news for me. Editors in London and Toronto and Washington wanted to know what was going on. For several years I made a decent living trying to explain that the Caribbean was not just a Cold War playground but a fragile David trying to tread its own path among lumbering Goliaths. I became a non-person for the US Embassy after I asked the ambassador, in print, to come up with evidence for the ludicrous story, then being spread across the world, that the Russians were building a submarine base in Maurice Bishop's Grenada.

But my stories would turn up beneath trite and condescending headlines like 'Shadows Over Islands in the Sun' or 'Leftists Ban Press in Sunshine Island.' The Caribbean stereotype was too deeply entrenched for the islands to be taken seriously. Only their relations with the world's Goliaths could give them editorial legitimacy.

So as the cold war wound down in the Eighties, and as one by one the Caribbean 'socialists' were felled, editors lost interest in the Caribbean. For me, the end came with Trinidad's attempted coup in 1990, when the Jamaat al Muslimeen held the prime minister and parliament hostage. For five days and nights the phone didn't stop ringing and I didn't stop working. And then Iraq invaded Kuwait and Trinidad's little trauma was instantly forgotten.

These frequent professional retreats were due, not to a failure of courage, but to an excess of discretion, the trickiest element to calculate when trying to fit in to somebody else's culture. When you leave your country of birth and settle down in somebody else's, you carry your own culture with you. For a couple of weeks' holiday, that doesn't bother anyone. But if you have the temerity to put down roots in your adoptive country, it sooner or later becomes an issue, whether you notice it or not.

It's okay for expatriates to retain their own culture and to regard their new environment more or less as a playground. There's usually a fat corporate contract, a nice salary and perks, a luxury house with servants, an office with a view, and a handsome gratuity. There are the regular cocktails around the illuminated pool, waiters discreetly carrying hors d'oeuvres and well-aged liquors, the great and the good mingling and back-slapping. The expatriate tribe gathers at the same bars, the same receptions, the same homes and parties, the same gym. Don't you just *love* this place, and aren't the people so *wonderful*?

But, as an expat, you have somewhere to go back to: home is always somewhere else. Your accent doesn't change; nobody really expects you to dance like a local and, after a while, you go home and dine off your stories, and get posted somewhere else.

But the longer you stay, the more complex things become.

Everything about you – accent, skin colour, body language, idiom, physique, tastes, memories, frame of reference, sense of humour –

announces to the population that you are a recent import. You make urgent efforts to fit in: to do the handshake right, to play mas, to debate the niceties of pan and soca, to deploy the idiom, to show up at the right parties. You learn the art of liming, adopt local dress style and creole diet, drink at local bars, shout as loud as anyone else in conversations, read the same magazines and books and listen to the same music as locals do. You let your accent soften and take on the nuances of local language. You give up your old passport and become a citizen of a new country. You no longer think of anywhere else as 'home'; the council crematorium is your chosen destiny. Taken to comical extremes, disapproving matrons in the colonial era used to call this 'going native.'

As part of the deal, Caribbean pleasures have to be traded for a degree of discretion. For anyone in the business of communication, it is an interesting challenge. You show suitable respect for local ways, you don't assume any privilege on the basis of being from 'away,' you don't hold down a job that a local could have, you make an effort at assimilation, and you don't cross too many important people. If you're from a society that long ago banished the death penalty and you hear a well-known personality on the radio calling for the immediate 'swinging' of the whole of Death Row as the answer to crime, you keep quiet – nothing an outsider can say will make any difference. A quiet understanding can be established. In Trinidad, it's called 'playing for a draw.'

It took me 20 years to learn this. It doesn't matter how much you identify with your adoptive country. It doesn't matter how passionately you seek its best interests, beg it to follow this course or that, to avoid this trap or the other. Things will unfold as they must. Society will go its own way, make its own choices, choose its own destiny, make its own mistakes; and it is neither gracious nor courteous to interfere.

If you believe in self-determination, there is no other choice. The answers, and the questions, must come from within. Especially with centuries of slavery and colonialism, and the experience of a whole Caribbean diaspora in the northern countries, looming over the discussion.

So you don't go on about why such enormous quantities of oil and gas revenues have passed through the treasury since the first oil boom, yet so many dire problems remain unsolved, so many systems still in shambles. Or why there are still people sleeping on the sidewalks on cardboard boxes. Or why we have come to the point where there is scarcely a window in Trinidad without burglar bars on it.

You don't discuss why, in this lively, creative and imaginative country, the politics are so sterile, the bureaucracy so lethargic, the electorate so resigned. ('We like it so,' people would say, defiantly, at one time.) Or why archaic British systems have never been radically rethought and restructured for a post-colonial era. Or why everything, however serious or tragic, is laughed off with a joke. Or why politicians swallow anything a foreign consultant might advise, no matter what catastrophe ensues, rather than trusting and building local resources. Or why villagers on the TV news still shake their fists over ruined roads and broken bridges just as they did 20 years earlier.

You don't make fun of the witch who croaks: 'Markbett, Markbett, Beware de Tane of Fife!' just because you have seen the play produced in a Shakespearean accent at Stratford.

So the best contribution I could make now, I thought, would be to shut up. When I put together a collection of articles and broadcasts to remember those 20 years by (the very thing that all journalists are advised never to do, as I later discovered), I called it *Going to Ground*. For me, that meant disappearing into the low-profile, backstage world of magazine editing and publishing, and keeping my opinions to myself. It was the only way of resolving the irony of telling people to trust themselves more and to listen less to outsiders.

My old students are well into middle age now, some of them corporate managers and directors. Meeting one of them in a Port of Spain street always produces a flashback to that school staffroom in the early Seventies. *Here, hold on for X will you, he's finishing his taxi run.* (A teacher on a *taxi run*?) A game of all-fours going on by the window, cards slapping down fast before the bell rings. *Fete match this weekend, Benedicts v. Bachelors* (married men v. singles, bring rum). Endless jokes, endless *fatigue* (good-humoured insult). One morning, blood on the grass in the morning sun: an overnight shootout between police and some 'freedom fighters' left over from 1970 and the 'black power' upheaval. A *petit-quart* of rum at a bar down in St James. A score of voices roaring over piles of ink-smeared copybooks. *Come lime by Y tonight … what yuh mean, yuh tired?* And me in the corner writing a review.

Regular. It means you're up for anything in this indefatigable country; tireless limer, drinker, smoker, fêter, sportsman, pan fanatic, calypso connoisseur, Carnival authority. They were regular, I wasn't.

'No, that foot first, then bring the other one together,' my patient wife would say at Carnival time. 'No, forget the feet now, don't move the feet, rotate the hips. Now the arms all wrong.' Expats saw Carnival as a glorious fancy-dress party with endless rum. Zealots would be in the panyards and mas camps day and night. The staffroom simply took it as a seasonal escalation of normal activity.

But I knew I could never get to love the lumbering Carnival king and queen costumes, the steel pans with their shrill clashing harmonics, the Panorama competition with its musical stranglehold, the calypsonians with their school-yard jokes, their gleeful degradation of women, their struggle to find anything worthwhile to say. The festival sucked so much energy away from the other arts, and colonised the national imagination to such an extent, that it is still hard for artists today to deal with the darker or tenderer emotions – love, loss, hurt, sorrow.

But behind Trinidad's relentless celebration lies something much older and deeper. One day, in the empty school hall, I came across one of my most difficult students, lord of the back-row rebels. He was bending over a tenor steel pan in such intense concentration that he didn't even notice I was there. He was listening to the individual notes, softly practising a melody, utterly absorbed in the music. I saw how deeply pan *mattered* to him, even if nothing else did, certainly nothing that could possibly happen to him in school. He was in touch with something that coiled back from this island through time to another continent, another culture, another world.

Perhaps there are things you can only really *know* in the place you are born into; the place 'where your navel string bury,' as they say in Trinidad.

Carnival

Jane Bryce

The turbo-prop drops from a clear blue sky and bumps to a halt on the runway at Piarco. The speaker system crackles its last message: 'Thank you for choosing LIAT and welcome to Carnival.' Clustered around the terminal entrance, a group of pan-players fills the air with sound. In my eagerness, I've come without the address where I'm staying, and the immigration officer allows me to write 'Auntie Brenda' on the customs form. Outside, a smiling woman welcomes new arrivants with a rum punch. The calypso belting out of the loudspeakers is interrupted by a commercial: 'Have you got your sunblock, your water, your Durex condom? Because in the heat of the moment, anything can happen. Make sure you have your Durex condom!' It's Carnival in Trinidad, and I am here, in Port of Spain. You inhale excitement just by breathing the air. It's as if a few million people – the entire population – have all caught something at the same time. I am on the edge of my seat in the taxi as it joins the mad swirl towards the city, and from my quickened pulse rate I know I'm catching it too.

In the Church calendar, it's the week before the beginning of Lent. The whole island is partying. Purists complain that old Mas has gone and Carnival has lost its meaning. There's no longer any need for slaves to mock or parody their masters, to roam the streets with unbridled licence. Instead, Carnival has been reduced to an occasion for bodily display and extravagant spending. But, next day, I am out shopping in the centre of town when a troupe of devils materialises in the crowd. The frame freezes, the busy street metamorphoses into a medieval morality play. Satanic emissaries with long black tails stride down the middle of the road, flicking at well-dressed shoppers with their whips. A devil chained by the ankle climbs a wall, writhing and twisting in the heat of unseen flames, until it's dragged by its chain out of the picture. It's stifling among the close-packed shops with people pressing into them in search of make-up, glitter, tights. But the chill the devil casts as it passes hangs in the air like the whiff of an underground drain.

Scene one: panyard. I'm taken aback when we arrive at a shabby concrete lot carved out of a residential district. It might be a car park, or a building site, or just a space where a derelict building has been knocked down. There's an open area in front of an awning, underneath which are the pans. What did I expect? Twenty pans on a float, like at Notting Hill? Or welcoming tourists at the airport with a touch of the 'authentic' Caribbean? Under the awning is an orchestra of maybe 200 pans – tenor pans, bass pans, little pans, big pans – 200 people with one totally rapt expression, all playing their different parts, subsumed in the music. Otherwise, only a rudimentary bar for the obligatory shot of rum or bottle of Carib, a brazier for serving corn soup. No chairs, no ceremony, just knots of people standing attentively in front of the players, like fishermen poised at the fringe of the surf. At first, all they hear is its overwhelming roar, but little by little their ears distinguish its orchestral elements – the long sigh as the sea gathers itself and flings itself forward to crash at their feet, the suck and whisper as it pulls at the sand, rattling the pebbles in its slow retreat. After the first impact, I surface enough to notice that, apart from the pans, there's a raised platform at the back on which stands a group of musicians with all sorts of extraordinary instruments. Someone's scraping a sort of circular cheese grater with a thing like a whisk. There are cowbells, shakers, every old bit of iron beaten and rung and clanged and clunked, all led by a guy with a metal gong which looks like a bit from a mechanic's yard, which he beats with a metal stick. It looks like a convention of scrap iron merchants. Actually it's the Engine Room: the rhythm section. It exerts an irresistible, tidal pull, so that I find myself winding my way inside the panstands till I'm standing right underneath it.

The noise is absolutely incredible. At my back, the incessant sound of struck steel, while all around me the aluminium poles holding up the stands are vibrating, the air's vibrating, my organs are vibrating, my eardrums play their own percussive rhythm. And you know what? It's all *acoustic* – the only acoustic music invented in the 20th century. It doesn't need amplification, the effect comes from the sheer, mesmerising volume of sound. As my temperature rises till my blood's at boiling point, I get the sense that, if I stand there long enough, the centrifugal force that holds my body together will spin out of control and everything will unravel, bits of brain and bones and blood all flying off in different directions. Half delirious, my skin cells humming, I stagger back out into the open and gratefully slurp soup out of a paper cup. The Carnival blend of coconut milk and corn and split peas and spices gradually calms the vibration and returns my body temperature to normal. But I have caught the contagion and it will have to run its course.

Scene two: Mas camp. We're playing with Minshall, a designer who has single-handedly redefined the meaning of Mas. His huge kinetic sculptures and fantastic imagination have inspired a band of ardent acolytes who would never play with anyone else. The other bands' costumes, consisting of bikinis, jockstraps and sequins, with a headdress or two thrown in, he dismisses as 'the sequin brigade.' His, by contrast, are distinctive and elaborate and, instead of following a theme, they tell a story. This year, it's the Legend of The Lost Tribe, in sections taken from the Qabbalah. A poster in the Mas camp explains to us that we are nomads wandering in the desert who have lost our way. We are supposed to flow across the stage on Carnival Tuesday like an endless river, or, as the poster declaims, each of us 'like a leaf blown by the winds of time.' We're in Beauty and Harmony, the section with the simplest costumes, but it takes minutes to unravel the yards and yards of white muslin, which wrap the body like a shroud with a flowing headdress. I secretly regret the bikinis and sequins, but the seriousness of the attending acolytes, the reverential atmosphere, silence me. I pay up and accept my costume.

Scene three: Panorama – the pan competition finals at the Savannah. They take a long time, because each complete orchestra has to be wheeled onto the stage and set up, play its piece, and get off again, along with a whole crowd of supporters. In the long gaps between performances, we stand around and lime, drink corn soup and beer and rum, eat shark bake and pelau, and mingle with the crowd. One minute I'm talking to a celebrated writer whose last novel I reviewed, then I'm in a group of people who are jokingly complaining about outsiders invading Carnival. A heart-stoppingly handsome man steps his whole six foot four inch self across the circle and gives me a bear hug, with the words, 'Don't mind them, we love visitors.' I have just been embraced by an invincible West Indies fast bowler I am accustomed to watching on television dispatching luckless batsmen with deadly accuracy. My delirium increases.

I'm sleep-deprived, but there's no time to sleep. We're playing J'ouvert at 2.30 a.m. J'ouvert is 'dirty mas' and takes place at night. It represents the devilish side of Carnival, a kind of communal exorcism, in which you daub yourself in mud or paint, and roam through the streets being devils for a night. How devilish depends on your choice of band, and the choice for us is between the one consisting of demented young men hurling black paint at you, or the one an experienced J'ouvert-player advises me to opt for, having done black paint and saying never again ... The mud band is the softer option. I stand in line, wearing very little, shivering in the darkness, waiting to be slapped all over with mud by a very rough man. I watch nervously as he dips his hands in a tub of gluppy stuff with which he seems to assault the woman ahead of me. I have an altogether new sensation in the gamut of sensations Carnival is throwing at me. I realise I'm scared. I've never done anything remotely like this before, and I haven't the faintest idea what to expect. Suddenly, I am next in line, slapped all over, smeared head to foot in mud, and stumbling forward to join everybody else behind the music truck. By the time a few bottles of Carib are coursing through my veins, I am ready to dance all night. We set off through the streets, dancing in a crowd, jammed up together, physical contact keeping us warm. Bodies bump and grind as we move forward, half-naked and anonymous, united by the music. After a while, I am aware that the arbitrary jostle has been replaced by a singularity of intent. Every time I move, someone behind me moves with me, not holding me exactly, but attached. I don't look back, but try a few times to shake off my escort. I step to the left, and so does he. I step to the right, he follows. His breath hot on my neck makes the hairs rise. I can no longer stop myself, and I turn my head, meeting the eyes directly in front of mine. There's no-one there. I mean, there's someone there all right, his face six inches from mine, his eyes staring, but so completely expressionless he appears possessed. He looks straight through me, as if my body too is nothing more than a vehicle, and our proximity just a physical accident. At the same time, I feel something hot and hard against my back and can't help being aware that all along the road dark alleys beckon ... at that precise and blessed moment, I am rescued by my more experienced friend, who sizes up the situation at a glance and deftly detaches me from my incubus. The devils have been exorcised. We walk slowly home together as the sun comes up, stopping for breakfast at a roadside stall. At the house where I'm staying, someone has been posted at the back door with a saucepan to sluice us off as we come in. I stand in a stream of icy water in the early dawn, gleefully relieved I went for mud.

Carnival Monday – a day to rest before the climactic marathon of Carnival Tuesday. Just for fun, in the evening, we pile into two taxis, vintage Sixties' British cars, with all-in-one leather seats and chrome and wood dashboards and mascots, and drive to St James. A street of rumshops hosts an ongoing street party, including pans – yes! I step out of the taxi, hear the music and turn, follow the float, and am lost … when I come to, I don't know how long afterwards, I'm wandering aimlessly in a crowd of people. Suddenly, an arm comes out of the crowd and pulls me over, and the owner says, let's dance … I check his face for human presence, and decide to stay. Hours later, immersed in discussion in a rumshop, I realise it is nearly morning and we have to be at the Savannah at eight. I don't know where I am or how to get home, but my new friend walks me there and sees me into the sleeping house. As I close the door behind me, I catch a glimpse of him still and silent at the crossroad, early sunlight streaking the far end of the street.

Carnival Tuesday. It's the last day, when everything comes to a head in a last orgy of all-day partying, the day of 'pretty mas,' the costume parades, the showing off and flaunting yourself in the street to music as you dance through Port of Spain. We struggle into our costumes, winding the yards of muslin into headpieces, wrapping ourselves in nomads' weeds, and set off for the Savannah, short of sleep, self-conscious and conspicuously white-clad in the grey of morning. As we approach the Savannah, we join rivulets of lost tribespeople wending their way to the same point – tall men with intricately woven turbans, women with fantastic designs painted on their faces and bare brown midriffs, little shells and feathers and amulets sewn into their costumes, some carrying elaborate staves hung with gourds and fetish objects. As we hunt for our section, someone mentions that there are two and a half thousand people in our band. Suddenly we realise what it's all about. We *are* the Lost Tribe, the people of Trinidad, with all their contradictions and violent disagreements. One man's vision comes alive in the coming together of so many of us in the costume of the band. Playing mas, I now see, is a collective statement of faith in the possibility of transcendence. At Carnival, the rivers flow into each other, just as the calypso says.

There is a long time to think about this, because nothing really happens for at least four hours, apart from standing in the sun as it gets hotter and hotter. We buy ice and wrap it in our headties to cool ourselves down. The high spot is meeting Minshall, a small spry white Trinidadian, around 60 years old, mas-man, wizard and leader of the Lost Tribe. Otherwise, time passes slowly, but it isn't boring because suspense is building moment by moment, and music's playing, and Tassa drummers are drumming, and finally we are in Beauty and Harmony and very slowly moving towards the stage. The first sections begin to go on, preceded by the Tassa drummers, then a long river of cloth carried across by a handful of dancers, then, very stately, the Patriarchs in their turbans, escorting a huge fetish totem. Then we hear the announcer say, 'And this is Beauty and Harmony, the largest section,' and we step onto the stage … a surge of adrenalin electrifies my body, sweeping me out there in front of all those people, and our griot is singing us across from the side of the stage and we're dancing with the cloth swirling all round us and the television cameras and the faces and up so high we are floating over Port of Spain. And then it's over, we've crossed, the next section is filling the stage behind us, and the Lost Tribe is flowing across like leaves blown by the winds of time. I stand in the cooling spray of cold air and water and watch my band playing, and the feeling is so intense I don't know what to do with it or even how to name it, except I'm playing mas in Carnival. My feet carry me to the end of the Savannah and as I hesitate at the edge of the stream of costumed revellers, I hear drumming and a Yoruba chorus praising Shango, god of lightning and electricity, and for a second, I'm totally disorientated. I have a hallucinatory moment when I'm back in a Nigerian village, attending a Shango festival. Then the song moves into an invocation of Shango's contemporary manifestations, and I find myself once again on a street in Port of Spain as a float passes with who but the Laventille Engine Room, and I step into the river and dance to the sound of a metal bar ringing on a crude metal gong. I dance all day through Port of Spain, high on adrenalin and rum, and the people on the float adopt me and give me bottles of beer. One in particular becomes my friend, and together we enter the garden of a house at the side of the road to beg for water from a very old frail lady who brings some in a bucket and we throw it over each other to cool off, my nomad's weeds are drenched and sticking to my body, but the thing is to keep going even though all I've eaten since yesterday is some honeyroasted peanuts early in the morning, and everyone talks to everyone else, and our band is like a family, and all together we arrive at Woodford Square, the whole band stops for a rest and people lie on the grass to recover before the last lap. It's getting dark. I'm part of the Laventille Engine Room entourage by now, and it turns out my protector is their singer and is known as Thunder, and last year they got to the calypso final. And on we go, and I notice Thunder has an enthusiastic following of ardent young female fans, and I comment on this, and he says 'I have my followers, but I'm following you,' and by now I don't ever want the day to end and any adventure that comes my way is okay by me, so I agree to go back to Laventille with the band and I climb in the truck and off we go.

There are a lot of people in the truck, apart from the musicians. There's an elderly woman who is quite silent and still in the midst of all the noise. Thunder tells me she's a priestess. She's there because this is an iron band, and iron belongs to Ogun. But thunder is part of the domain of Shango, and I think of the sparks that fly when iron is struck, and the electric surge that propelled me across the stage, and I realise there are a lot of powerful forces in this truck. I'm standing next to a young woman and when she hears I'm from Barbados she tells me she's been there, so I ask what she went there to do, and she says, 'Oh I was carrying drugs to sell.' And it dawns on me that I am in a social situation for which I'm ill-equipped. I have no money left, I am wearing the remains of a carnival costume and I'm going to a part of Port of Spain that I know only by its reputation. But the adrenalin is still coursing, and when we stop somewhere still in Port of Spain, I help the band unload the truck and pack all the instruments into some battered looking vehicles, into one of which I get, along with Thunder and two or three other people. We are heading for Laventille when suddenly Thunder stops the car and gets out, tells the driver to wait a second, and disappears. I am too high on rum and exhaustion to notice but he's away a long time, and the driver gets restless. We're parked in the middle of a street and Thunder has still not returned, when for the first time, the driver seems to notice me and asks who I am. From his expression, I can tell this is a good moment for me to get out of the car and let him go home, so I do. But what to do? I'm in the mood for an adventure, and don't feel like giving up on it so easily, so I sit on a wall and watch the trucks going by still playing music, and my friend the music expert drives by and sees me and stops. So I go with him to a bar round the corner, and he's very sympathetic, but he says it's a good thing I didn't go to Laventille, because it's a dangerous place and it's all for the best, and soon my more experienced friend from J'ouvert comes along, and she's going round the corner to her auntie's house, so I go with her. And instead of my adventure, I end up sitting safely in the auntie's living room, and then they see me back to Auntie Brenda's, and I have this absolutely enormous sense of relief at being home and I fall into bed and sleep till the next morning. Everyone tells me it was a *very* good thing I didn't go to Laventille, as anything could have happened and now I feel Thunder did me a favour by disappearing. On my way out through the airport, I buy the CD with his song on it, and listen to it when I get home, and laugh.

Misreading Wallace Stevens

Olive Senior

'The birds are singing in the yellow patios.'
(Wallace Stevens: *Like Decorations in a Nigger Cemetery*)

On a day beloved of travel writers
the yellow of tropical, the pale green
palms upturned

the vivid birds preening
in patios overlooking a blue
denial

the world arranged just so
for the viewers.
Unseen

like decorations
in the cemetery right under
their noses

the graves
outlined in white bleached
coral, the conch shells

splayed like bones. Unseen
the mirror's solicitations
to keep the spirits

spellbound; the flowers faded
and torn, the crockery
decorations

broken and worn
like the folk
buried there.

In a moment of heightened interest
in something totally trivial
the visitors

are caught spellbound
by the sound
of a funeral

procession. A brass band.
And a choir of birds singing
in the yellow patois.

How exotic! the travel writers thrill.
How perfectly chic!
Understanding

not a word, they immediately
arrange for translation and
publication – each one

carrying home
a trophy recording and a wonderful
necklace of birds' feathers.

The funeral procession
passes into
the cemetery out of sight.

Unseen the black souls
now dressed
in white

singing in the yellow patois
accenting
towards light

How I Lost My Camera in Havana

Simon Lee

Fidel was there to greet me when I landed at Jose Marti airport humming *Soy un hombre sincero*. He was everywhere at once, declaiming from the television screens. I listened respectfully for a five, understanding nothing but enjoying El Jefe's rhetoric. Then, saluting like a Sierra Maestra veteran, I mamboed through Immigration, jumped in a taxi and headed for Havana, city of my dreams.

I'd been on the way to Havana for 30 years, ever since Che upstaged Jimi Hendrix in the heirarchy of super heroes in the swinging, shagadelic, revolutionary Sixties. Viva Che! And there he was, beret and beard, *la revolucion incarnata*, gazing from posters high above the dark streets of the outer barrios. In some places he faced off with the Pope, who was due in the next few days.

Now that's what I call a real welcome. I hadn't been in Cuba an hour and I'd already seen Fidel, Che and even El Papa. As the taxi glided among the shadows of baroque-encrusted colonial mansions, floated through the Plaza de la Revolucion and down La Rampa towards the Atlantic-blasted Malecon, I had to pinch myself. No this wasn't a Tomas Alea movie. This was Habana *verdadera*, Habana *libre*. I'd actually made it and I had my camera along with me to capture it all.

In a fit of extravagance matching my mood I checked into the Hotel Inglaterra, whose regal nineteenth century atmosphere, which began with the mosaic tiled dining room, was anything but revolutionary. Next door was the Gran Teatro, its cupolas bursting exuberantly from their roccoco cleavage. Far too excited to contemplate sleep, I headed out into my first Habana night. Opposite the lobby, in the Parque Central, a fleet of ancient American taxis idled for passengers. Stopping briefly to admire their sensuous lines, I plunged into the Calle Obispo in search of music. Passing La Floridita where Hemingway invented the Daquiri, I picked up the strains of *son* floating down the ill-lit street.

La Lluvia de Oro was packed with Habaneros and tourists hanging on the every note of the all-female Grupo Cafe. Morenas and mulattas pulled willing dance partners from their seats to execute intricate steps through the swirl of cigar smoke. Inspired, I leapt to my feet, camera flashing and film finished in minutes. By early morning, with a couple of mojitos under my belt, I was in a cavernous studio off the Prado, singing with Grupo Cafe on a recording of the classic calypso 'Rum and Coca Cola'. *Ay compay*! I had the Habana fever.

A few hours and cups of thick sweet black Cuban coffee later, I was on the roof of the Inglaterra, the golden dome of the Capitol blinking to the right as I snapped the city's morning dance. Back on the ground I chose a gentle blue De Soto taxi and we went sailing along the Malecon, where breakers smashed into the sea wall and spray arced high over the road, rebounding off the peeling facades of deserted mansions. My camera clicked deliriously all the way.

On we drove through Vedado, across the Almendares River, past the Necropolis Colon where Spanish administrators and Cuban dons slept side by side in the eternal solitude of their marble mausolea. Habana is gloriously vast and, by the time the De Soto had chugged through Miramar and to my lodging in Playa, even the camera was drowsy. My host Raul directed me to my bed but it seemed mere seconds before he was knocking at the door to invite me to sample Havana Club rum and smoke lethal unfiltered H.Upman cigarettes with his doctor buddies.

Then they launched me in the direction of a rumba session at the Writers' and Artists' Union. The courtyard was writhing with student couples, rumbaing acrobatically to the sinuous Afro rhythms of the drums and choral chants. My camera was busy too and even had stamina for an all night performance at the Salsa Palace, which we left when the rest of Habana was eating breakfast.

Besides dreams and pictures, I had assignments in Habana. The most important was music, so I was delighted when a veteran journalist offered to introduce me to his friend, Cuba's leading musicologist. We went looking for him at the UNEAC, where the rumba had played. The courtyard was now filled with poets and singers, actors, painters, writers and of course Helio the musicologist.

His English was a big improvement on my Spanish and he gave me a crash course in the history of Cuban music. Rapidly our table extended as he called friends over – a leading percussionist, a bolero singer, the great poet Ambia, a celebrated actor. An impromptu fiesta ignited as the rum flowed and I was able to catch some of it with the camera. When UNEAC closed, the party continued across Habana singing boleros as we went, until the money gave out about three.

I hit my bed in Playa with a sense of achievement. Not only had I made a great start on the music research, but I'd met some fascinating artists and taken some hot shots. Rummaging through my backpack in the morning I couldn't find the camera. Devastated, I ransacked the room. Nada.

I took the bus south to Trinidad hoping the camera would reappear by the time I got back to Habana. I saw one just like it in Trinidad but resisted the urge to snatch it. But mine had really gone, claimed by the revolution or the Habana night. The night before I left, Raul presented me with a pen and a journal 'from your Cuban family.' As we sat toasting with old Havana Club I laughed and the lost camera finally dropped out of mind. 'No problem Raul, it just means I have to come back to Habana.'

Listening to Charlie Zaa

Robert Edison Sandiford

So here we were, The Mrs and I, sitting in the middle of the Rio Piedras, an outdoor mall in San Juan, Puerto Rico, sharing a soft vanilla ice cream in a sugar cone and listening to the sounds of a Latin pop singer with the unlikely name of Charlie Zaa.

We had spent too many hours cruising the shops along the street and were looking for a place to cool off before heading back to our pick-up point. The sun was hot, and The Mrs chose a spot by a music store.

In the store's window was a television playing music videos of Zaa's songs. Above us hung a poster of Zaa.

The poster was a blow-up of his album cover. A head shot, it showed the singer in black and white, slightly hunched over and looking off to the side, with a scarf around his neck covering the lapels of his tuxedo.

With his dark hair and daring looks, Zaa was reminiscent of Frank Sinatra in his prime. In fact, the whole album, entitled *Sentimientos*, was evocative of the big band era.

The more I watched the videos, which were shot in black and white, too, the more I admired their quality. And the more I paid attention to the rhythm of the words and the melody of the music, the more I liked their playfulness and passion.

By the time The Mrs was ready to leave, I was humming Zaa's songs, mouthing the lyrics and ready to buy *Sentimientos*. I was also somewhat surprised at myself.

The least of my concerns was not speaking Spanish – I didn't own a walkman or stereo, either.

I used to commit such acts of spontaneity all the time in Montreal – still do when I'm there visiting the homestead.

But I realised I tend to feel – or, more accurately, am made to feel – a bit weird for acting on impulse in Barbados.

Regardless how beneficial or pleasant the action, such behaviour is often perceived as subversive. A lack of choice or funds can also hinder to no end a person's ability to be wild and crazy in the best sense imaginable.

The truth is, though, that in a society where there is great pressure for people to conform it's difficult to be dynamic – to follow your instincts, follow your heart. The status quo is supposedly the way to go.

What brought on the desire to purchase Zaa's album – besides the classy packaging and infectious music – was simply the atmosphere.

It wasn't that I felt 'less inhibited' as a tourist or that I was inspired by stereotypical notions of how more 'free-spirited' Latin Americans are.

I appreciated the right to be just another face in the crowd, remarkable because of who I am, not because of what I appear to be; unique, perhaps, yet neither more nor less noteworthy because of the colour of my skin, the brand of jeans I wear or the way I walk.

Just another guy sharing an ice cream with his wife and listening to Charlie Zaa on a busy street, trying to take in all the various sights.

Goods and Chattels

Marie-Elena John-Smith

She did not usually go to see weddings – that Friday afternoon ritual of schoolchildren, old women and the idle. She didn't care much for the pushing and shoving and the shouting outside the cathedral, and she seldom got to see anything. A schoolgirl like herself would almost never be allowed any of the coveted places at the front of the throng. Those were reserved for the professional wedding-watchers, self-appointed to keep up a running commentary on the apparel and demeanor of the invited guests, the members of the wedding party, but most of all on the bride.

She much preferred the visits to the brides' homes the afternoon before, straight from school and still in uniform, when she would escape the boredom of the cloistered lives lived by the Lebanese children she supervised in exchange for a Catholic education and a place to live in town. She would hang back as their nannies came to pick them up and walk them the three blocks home, shading them with parasols. She would pretend to help the teachers sweep the class, straighten the desks, erase the blackboard. Then she would join a gang of girls of her approximate shade, the gang of the medium-browns (although she was the only one who glowed) where she was something of a celebrity by virtue of her absolutely straight Carib hair, which did not exist among any of the other girls in any of the various degrees of brown. Such hair was found only on rare occasion in the almost-white gang, a gang to which none of the browns, from dark to light, had access.

The other girls, on these Friday afternoon pre-wedding visits, always headed straight for the bedroom, where they would spend up to a full hour with everyone else come in from off the streets, scrutinising the carefully labelled, opened gifts displayed on the bed, and passing judgment on whether or not enough money had been spent, considering the giver's status. Some of the older women would go so far as to examine the manner in which the display beds were dressed, lifting up the coverlets to determine whether or not the sheets were of Irish linen and if they had been hand-embroidered.

She found the analysis in the bedroom to be boring – all the talk of crystal and silver and china, bedding and curtains and runners – and she preferred to wander around the house, catching glimpses of how people in society lived. Her exposure to town people was limited to the Lebanese, who had come with their ways, the rough ways of poor Arab farmers, and had not yet acquired breeding, did not yet know the art of beautification, of grace. Their attitude of dominion was unsubtle and coarse, unlike the smooth aura of entitlement that the Europeans had passed on to the most privileged of their slaves, those that shared their white blood. For her, it was all brand new and wondrous.

She would watch the mother of the bride, walking confident and straight-backed, gesturing to her servants absent-mindedly, taking their presence for granted in a gracious sort of way, turning her head regally to accept the gleaming silver trays delivered in advance of the wedding by the maids of the invited guests. Especially, she liked to watch the mothers open the presents borne on those polished trays. Their gold *pomme canelle* earrings would swing like early wedding bells, their thick bracelets would jangle as they bent to pick up the teapot, the platter, the monogrammed bed sheets, holding them aloft for all to see before bearing them off to the bedroom for display.

The brides' mothers were omnipresent on those Friday afternoons, but if she stayed long enough, she would also get to see the real treat: the daughters. What struck her about these girls was that, without fail, they were distressed, pale and trembling with the swollen-faced look of days of crying. On occasion, they would even streak from one back room to another, tears visible, sobs audible. 'Tears of joy,' 'over excitement,' 'nerves,' the family members would murmur for the benefit of the people off the street. The family servants, proud of the girl's virginity, or attempting to dispel rumours, might also use the opportunity to circulate in the gift-display bedroom, glee unconcealed: 'She 'fraid what she going get tomorrow night!'

She believed those explanations. She was the only one who did not understand that, in the days before the wedding, these girls were finally forced to come to terms with the end of a life in which they had control over what they did, when they did it and who they did it with. They would relinquish their ownership over their own selves, and they would swear in front of God to obey their new lord and master until death. These society girls cried because they knew that they were about to become a servant: worse, in fact, because servants were paid and could leave when they wanted. They were crying because they were about to become somebody's slave.

The women who had come in off the street, with the exception of herself, were too familiar with slavery to contemplate doing such a thing to themselves. For the next century or more, these Caribbean women, with their lack of interest in marrying their children's fathers, would generate a steady traffic in befuddled missionaries, curious sociologists and excited anthropologists. Official terms would be coined. *Visiting unions*. That was what the scholars called the Caribbean way of making babies: the men would visit the various homes of their women and children – they did not live with them. And when that man stopped visiting for his union, the woman would unite with another visitor to have his children. '*Female-headed households*' and '*matrifocal societies*' (such difficult terms for such a simple thing) – these were the catchwords with which the pundits would discuss the phenomenon of Caribbean women raising children without the yoke of the men.

Theories would be put forward as to why they did this, studies would be undertaken, and the scholars would line up into two antagonistic camps. One set would say that it was all about handed-down African culture, and that the visiting unions phenomenon was essentially an adapted version of polygamy. The other group would blame the laws that had prevented slaves from marrying and from staying together as a family.

All the big-brained people developing their theories and writing their arguments and counter arguments should have just talked to any of the women to understand that the reason they did not marry was simple. It was that the descendants of slaves had a natural aversion to slavery.

From Oxford College to Baby Doc's Haiti

James Ferguson

'Why Haiti, for God's sake? They'll probably eat you at some voodoo ceremony.' My donnish neighbour at the Oxford high table dinner was puzzled by my choice of academic excursion. I'd applied for a grant to travel to what Graham Greene had unreassuringly dubbed the 'nightmare republic' to pursue my postgraduate research into French history. (I was, for a reason I've now forgotten, writing a thesis on the Haitian revolution and French literature.) Amazingly enough, the money was forthcoming from some university bequest and, suddenly, the prospect of throbbing drums and headless chickens seemed uncomfortably close.

It was my girlfriend (now wife)'s fault. She'd persuaded me that I'd learn more about Toussaint L'Ouverture and the first Black Republic on the spot than in the cloistered safety of Oxford's Bodleian Library. We'd survived a short, expensive and very hungry trip to Algeria the year before, so thought that another taste of an ex-French colony would be instructive, if not exactly fun.

The books I consulted over the next weeks were hardly encouraging. *The Comedians* isn't a tourist-friendly advertisement, what with Tontons Macoutes, corpses in swimming pools and the like. The Berlitz guide helpfully pointed out that in Haiti 'they bury the dead under heavy tombstones to keep them from returning to haunt the living.' A trawl of news cuttings and reports revealed that Baby Doc Duvalier's regime was among the worst human rights abusers in the Americas.

So, in a state of mild apprehension, we flew to Jamaica in August 1985, and spent a week or so in Kingston and in Port Antonio. It was a culture shock of sorts, especially as my idea of foreign, Algeria aside, was limited to France, but Jamaica somehow seemed more rundown and brooding than exotic.

Nothing, though, could have prepared us for our first impression of Haiti. If the road from Kingston's airport into town goes through some dangerous-looking districts, the way into Port-au-Prince was more like shifting a century or two, a snapshot of third-world chaos. There were as many animals as vehicles on a surface that was as much pothole as tarmac. Ramshackle shelters made from palm thatch lined the road, interspersed with half-finished breeze-block boxes. Piles of burning rubbish produced a sickly sweet smell that drifted into our antiquated taxi. People were everywhere, children playing in nasty-looking puddles, women squatting by piles of fruit, and everywhere the frenetic and noisy activity of the Haitian capital. In fact, it was the noise that had the greatest impact on the initiated: blaring radios, whooping car sirens, the hammering and thumping of countless roadside workshops and the hubbub of people everywhere. This was not helped by the fact that the taxi windows could not be wound up.

For a terrible moment it crossed my mind that all of Haiti might be like this, that we were condemned to months of unremitting cacophony. But soon the taxi began to climb into a more salubrious world of high walls and lush gardens and pulled up outside a large white building of Victorian appearance. This was the Santos guesthouse, an elegant but inexpensive establishment that seemed mostly to cater to the many aid workers who have always been drawn to this land of spectacular poverty.

But happily, the Santos promised calm and good taste rather than poverty. Set in the upper middle-class hillside suburb of Turgeau, it evoked the civilised tropical existence I had hoped might exist among the squalor. Stunning Haitian paintings and sculptures complemented solid mahogany furniture and a cool entrance hall, watched over by Madame Santos, a stern but kind member of Haiti's light-skinned minority. A small pool was shaded by a breadfruit tree. Breakfast and dinner were served in a large and airy dining room.

From this haven of *demi-pension* tranquillity we made excursions down into the teeming confusion of the capital. The library – the pretext for this academic foray – was in the middle of town, and my perusal of disintegrating books took place amidst a cacophony of hooting cars and yelling street sellers. But this was peace and quiet compared to the real heart of the city, the few blocks around the main Dessalines Avenue where a permanent street market attracts an almost impenetrable mass of humanity. This was the place for money changing, our dwindling stock of dollar bills replaced with vast and rather smelly wads of gourdes by scrupulously honest street dealers.

It struck me in downtown Port-au-Prince that people with no money spend an inordinate amount of time engaged in buying and selling. All along the crumbling sidewalks were stalls, often blocking anyone's way into the slightly more appealing shops behind. Vast piles of plastic bowls vied for attention with counterfeit watches, heaps of green bananas lay next to mountains of second-hand clothes shipped in from Miami. Even more cornucopian was the Iron Market, a stiflingly hot Victorian-era structure stuffed with paintings, religious artefacts and determined salesmen, from which I feared I would never re-emerge.

Poverty in Port-au-Prince was sometimes shocking. Outside the cathedral emaciated beggars seemed close to dying; mothers thrust babies at the few tourists; a sprawling slum area by the sea, La Saline, was an endless jumble of cardboard shacks and open sewers. This was before the advent of the lethal gang warfare, political and drug-related, that has made La Saline a terrible place to live, but it was bad enough then.

But the city was also beautiful. Gaunt mountains, skeletal through deforestation, surrounded a perfect horseshoe bay. Eccentric filigree mansions half-hidden by bougainvillea stood on the hills. Elaborately decorated minibuses invoked divine protection, while lovingly hand-painted signs advertised restaurants and hairdressers. From high above in the bourgeois suburb of Pétionville, Port-au-Prince looked gorgeous, especially at night.

We hired a car and drove to the once-prosperous and nostalgia-ridden south coast port of Jacmel, full of crumbling gingerbread mansions. We visited the northern city of Cap-Haitien, the 'Paris of the Antilles' before the French were thrown out by the slave army. Here, in a scene Graham Greene might have relished, we met a Baptist coffin manufacturer from the US Midwest who had come to do some good work. We explored the Artibonite Valley, the southern peninsula and the area near the Dominican border, where a huge saltwater lake was home to crocodiles. We even spent some time in Gonaïves, possibly the ugliest place in the world, where a US vessel was later to dump a load of toxic waste onto the beach.

And, of course, we did what every visitor to Haiti should do, marvelled at the Citadelle, the impregnable mountaintop fortress built by the mad King Christophe to withstand a French re-invasion that never happened. The Citadelle, almost reaching the clouds, and reached by a slow horseback ascent through the most beautiful country, was spectacular beyond belief, a vast stone monument to paranoia and cruelty.

We had people to meet – academics, a couple of cautious 'opposition' politicians, friends of friends – and they were always hospitable and proud of their country, despite its all-too-obvious problems. Some laughed openly at Baby Doc, whom we saw one day (or so a friend said) crashing through the water off the Club Med resort in a speedboat. But the sense of dictatorship was palpable. Pictures of Duvalier *père* and *fils* adorned public offices and foreigners were advised not to walk too close to the twitchy guards outside the gleaming white hulk of the Presidential Palace, where, we were told, Baby Doc's pale-skinned wife Michèle had a refrigerated room in which to wear her furs. We didn't actually see any Macoutes (or any who admitted to being such) but were slightly alarmed one night when a large black car drew up next to us as we walked home and a be-shaded gentleman introduced himself as Mr Champagne and said he would call on the hotel the next day. Nor, I admit, did we attend the almost obligatory voodou ceremony, although in Jacmel the drums were clearly audible. I've never liked ceremonies of any sort.

Ordinary Haitians were unfailingly kind and friendly, if sometimes a little hard to shake off when scenting dollars. The old cliché about dignity amidst poverty came to mean something, as did the other one about creativity. Artists produced idyllically lush landscapes poignantly at odds with the dusty reality, sculptors fashioned mysterious icons out of recycled metal.

And Baby Doc, though he didn't know it, was living his last months of luxury in his white palace. The following February he was unceremoniously chucked out by his generals and the Americans after a popular uprising looked likely to lead to real revolution. Things were supposed to get better, but they didn't. When I visited again in 1987, the army was in charge, there were no tourists, violence was rising. I later heard that a politician had been shot dead in the hall of the Santos and that Madame had packed up and left for Florida. Surely the situation could get no worse, people said, after the cycle of coups and counter-coups that racked the country throughout the 1990s. But, as we know, it did.

PERSONALITIES

The Creole Chant

Annalee Davis

I am the complex creole
My context is the Caribbean

An archipelago crocheted into a cross-breed
Of carnival, class and commess
Cognisant of Columbus
And the Commonwealth
That created these confused colonies
Correctly criticised for the callous treatment
Of the Amerindian
And the reconstitution
Of a Caribbean caste system

Several centuries later
My coronary artery crackles

When I think of the creatures
That created this cacophonous confusion

And when we collide
There is more chaos than community

Some feel like foreigners as though characteristic
Of these now ex-colonies
– our natural native islands

But I have a creed that I wear
Like a crest on my chest
My credentials are that I am created equally
Credible from my cranium to my coccyx

I cleave to no church, temple nor country
I sing the canticles and practise a yoga
I breathe
I chant

I made my jappa and wrote a creed
I owned a crucifix
And acknowledge the crescent

I anoint myself with a communion of
Cinnamon, coffee and cumin
Coca, cotton and cane
It is with composure and compassion that
I conceive my compatriots as compatible
Whether Cuban or Guyanese
Christian or Muslim, Hindu or Jew

I contemplate a Caribbean conservatory
That is a consanguineous conscious commune
Confidently confirming a conglomerate
Who speak patois, papiamento, spanish and creole

As a complex creole
Confronting this crossroads of centuries
I cannot condone the corruption
Nor those who configure the conflict –
I out cast them from society

I contradict the unicursal way
And commemorate the cobweb we have become
I come to you
Not as a comedian

Nor as a clown
I come to you as a coalition
Of combustible matter
A civilised collective
Sometimes caustic, but never counterfeit
I am a cordless creator
Of culture
Conveying my codes
To a society that isn't convinced
Of the credit of cultural producers

And now I wear a coronet
A continuous circular

In my cipher
I chuckle
I weep

I celebrate the chorus of the creole chant

Signing for a Madman

Andy Taitt

The attendant at the gate shouted a greeting to me even while I was checking that I had turned the car radio down.

'Mr Taitt!'

I was glad to see him. It removed the need for a lot of explanation.

'I come to sign for Jomo on Block A.'

'OK.'

'I know where it is.'

I drove past, turned left under the flamboyants, tamarinds and mahoganies and reversed onto the grey earth and dry grass.

Even as I was parking, the first inmate approached. He waited while I rolled up the windows and locked the doors.

'Good evening.' He was white. Even white people go crazy too.

'Good afternoon.'

'You got a dollar?'

'No, buddy.'

'You got cigarettes?' This guy didn't seem too crazy after all. He still had his priorities straight.

'Don't smoke.'

'Oh. Alright.' More points in his favour – he recognised a lost cause quickly.

I crossed the roadway and went through the gap in the low limestone wall. There was a rectangular patch of lawn with an asphalt path running along the low wall and at right angles across the lawn. The dirt path ran more conveniently across the grass. After three months without rain there was little grass and a lot of dust.

To my left was the entrance to the building. A grey painted wooden door – the paint long dried to dust on the jalousies – was set in a hexagonal entranceway. There was an air of surviving grandeur, out of place in the dust and the quiet decrepitude.

The iron gate I was heading for was to my right.

A woman whom I had seen earlier was now ahead of me heading for the same locked iron gate. It was one of two iron grille gates about eight feet apart. The first was at the top of a flight of four steps and, to see along the corridor beyond, it was necessary to bend over. At the far end of the corridor, three attendants sat playing dominoes with an inmate.

The lady said to me, 'They see you standing up here and they won't move at all.'

I bent over and looked in. But just then an attendant got up. A man came angling across the same piece of lawn I had not long walked across. He waved gaily to a passing nurse and she returned his wave just as gaily, her manner saying this was the only way to deal with this crazy coot. He looked up and spotted fresh game. He headed straight for us, once more waving. I had learnt by example. I waved back to him. He came right up and made an interrogative gesture with his hands. Too crazy to talk, and with an idiot grin all over his face, but he had enough of a grip on reality to recognise that money makes the world spin. I shook my head no. He got the message but thought it worth another try. I shook my head with more finality. He watched me, crestfallen.

The attendant got to the inner gate and apologised for not coming sooner.

'You see me ever since and you won't move,' the lady said.

He mumbled an apology as he came through to the outer gate and started to open it. 'Who would you like to see?'

'I come to see my son, Arthur Hade.'

'Haynes,' he repeated looking doubtful as the name rang no bell.

'Hade,' she repeated. 'H–a–d–e.'

'That's an unusual name,' he informed her. 'And you, sir?'

'I come to see Jomo.'

'And what is your name?'

'Andy Taitt.'

'And what is Jomo's name?'

'I really don't know, you know. Randall Waterman, I think.'

All this time he was locking the first iron grille behind us, before he opened the second. He handed me over to another attendant and went off with Mrs Hade. I told the new attendant I had come to sign for Jomo.

'You sure you know what you doing?'

I was not. I was never sure what I was doing when I came to sign for Jomo. The hospital authorities said he was fit to go and, as long as he kept taking his medication, he would be all right. His own family, however, did not seem to agree. They would never come to sign for him. Jomo thought his brother was behind it. They had bought a piece of land, he claimed, and the brother wanted to work it all himself.

Jomo himself had done no wrong. Jomo never did any wrong. True, he might have thrown out the plate of food with good reason, even if his family thought his reason spurious. True, a man had attacked him one day down in Temple Yard and had chopped him with a cutlass – for no reason. Jomo had come in the shop one day and showed us the chop. The clean flesh sat exposed to the air. Jomo's only attempt at treatment had been to go to the beach. 'Let ital ways take their course.'

'Bookman,' a voice shouted at me. I saw a face that I vaguely recognised, a tall young man did a crane-style kata for my appreciation, a proud smile on his face.

'Teacher, Teacher,' another voice. 'You remember me, right!' he asserted. 'I was in the hospital when you had you eye.'

I remembered his face. I had seen him hanging out with my friend George who had first introduced me to this place.

As we walked along, various other characters sidled up to us or approached us directly. I must have looked sceptical because the attendant assured me that they would not trouble us. I knew that, but weren't these guys here because you couldn't predict what they would do next?

'Andy Taitt. Bookseller, the Book Place.'

This one obviously knew me.

'I been in your shop sometimes,' he said, with a discernible English accent. I looked at him more closely. You don't want to stare, but I never forget a face and this one wasn't stirring my memory.

Jomo was encouraging me along. He wanted to get out of there. So I went into the little alcove they were using for an office.

'Parris!' the chief nurse called. When there was no answer, he called again. 'Parris! Man, come here, man.'

Parris came in. 'Man, why you call me? I busy out there doing something.'

'You busy? You busy! You busy doing what? Playing dominoes?'

Parris smiled sheepishly. 'Man, you see how you treating me. Man, you in got to treat me so, you know, man.'

'You get treat how you behave. If you don't behave so, you don't get treat so,' the chief nurse said, triumphantly. 'You can't pull them tricks, boy. You would get catch. Carry this fellow in there and fix him up.'

One of the nurses led me over to the corner to sign.

'You have to sign this form. This says you are responsible for Jomo and you will make sure that he comes back when he should.'

I had gone through this before. I made my position clear.

'I really don't know much about Jomo, you know. I know the man from coming in my shop. He tell me his family won't come and sign for him. I feel if the doctor say he good enough to go then he shouldn't have to stay in here just so. After all, he is human being. But I can't really be responsible for him. When he leave here I don't know where he going. I can't promise to bring him back.'

'That is alright. That is alright.'

Another nurse said, 'He know that, man. He sign for Jomo before.'

The first nurse said, 'Well, you not really responsible in that way. That is just a legal requirement.' He made that sound as if a legal requirement was something you trifled with.

I said, 'That is what I want to make clear. I can't be responsible for him. I can't make sure he takes his medicine. I can't do any of that stuff. I only signing because you guys say it is alright for him to go.'

But they were anxious to get rid of Jomo. They simply needed the space and with him gone, there would be one less body to take care of.

Besides, like me, they knew and liked Jomo. He was intelligent; he meant well and was kind. He understood his situation and recognised that the staff was not responsible for his being there. While he was there they took good care of him and respected his humanity. The only trouble was that he tended to lose control sometimes – in fact, too often.

The actual signing took very little time. I was anxious to get to the university bookstore before all the good books in their sale got taken. When he heard I was going on campus, Jomo asked if I was going to school there. He respected learning; I had first met him when he started coming in to buy books on Africa and rastafari.

Jomo went off to get his things, and the nurse asked another one to show me out. She was one of the few female nurses I had seen for the afternoon. We walked along the corridor I had used on my way in. The crane man did his kata for me again. I was fairly certain he didn't know me. I was a generic audience.

The playwright appeared again. As he started to talk to me, the nurse took a right turn rather than continue along the corridor to the double iron grille. This new exit was another double iron grille. It made sense. The two gates were never unlocked at the same time. Nobody could hide behind the grille and surprise a nurse with a key. It sounded like a lot of trouble in a place where people walked around freely but once, on tour with a group of school children, we had been told that there were criminally insane being held there by the courts for murder.

The nurse closed the first gate behind us.

'One of the things I want to do is to write a musical based on Timmy Callender's *How Music Came to the Ainchan People*,' the playwright said. He said it as though he would have liked my help with the idea. It sounded like a good idea. But all these guys here had already crossed the fine line. Another of my friends, who wasn't here, had discovered that the way to make a quantum leap in consciousness was to pull out all his teeth.

I wasn't certain of my way out of this new exit. The nurse – young, slender, friendly – said all roads led out of there. I suppose as many as led into here. She locked the grille behind me.

I stood for a moment to get my bearings. Turning left would put me back in my original direction and take me to the front of the building, but there were annexes and extensions everywhere and the way out was circuitous.

Of a sudden, it struck me. I had not noticed on my way in but then I had been concerned with getting in and seeing Jomo and getting out as quickly as possible. This whole compound was beautiful.

Everywhere solid, grounded 19th century buildings of coral stone. These blocks had been cut by hand with carpenters' saws. Low squat annexes ran off on every hand; ugly in a way, but beautiful with history. Just at the time of day when the sun started to lose its heat they sat and reflected light quietly in the afternoon sun, their glow in contrast with the cool shadows they cast.

Walls of double courses of limestone blocks separated areas of lawn in squares. Everywhere tamarind trees and ancient mahoganies shaded the compound. At the end of the dry season scarlet flamboyants outshone everything else, their incandescent branches spread out low over the ground, the earth beneath burnt red with their fallen flowers.

The noises of the traffic were deadened by the buildings. Blackbirds whistled and screamed in the trees. Sparrows hopped on branches and on the ground, doves cooed serenely. Cordia trees stood up straight and straggly and orange.

This place was wasted on crazies. They were too busy fighting their own private demons to bother about a place like this. Somebody meant well in putting them here; their not bothering about the surroundings meant they would have one less thing to bother about. But those of us not yet crazy could probably be saved from going crazy if we could come here and not bother – about them, about us, about anything.

But I was bothering about them still. Eventually I found my way out. First, I walked through a doorway: an old man was standing with his back towards me. I didn't want to sneak up on him too quietly in case he wasn't dangerous except to people who invaded his personal space unexpectedly from behind. He was also white. That bothered me even more. He looked happy being there. That too was bothersome.

I got past him without mishap, but my sensibility came under attack one more time. There was another young white guy inside there, gazing into space. This was becoming too much. Black people go crazy and they have every right to. Their lives are hard and they have to scuffle to stay alive. They're poor and the pressure drives them crazy. You see them walking around Bridgetown doing crazy things, making other people miserable. The bus stops outside the green iron fence and they wave at you; if you walk past they beg you for money or cigarettes. Yes, black people go crazy.

But you never see white people doing all that stuff. Now, in one evening, I had met three. And when I looked around the room, there was another white guy with a pale round face, weak eyes behind round plastic imitation tortoiseshell glasses sitting on a bench.

Getting into my car, rolling down the glass, buckling the seat belt, a voice reminded me that these guys all had serious problems. None of them wanted to be there or had put themselves there; if they had, then they were in even worse shape than they looked. I would have felt sorry for them if it would have made any difference to them.

In the meantime I was glad to get out of there. Something that they couldn't do. If the price of enjoying those serene surroundings was going mad, they were welcome to them.

A Morning at the Library

Philip Nanton

'... I really must go, Janice. I have to prepare a talk to tell them all about the library at 11 o'clock this morning. Dr Cumberbatch is bringing Lady Susan and some other high-falluting persons whose names I don't know but who have plenty of money to spread around. So, that is why I can't stop. It's about the library ... the talk I mean ... along the lines that I told Mrs Barnstaple how this is a specialised place. People who come here are supposed to be able to consult files, old books, manuscripts, to do their research, that sort of thing ... I was not having any of that! I told the Honourable Secretary when she asked me. Look here, I said, you can't talk to me like that. I started as an office secretary doing filing and that sort of thing in a branch library out at Oistins a long time ago – before you were born in fact – and I worked myself up until I became Chief Librarian. I served my time. Then I couldn't take all that travelling to this country and the next; conference on this, conference on that. I had enough. So I took retirement. But I came back to work here. I like the hours ... Peter? ... he got a good handshake he tells me. He's using it to set up a business ... I can't say. He says to me: "Mother, if I tell you, someone else will be doing it tomorrow." I can't argue with that. My daughter ... two ... six months now. Just a minute, Janice... Marjory! They're not supposed to send children to us here just so. You know that, man, oh cripes! We have to put a stop to it. I keep telling them it's the Museum that they want, not the Library. Hold on Janice … Good morning. Can I help you? … Janice, hold on eh … First, you have to fill out this green card … I don't know why they ask that. I suppose it's to find you if you don't pay. I'm only joking … I have to keep a strict record of everyone who comes in and goes out of here, you see, so I need to know who you are. Yes, you have to pay. It's only a small fee … Each time you come here, unless you join for the year. Are you local? You look local. I don't know that name. Yes, you still have to pay. But you could join for the year, you know … Marjory! Kindly show this gentleman … what did you want again? Show him what we have. Look under 'cannibals' … Janice, Janice you still there? Child, you know … Janice, tell me now, the fair, are you going this year? Well, my dear, I am up in arms and steaming. They put me on the stall ALL day. Can you imagine? And when will I get my lunch? I shot straight back at them. Look here, I said, that's not my job. I normally don't do that. It's my responsibility to take the Governor around to see the stalls, every year without fail. That's what I do. Now, how can I do that if I am on the stall all day? Someone else will have to take over the stall because I always take the Governor around … Marjory, did you find the file for Dr Cumberbatch? … Sorry Janice, we had a problem here to find a file all week … Marjory, where did you look? You found it under what? … Janice, it has been chaos, child. We lost this file. And you know who will get the blame. We know Dr Cumberbatch is coming and she wants to look at the files on hurricanes. Well fine, but could we find them? Could we? You see, we have these volunteers … well, between me and you … anyway, we looked under 'wind,' nothing. We looked under 'cyclone,' nothing; 'disaster,' nothing … 'calamity' my dear … So, anyway I said, look here, I am taking the Governor around the fair and you all will just have to find someone to run the stall while I'm away. It's just like with the Cuban Ambassador. I phoned the embassy WEEKS ago. Did they want a stall? THEY will tell me if they want a stall. Well fine, I say. NOW they come back to me THREE days before the fair. It's the Assistant to the Ambassador. They are VERY upset. Why have they not got a stall? I'm not having any of it. I told them. They will have to take it up with Fair Committee. They are outside now. No, the visitors we are expecting today. Dr Cumberbatch, Lady Susan and her consort, my dear … suits and hats … white stretch limo … I can see it … and I haven't finished the talk … I better go.'

Luis

Jane Bryce

I met Luis in Havana. La Lisa, a working class district on the edge of
the city, is a 20-kilometre ride in a battered taxi from the centre of
town, a district of shabby apartment blocks with outside staircases
where life is lived on the street. I was visiting a family on the fourth
floor of one of these. Juan, whose family it was, led me up the stairs
and along the outside landings which punctuated each stage, past the
doors of other apartments. On the third floor, a door stood open,
casting an oblong of light onto the concrete. It was like the mouth of a
cave, and I glanced inside. A man was there, under a bright electric
light, and as we passed he called out to us. 'My godfather,' said Juan,
and we went inside.

I saw an elderly man in a wheelchair in a sparsely furnished room.
I smiled and uttered a few of my limited store of Spanish words. He
answered me in broken English, inviting me to sit down, telling me his
name was Luis. As I sat, I noticed that Luis had no legs. On the wall
was the faded photograph of a woman. Gesturing to it he explained,
'My mother, from Scotland.' The only other picture in the room was of
Fidel. Apart from that, there was a bookcase with a few scattered books
and a table with a strip light attached to it. I asked what he used it for,
and he said, 'Reading and writing.' Wheeling his chair over to the
bookcase, he brought me a book to demonstrate. It was a Yoruba

grammar book, printed in 1914, no doubt to assist colonial servants being posted to Nigeria. From this book, Luis was teaching himself Yoruba.

Luis was a babalawo, a master of the word. A legless priest, confined to a priestly cell, learning a language he could share with no-one. Marooned on an island three floors up, relying on passing ships for sustenance. I asked how he lost his legs. He said, jumping off a building, trying to kill himself. 'Unfortunately, I survived.' His eyes were humorous and his voice warm, belying the bleakness of the words. In that case, God must have wanted you to live, I suggested. Luis flashed me a look and laughed. 'No, the doctors,' he said. 'Now I am in prison.' He wanted to kill himself when his wife left him, he went on, taking the children with her. He must have read my expression, because he deftly turned the conversation. 'Do you have a child?' Gratefully, I nodded. 'Oh then, she must be as beautiful as the mother?' It was my turn to laugh. 'Mas linda,' I said, drawing the picture out of my bag. Luis looked from my daughter's face to mine and nodded. 'Mas linda.' We both laughed.

Luis fought for Castro in the Congo and Angola. He had lived the revolution, and was living it still, cheerfully tragic in his contradictions. Juan, who had gone on, leaving me with Luis, now came back and asked me to go upstairs. I stayed up there for some time, eating, and looking at school books. As I came back down, I paused once again at the open door, and Luis was waiting for me. He called me to come in. He was holding something, and explained he wanted to make me a gift. On the paper he gave me was the picture of a rose, and on the back, the place and the date of our meeting, and the words: 'My modest given to you, for remember me. God blest you. Luis.' I held the paper in my hand and felt for a response. The apartment was as empty as a prison cell. My eye fell on the Yoruba grammar, and by some trick of association I saw the grove, and the lazy brown water of the stream. 'Osun is my goddess,' I said, 'and she would like me to give you this.' I knew as I put the note in his hand that it was nothing, but like him I had nothing else to give. But it wasn't the money that excited him. At the mention of Osun, his eyes caught fire, and he turned his chair around and led me to a cupboard at the back of the room. Flinging open the door, he revealed two small shelves of paraphernalia, which at first I could make no sense of. They looked to my eyes like old bits of junk, dirty and worn – bits of iron, a clay pot, other objects of indeterminate status. Luis was watching me closely. 'For the worship of Osun,' he said, and pointed, 'for Sango, for Elegbara.' His voice was husky, and I looked again at the ritual objects. I did not understand their purpose, while for him they were infused with meaning. But now I understood something else, which before had been lacking. Luis did not inhabit his prison cell. He was elsewhere, seated in the shrine at the centre of the grove, throwing cowries to divine the future. He had not been surprised to see me. The children of Osun will always find each other, brought together by the currents that flow around the earth.

It was time to leave. *'Ese gon, baba,'* I murmured, 'thank you.' I could tell from his response that he wasn't used to hearing Yoruba spoken. Its meaning is in the music, which he couldn't hear. He had, after all, only the book to teach him, and silence where the music should have been. I left Luis in La Lisa, and returned to central Havana. The air was thick with an indefinable smell, a miasma born of effluent and the noxious exhaust of a million cars, choking the city. As I neared my hotel, a faint breeze blew across my face, bearing the smell of the sea.

Our Worship Sir

Oonya Kempadoo

Was Court Number Two I had to go, up in front, close behind a Jacket
Mister. The man broad and the books on he desk reaching he chest. He
busy looking, turn-page reading and pulling he fat nose. The room small,
like a classroom and the teacher sitting up in the box with a old fan by
him. Two Police chuked-in to one side with they dwarfie school desk and
chairs. Scratches all over the benches, corners rubbed down by nervy
hands, varnish wear-off the edges. Could hear people dragging they feet
and talking outside. The place smell hot and dusty like a classroom too.
Wood, old paper, shirts soaking sweat, only thing missing is chalk. More
Police, about four fresh ones at the back of the class, on a bench along
the louvres, whispering and signaling to the one standing by the door.

'Gilbert Ramsey! Gilbert Ramsey! No appearance Your Worship.'

'Pauline George! Pauline George! No appearance Your Worship.'

'Twenty-ninth'a June.' Teacher look at the lady sitting behind a
desk by him.

She look up at him and raise-up her pencil-in eyebrows 'Yes, I hear
you.'

She keep them raise-up and write the date, scratching she head
with the top'a the pen, fingertips round off from housework like
Lynette own. Teacher call another name, the Police at the side repeat
it then the one at the door bawl it out.

'Terence Samuel! Terence Samuel! Present, Your Worship.'

The fella come and stand next to me, Mr Jacket still reading and writing on some yellow paper.

Teacher flap he hand to the Police by him, 'Prosecutor?'

'PROSECUTOR' mark-up on he fat black book so everybody could know is his. Voice deep-deep to fit a man looking like he. Short and red he head like a rock, chin square-off and forehead squashing down he nose. Lips well shape out and shave clean all round. Big Pro. He voice come from down by he belt, boom round in he broad chest spanning he uniform button tight. Black and red hat resting on he desk.

'Sir, sorry we're unable to proceed today ... '

'Come back on the twenty-sixth'a June ... '

The fella go back outside fumesing. They wasting people time.

Miss Eyebrow inspec'ing she big grubby diary, taking she own time. A rough-up fella on the bench next to me, closer to Big Pro. Scar-up all over he head and neck. Piece'a ears gone, a old Tom Cat – head and neck in one, shoulders tough and thick. A damage-look in he small eyes, like he brain get beat-up too. He take he two big-skin hands and scrub he shave-head and face, set back looking out the louvres to the sea.

Outside, the sea chilling, looking close like a wall going up to the sky. Hot sun scorching rooftops in town, a red-tin desert. Bus sounds and music from the market square, stifle and smothered. Fort Granby outline 'gainst the sky and lower down, the tall church tower with the balls balance right on the ends'a the points. A old lady come out'a she kitchen squinting and go down she back step, one at a time. Heat whiten she hair more and dance like glass off she galvanise roof. Broad bright-green banana leaf waggle 'gainst the louvres, dodging a hot breeze driffing in – the only living colour 'part from the sea. Tom Cat stretch and yawn. Time stretch 'eself too. Wasting.

Next case is Tom Cat own. When he name call and he stand up, the back'a the class start sniggling and holding in laughs. He pants tight tight and pinch-up in he bumsey. He crook knees and pull it out, fix he balls and spin a finger in he nose-hole.

Big Pro smiling already, call in the wic'ness – is a oldish man with a owl face like a round heart, eye and nose slanting to he chin. Fit heself on the stand easy, shoulders and body small under he head, a ole time turquoi pants pull up high on he waist.

'Yes Sir, I was inside me house waiting fuh he that day. I was hiding.'

'You was hiding inside *your* house?'

'Yes Sir! Cause I tired'a he coming in my place a'ready. Break-in, taking anything he want – pot ... food ... I tired'a he coming and tief, mash-up all me door. So I was waiting fuh he, and I would'a chop he up if I ketch he!'

The old man excitey, itching on the stand, watching Tom Cat, pressing he lips in a line then juking them out. Hopping.

'I would'a chop he up!'

Tom Cat don' even look at he. T'umb he next nose-hole staring out the window. Big Pro cool down Owlie, them jokers in the back laughing and they go on bout 'if he know this man ... how long ... what time he come home from work.' Tom Cat brace forward on the bench and put down his head to sleep. Big Pro tap him to set up. They go on. In a silence, when Teacher busy writing, Tom Cat let out one loud fart. Miss Eyebrow duck she head sniggling and Big Pro jump back, questioning he hand at the man.

Tom Cat start fanning. 'Is dem food allyou giving people inside'a there. Wha' you expec?' Steups. Fanning the sink fart slow over to Big Pro.

Big Pro turn he head shaking it and laughing in he chest. Them other jokers in the back like nothing better. Teacher grunt – ready to continue.

'From where I was hiding in me bedroom, I see when he pass close to de house. He was coming to break-in me door ... Eh? No I couldn'a see he do dat. The door was board up. I had was to nail it with some board cause he had break-out de lock before. From de outside I nail it. But as he open de door and reach inside – I pelt a chop behind he with me cutlass. I would'a chop he tail!'

The old man grapping the air and firing chops, watching Tom Cat in he face, 'You get away, yuh lucky! Chop he up!'

'... No I ain' see he open de door. But he must'e rip out de board with he bare hand! As he reach inside ...' wild chops again.

'Where did the door lead to in the house?' Big Pro rumbling laugh.

'De bedroom, de bedroom.' Owlie turn he hand like he turning a page, gimme next question.

'How far into the house he reach?'

'Ha! He didn't have time reach far, cause as he land inside – I fly behind him. And he run! With de speed he run, he one foot'a shoe left behind. Huh, I would'a kill he ...'

Teacher eyeball him and he ease off.

'What? What he left behind?' Big Pro smiling at he friends in the back.

'He one foot'a shoe!'

That bounce round in the back 'one foot'a shoe, one foot'a shoe!' Big Pro beamsing. 'Where was it?'

'Outside. Heh. The jump, he jump out'a dere, de foot'a shoe end up just outside de door … Well, I went and bring de Police and when I come back I notice de knife rest-down by de door … He had intentions!'

Tom Cat not rumpfled by nuthing, rest he elbows on the back'a the bench and watch the old man stewing. Teacher pick up he papers and signal. Akse Tom Cat if he have any question for the wic'ness. He don' have none. Teacher read out the whole long story, everybody tired'a hearing it, Owlie blinking and tucking he chin after every line.

'Correc,' correc' …'

They shoo Owlie from the stand and he prance down. 'You too tiefing! Big tief you.'

Passing cross in front'a Tom Cat he steupsing loud loud, bending forward and longing he mouth, flouncing heself. Big Pro had to tell him to have better conduc.' Set he down behind we. They looking at notes again. Miss Eyebrow still smiling bout the belch, Teacher playing stric.'

They only give Tom Cat a small charge '… US$250. You get off light today.' They know him well, tired'a seeing he face in court.

Tom shake he head like he get a lump'a idea 'Sir, yuh can't give me a lickle sentence instead'a de fine? I had intentions! I did break-in de door. But you can't gi' me a sentence? I prefer a lickle sentence than to pay de money …'

Teacher huff a half-smile and lean back, looking away.

'… a lickle two months Sir.'

Nobody ain' taking him on. He set back down scratch he head and steups, grumbling. 'I ain' know where allyou expec' people to find money to pay. Humph.' He brace back watching the sea.

Mornin dragging 'eself into the next case.

'Lucille Smith!' A woman get up from a bench behind.

Teacher take off he spectacle, rub he eye and wave she to the stand. She squeeze past, brushing she bumsey on Big Pro desk to step up onto the small box.

'Hold the Bible with yuh right hand,' Miss Eyebrow say from behind she desk.

Make the woman swear to tell the truth. She answer 'I do' soft-soft, put down the Bible and don' know where to look. Put she hands behind and lean back on the government-cream wall. Pro get up slow, scraping the chair and running he finger inside he belt, clearing he chest. Teacher put back on he spectacle and look out the window. He is a Indian-mix man, must'e from Trinidad. Hair stand up, comb back sharp, make he look stric'er. Serious face, eyes quick, he hand tired'a writing.

'Tell the Magistrate your name and where you live.' Pro rumble, swelling he chest and rolling he hand towards Teacher.

She start, Teacher writing it down, the woman talking and looking up at the ceiling, roll she eye to Pro when she finish.

'Do you work?'

'I does vendor work. I have a boutique in Store Bay. Right by the road.'

'Slow down, the Magistrate has to write down everything you say.'

She watch she shoe again and Pro turn to the window and breathe in deep. Important.

'Do you remember the day of the sixth of October 1998?' He stay looking out the window.

'Sixth'a October?' The woman rolling she head quite back now. Pull-in both'a she lips and bite them, look down, check each side'a she jeans-pants.

Big Pro turn to her.

'I t'ink so, heh.' Shame and smiling, getting on like a li'll girl. She almost big-size like Pro. Hair paste back neat, face shining with Vaseline, t-shirt with a gold print spanning, she waist big as she bosom.

'You think so?'

'Oh yeah, yeah I rememba. Un humn yes.'

'Where you was at six-thirty am that day?'

'Six-t'irty in de evening? I was home.'

'No, A.M. In the morning.'

'Oh A.M., right.' Tap she head, hold on the stand and brace forward. 'Yes, in de morning,' she get it, 'I was home. Dat was when Georgie come and tell me dis fella break-in me shop. Georgie does live by me, he ketch ...'

'Hold up! Hold up.'

Them Police in the back chucking small laugh at the woman stupidness. Big Pro heself smiling at Teacher and swelling up he chest to continue.

'You can only say what you saw, only that.'

She watching the fella next to me and he staring back, bold-face.

'Where is your shop located? ... So it's in a part of a big building ... and the building is made up of what?'

'Well, it have some offices and a minimart and ...'

'No, I mean wood or concrete or what?'

'Wall. Is a wall building.' She look at Pro like he should know better since he know the concrete building heself but Pro looking at Miss Eyebrow and they shaking they heads together.

'And the shop is part of this building? How many openings?'

'Opening? I didn't leave nuthing open.'

Gaffles from the back.

'No. Doors.' Roll her on with he hand and turn back to the window.

'Well, it have a sliding door to the front and two half'a door to the back.'

She feel good with she answer, nod and plunk she hands behind she waist. Look down at Pro sideways. She ready again but 'two half'a door' echoing round the back'a the room. A police hold up three fingers and slapping the bench. Pro smiling round. Teacher have to watch the sea for patience.

'So how many doors? Two half'a doors is the top and bottom of one door and the one in front makes two?'

'Yes!' Like this big police couldn't count. 'Two half'a door ...' she pointing top and bottom ' ... and one in front ...' thumb she hand over a shoulder '... two door!' She stance waiting, eyes turn up to the ceiling.

'Now, the doors, how do you secure them?'

She wing a look at he and don' answer.

'How do you lock them to secure them?'

'I does just lock them.' She do a key action in front. 'Is a sliding door, I just lock it.' Turn she key again, more firm.

'No, *how* do you lock it?'

She realise he simple now, that's why he smiling so stupid to heself and the fellas in the back laughing at he. Turn square to him and she hand draw it out 'You does have to pull one side across so, to meet the otha side ...'

Everybody laughing 'cept Teacher and Mr Jacket.

'... and then you does just lock it.' She turn the key again. So simple. Turn up she hands.

'*What* you locking it with? A padlock, a chain?'

'A key! You does lock it with a key!' Do it slow so he can see clearly. Teacher glaring at Big Pro.

'Okay, okay. And the backdoor, the same?'

'Yeah. A next key.'

'Okay so the locks are built in. And what is the front door made of?'

'Glass. Is a glass door.'

'The whole door?'

'Yes. The whole door is glass. Is a glass door.' Draw a big box with she two hand.

'Anything else the door is made up of?'

Teacher take off he spectacle and put down he pen.

'Is a sliding door. It make out'a glass. The whole thing is glass, you could see plain through!' She can't believe that Pro don' know what a sliding door look like. And them jokers starting up again in the back.

'But what is *around* the glass!' He smiling again at Eyebrow. 'The frame, what is the frame made out of? Wood?'

She give up trying with him, look to Teacher for help. 'How it can make out'a wood? Is a sliding door. I sure everybody inside'a here know what a sliding door make out'a. Is not wood.'

Teacher refuse to look in she eye.

'Well what?'

'A silva t'ing what does be round them kind'a door!'

'A metal?'

She fed up. 'Yeah. A silva' metal.' Paint it heavy-hand round the door. Done with that.

'Okay a glass door with a metal frame.' Pro trying to get back to serious.

Teacher pick-up he pen but he ain' writing. He looking at Big Pro like he sorry for him. Mr Jacket was listening all the time, acting as if he reading, now he watch Teacher and turn-up he two hand at him. Teacher fedupsy look pass him straight and go back to the sea.

'The backdoor now. What is that made ...'

The stupidness I have to stay here and listen at, just to wait for mine to call.

'... Do you know Wayne Martin?'

'Yes I do.'

'Where is he?'

'He was breaking into my shop.'

'No, I didn't ask you where he was that day. Now. Where is he now?'

She was already looking at the fella next to me, rocking sheself. And he staring back again, nuthing on he face.

'Where is Wayne Martin now?'

Juk she chin at him and rock some more.

Mr Jacket stand up 'Your Worship ...'

Big Pro say she have to *say* it.

'But look he right dere!' She fly out a hand at the fella. 'Right there. Eh eh!' She waiting again but Teacher and Mr Jacket take enough.

'Yes I think this is wasting time. The other witness is here?'

'No Sir.' Pro mumble, fingering he hat.

'Well, we'll continue this another time ... and talk to your witness before ...' Flap he hand from Pro to the lady '... try and ...'

Pro hold he hat and look down like a small boy. Teacher still flapping he hand and fretting. 'Come down from there ... You can go.'

She still waiting.

'You can go and sit down.' Chase her from the stand and close he eyes, turn to Miss Eyebrow for her to find a date.

Pro and Miss Eyebrow and the rest'a the class shame for the woman, how she can't even answer a few question. But she ain' shame, she don' feel no how. Must be Pro that do something wrong with he big stupid self.

Midday reach. After I setting there all mornin, all they do is to call me name, make me stand up, Pro rumble something and then they tell me I have to come back again. Again. I have to come and waste time. Set down on a hard bench, in a stifling pokey room breathing full'a hot people and listen to all'a that. For a stupid t-shirt. I have to come back again.

Vroom! Vroom!

Klaus de Albuquerque

Masefield Osborne had resided all his life in a little wooden cottage in Belham in the island of Montserrat. He lived with his 80 year-old mother. Masefield was a short wiry man in his late 40s, the kind of man whose age is hard to guess, and who looks the same with each passing year. His most distinguishing feature was a spritely walk. Few people could keep up with Masefield, and he never walked anywhere without driving.

Every morning, except Sunday, after a breakfast of condensed milk sweetened tea, and bread and cheese, Masefield was on the road driving. A familiar sight to all islanders, people would wave to him while driving by, or would wish him good morning when they walked past. Masefield got his share of good natured comments which he took in his stride.

'Luk at Masefield dere. He drivin his caar again witout license.'

'Masefield, watch out dere. Doan exceed de speed limit.'

'Masefield, wat type of petrol yu does use?'

But Masefield just raced on up Happy Hill, smiling, waving, and 'vroom vrooming' away. He could not respond while his engine was running. His steering wheel was a short, well-worn two-foot stick. It doubled as a gear shift. He had one of those old bicycle horns hooked onto his belt which he would blow occasionally when passing stopped cars or if there were goats on the road.

Every morning, precisely at 8.15, Masefield would back onto Belham road, first using his stick to shift into reverse gear and then two-handing it chest high to steer. He would brake by scraping his well-worn tennis shoes on the tarmac, then shift to first gear with great flair, ease off the clutch by lifting his left foot, and then gently coax his car forward with the appropriate engine noise. Since Happy Hill had a steep grade, Masefield used first gear all the way. With his stick held in both hands he steered round the curves. He had to 'vroom vroom' all the way but always got to the crest noticeably unwinded.

Periodically, Masefield had to stop behind a parked car. He would come to a complete stop, shift into neutral, then vigorously shift back into first while gently lifting up his left leg to ease off the clutch. He would blow his horn and proceed. Cars behind him seldom blew their horns. Masefield, although he had not yet devised a rear view mirror, knew instinctively if there was someone behind him wanting to pass. He would wave them on if the road was clear, or signal them if a vehicle was approaching. His hand signals were impeccable – the envy of every driving instructor. Drivers responded by blowing their horn or waving as they drove past.

From Happy Hill to Salem it was a fairly flat stretch. Masefield would shift crisply into second gear, humming smoothly, and concentrating on the bends. He covered this stretch at a kind of trot. It was here that the Nepalese hydraulic engineer, Mr Jayarpanda, would pass him every Monday, Wednesday, and Friday. Masefield would try to avoid eye contact with Mr Jayarpanda, as the latter was liable to take both his hands off the steering wheel of his car and wave madly at Masefield. Mr Jayarpanda was the worst driver on the island. Sometimes Mr Jayarpanda would stop Masefield and, with a concerned expression would ask Masefield in his funny accent:

'Why you always make like you driving? I can take you in car.'

Masefield would always politely refuse and head towards Salem, revving his engine to remind Mr Jayarpanda of the raw power under his bonnet. Mr Jayarpanda was new on the island and had yet to understand the kind of human eccentricities that made small island life tolerable.

As Masefield approached Salem, he would double de-clutch in great style and shift into third. It was 'vroom, vroom, vrooooooom' all the way into town. At Salem he would stop and talk to a few people.

'How is your mudder keeping, Mase?' an old woman would ask him.

'She be fine but hartheritis bother her now and then,' he would reply.

Some young boys would gather around Masefield when they were out on school holidays and beseige him with questions.

'Mase, how com your caar doan have no speedometer?'

'Where your brakes?'

'Where your lights?'

'Why polis doan stop yu?'

Masefield would answer these questions patiently – he had a built in speedometer in his head that told him how fast he was going, his shoes were his brakes, and he did not need lights as he never drove at night.

The police Land Rover would generally pass Masefield most days and the occupants would smile and wave. If Corporal Cooper was in the Land Rover he would always yell:

'Mase, me hav to check your license some time. When yu goan bring your vehicle for inspection?'

Masefield would wave them on and mutter under his breath, 'Go catch tief an lef me alone.'

Masefield would cruise the final stretch between Salem and St Peter at great speed 'vrooming' all the way. It was a wonder his vocal cords held up so well. After a short rest under a canip (known as guinep elsewhere in the Caribbean) tree, Masefield would turn around and head home. When canips were in season, he would knock a few down to eat. He always threw the green outer shell and spit the seeds off the road. He never ate while motoring.

The unsuspecting tourist driving a rental car would sometimes stop Masefield to ask for directions. This was quite inconvenient since Masefield had to stop, shift into neutral, and then using his stick pull up his hand brake. His last act was to switch off his car engine to allow him to talk. In his unfailingly polite manner he would explain how to get to Galways or Kinsale.

Masefield would reach home about 1 p.m. He would slow down, shift into first, and carefully indicate that he was turning left. He would drive into his yard, park his car and put his stick on the small verandah beside the door. His mother served him a large bowl of soup every day with dumplings, Irish potatoes, carrots and calalu. She would use Maggi cubes for the soup base.

Saturday was market day. Masefield would drive carefully to town being very mindful of the traffic and pedestrians. He would blow his horn often and this would sometimes elicit comments.

'Mase, how com yu hab a bicycle horn on yu caar?'

Mase would park his car with great precision – pulling ahead of a parked car and then reversing into a space. He would take the basket from around his neck and head for the market to buy fruit, ground provisions and vegetables. He would sometimes find a live fowl-cock for Sunday dinner. The fowl-cock's legs would have to be tied. It was an odd sight seeing Masefield driving back to Belmont, basket on his head with the fowl-cock peering out. The supermarket was his last stop for bread, tea, condensed milk, cheese, butter, maggi soup cubes, macaroni, sugar, flour, raisins and Uncle Ben's rice. His mother had a little garden where she grew calalu, carrots, pigeon peas, Irish potatoes, tomatoes, green onions, thyme, and pumpkins.

On Sunday Masefield walked to church holding his mother's hand. The car stayed parked all day. For Sunday dinner his mother would prepare a fowl-cock stew with rice and peas and ducana. Masefield never went out at night and was never known to take a drink. He had been a good student at school, worked for five years with the Public Works Department, and quietly resigned one day.

Six months later he took up driving. At first, this attracted a lot of comments with people calling him 'maad' or a 'crazy-ant' and suggesting he see Dr Kelsick. But soon islanders realised that Masefield the 'driver' was the same Mase they had always known. The 'crazy-ant' comments gave way to accommodating Masefield's make believe 'cyaar,' and to good-natured teasing.

In 20 years, Masefield never missed a day in his six-day driving schedule, except for a two-week period when he was recovering from a nail-chook (puncture) to his foot. Normally a very careful driver, Masefield was distracted by a stalled lorry one day as he was coming down Happy Hill headed for home. As he passed the lorry, he turned to look back and unfortunately his left foot stepped on a board with a nail. Masefield had to switch off his car and limp home painfully. The next day with his foot swollen, he hobbled to the hospital where Dr Persaud cleaned and dressed his foot, gave him a tetanus shot, and advised him not to drive for two weeks.

The next few days people who used the Belmont road regularly asked, 'Yu seen Mase, wonder wha happen to him?' Those who knew would respond, 'I hear he get a nail-chook.'

Even Corporal Cooper stopped in to see him at his cottage. When Mase returned to his regular route he was greeted by enthusiastic waves and shouts of, 'Glad to see yu back.'

Shades

Philip Nanton

Shades is what I does call him. He doan take them off, neva, neva, neva. De colour of de plastic that he see tru' is green-gole – the way he must does see the world. He beard twis' up in one lang, lang everlasting grey plat. An watch de shoes. Ah say watch de shoes. They probably wan time belang to somebody else. Cast arfs. The back mash down and cut arf, coolin' de heels. And de bottom sole wear right dung on de two outside and dey stop steep steep. So he stand, on two tiny wooden hillocks. Yes, I does know hillocks. I did read hillocks in a book one time and I like de word hillocks. Hillocks, hillocks, hillocks ... Dat wha' mek the shape of dese slopey, slopey shoes.

He does wear neat, neat overalls, yu' hear, and dey clean clean of a marning. If dey clean! Cut yu' han on de crease if yu' pass over it. Dey almos' bright, with shart, wide sleeve-hole fo' de arms. In dey tell yu' dat he lean an' strang. A nasty old money belt tie up an' hold everyting together in de middle. But de teet man, is de teet a wah gi' he way. When he talk, which is everlasting unto marning, de yellow flash wid de gole, it a mout o' Credit Union investment wha' miss de necessary dental work fi cover depreciation.

He stand in front a li'l wooden table on the road side with slats on tap, in dese he ha de funnel, strainer and plenty see-through battle. Two crocus bag hang off de front of de table, empty mout' waiting.

By de time I does reach to him of a Sundi marnin' is usually one big show. He audience stan around on de pavement, near the edge o' the road, mek a half-circle. Sun hat no arse bu' wha fo' do? Stan' up dere and tek she blows an check de scene. But I does always say Gard is good and patience is my right arm, which is a virtue.

When it come to cutting nut now, some hold the nut near they chest. Some chap it on the ground. Mr Shades stan wid he back always facing de audience cause show going on. All we seeing is overalls, hillock shoes, the rasta tam and the plat swinging side to side. De legs wide apart, an de knees ben' like he riding invisible horse. De lef' han' raise to him ches.' He hold de nut in the palm of dis hand – almost show off like. As he spin it like a basket-ball player, he flick it with thumb and wrist. Wid de right he chap, backhand, wid a sharp, sweet blade cutlass. Spin chap. Spin chap. Spin chap whip, whap, whap. Husk flying all 'bout de place. Sometimes with the last chap de right leg cack arf and raise up a li'l off the ground for the *coup de gras*, a say *coup de gras*, I a Frenchiefied creole family lang time.

But each nut tek at the most only tree, four chap. Den he turn de right wrist over and gouge tree small nick wid de cutlass point, plick, plick, plick; flick and is water fo' days. Then you hear de talk 'Is nat anybody could chap nut. Some cut down. Some cut cross. It have one man in St James he does cut all behind he back. Pussanally I say dat is axing fo' trouble. I use backhand ... I coming to you now, daddy. (Spin chop) ... ease m' up in d' cyar man, is m' trade (spin chop) ... Ssssst! Ssssst! Look she passin' dey, she looking nice ... she look too sweet ... Want some nuts darlin'? ... I gat plenty ... Gi meh a piece nuh ... Ah say gi meh, gi meh nuh ... Daddy is a reg'lar, is he bottle. (Spin chop) Daddy, buy meh a Guinness nah? You want d' bottle, daddy, ain't? (Spin chop) ... Daddy say he want he bottle. You in d' cyar wan' bottle now. Dis nex' man a look a nut. See m' troubles. Spar, take a jelly, nuh. Ah know yo' would a like it ... Cool it ah coming jus jus now.

We nat family. Definitely nat family. But he always call me 'Daddy.' At fus' me nah know how fi take this name he a gi me. We look de same age, so I believe he making sport, easing up from all dat chapping, nut spinning and right foot raising. Then again, 'daddy' could be respec' like, so 'daddy' is the mos' I can expect from he. I buy dat.

As I says Gard is good an patience is me right han' which is mercyful but de problem, though, is wid de line. Sweet Jesus I doan warn t' call no bad word near people yard but is damn 'tupidness. When you an' me an' more stan' round Shades, an' a next baddy come up again, who know where de line start an end? Shades heself doan even know. He chap a nut gi it one fella. Knock it back. Money in de pouch. He garn. Nex, car pull up. Lady jump out. 'Rasta, it have nut?' Boot fly open, five six nut fling in dere; behind she hear harn blowing in she arse, money cross palm, she garn. Fo people like me, patient, Gad fearing battle people, is we dey scrunting to raas ...

... You have a point but I suppose that he DOES try. But to give the process its specificity, as this is partly an issue of business management, it's the 'bottleneck around the point of sales.' That is the problem. A little like the 'united colors of Benetton,' juggling its short diverse lines. Probably not how he in the green and gold shades would put it, but it means much the same. It seems to me that ... 'Shades' ... that is his name, is it? ... very apt ... well, Mr Shades has a constant juggle with slightly different client interests. First, there is the passing trade. They take it straight from the nut. No messing about here. They pay, throw their heads back, down the water and drop the empty nut to join the debris already there on the ground and they're off. Some of us, you and me, we are strictly bottle people. We are the illegals. We are the ones sneaking out on a Sunday morning. We're evading the health and safety requirements of the official world. The government wants to stop this behaviour because private recycling is considered, not to put too fine a point on it, unhealthy. But business is business and like dodgy accounting practices, noise pollution, unprotected sex, blasphemy, and Lord knows how many other misdemeanours which have been officially outlawed or frowned on, it has not stopped.

In fact, Shades keeps a handy supply of empty plastic bottles for those of us who are even too lazy to bring our own. It takes five or six nuts to fill each of our bottles. We do nod to hygiene because Shades always rinses the top, screws down the whole thing and anoints the full bottle from another, filled with tap water, before he hands it over with 'arrite dar, mo time' or some such. To keep us stoics happy while we wait for all this to happen, he shaves a spoon off the edge of an empty nut, cuts it open and we enjoy some free jelly while we wait.

But what makes us patient bottle people restless and very, very upset, is the car drivers. They treat the business as a bloody MacDonald's drive through; except, of course, it's on the edge of the main road. They expect quick service. They use the excuse of the build up of traffic, the honking of horns. They rely on the exasperation rising behind them as they hustle a quick bottle or a boot-load of nuts. So, when there's a rush on, this is Shades' big problem. Who to serve first? The casuals, the stoics or the car drivers? How to practice management skills and keep us all satisfied? Truth is, he doesn't always do it very well. Sometimes he can't chop fast enough to fill a bottle, slake a thirst and argue with a car driver.

There is probably a training course for this log jam somewhere in the world and probably a management guru with a sharp suit, power point presentation and solution waiting to deliver it. For the moment, we have to do without their help. Simultaneously, I want my bottle, the nice lady in the car wants her nuts in her boot and bald head next to me could commit murder for a drink. It's most unsatisfactory …

PERFORMANCES

Soufrière

Shake Keane

Part One of *The Volcano Suite*
(written after St Vincent's volcanic eruption in 1979)

The thing split Good Friday in two
and that good new morning groaned
and snapped
like breaking an old habit

Within minutes
people
who had always been leaving nowhere
began arriving nowhere
entire lives stuffed in pillow-cases
and used plastic bags
naked children suddenly transformed
into citizens

'Ologists with their guilty little instruments
were already oozing about the mountainsides
bravely
and by radio

(As a prelude to resurrection and brotherly love
you can't beat ructions and eruptions)

Flies ran away from the scene of the crime
and crouched like Pilate
in the secret places of my house
washing their hands

Thirty grains of sulphur
panicked off the phone
when it rang

Mysterious people ordered
other mysterious people
to go to mysterious places
'immediately'

I wondered about the old woman
who had walked back to hell
to wash her Sunday clothes

All the grey-long day
music
credible and incredibly beautiful
came over the radio
while the mountain refreshed itself

Someone who lives
inside a microphone
kept things in order

Three children
in unspectacular rags
a single bowl of grey dust between them
tried to manure the future
round a young plum tree

The island put a white mask
over its face
coughed cool as history
and fell in love with itself

A bus travelling heavy
cramped as Calvary
thrust its panic into the side of a hovel
and then the evening's blanket
sent like some strange gift from abroad
was rent by lightning

After a dream
of rancid hope and Guyana rice
I awoke to hear
that the nation had given itself
two hundred thousand dollars

The leaves did not glisten when wet

An old friend
phoned from Ireland
to ask about the future
my Empire cigarettes
have lately been tasting of sulphur
I told her that.

Oval Lime

Simon Lee

A few tentative blasts from a conch shell echo across the empty pitch. Dawn begins to creep above town and a slight breeze promises to shift the rain clouds.

3.56 a.m.: I PEER hurriedly at the luminous video clock and a rush of panic carries me out into the pre-dawn. Monte Grande sleeps under a fine drizzle. The rain will stop, it has to stop, I'll get a ticket we'll lick down Pakistan and … What if I don't get a ticket, will they carry the match on TV? I hear there are thousands sleeping outside the Oval.

4.30 a.m.: Independence Square and I get lucky; counting my change from the maxi man in the pale neon light I discover he's given me a $20 for a $1! He's gone already and that lucky feeling soon evaporates when I wake the sleeping taxi driver in Woodford Square and he complacently informs me that when he dropped his first fares at 3.20 a.m. there was a crowd half way round the Oval queueing for Grounds.

5.00 a.m.: At the cricket shrine, I studiously ignore the line tailing back out of sight and, mustering my best bold-face style, approach the gate immediately opposite and thrust my press card through the small hole. In the midst of my silent rehearsal of pleas to be allowed to buy a ticket comes the loud click of padlock released, the unravelling of chain and the heavy gates miraculously swing open. Speechless, I stumble into the floodlit Oval suppressing the urge to jump and yell in delight. I quickly lose myself on the other side of the ground before the mistake is discovered and I am unceremoniously ejected!

5.40 a.m.: My sleepy eyes – now accustomed to the glare – take in the crowd which is already arranging itself in the stands. A few tentative blasts from a conch shell echo across the empty pitch. Dawn begins to creep above town and a slight breeze promises to shift the rainclouds hovering in the St Ann's hills. Armed with coffee, I climb to the top of the Sir Learie Constantine stand, the road below full of anxious traffic.

6.15 a.m.: Down on the cycle track a Trini section is quarrelling, with rum-inspired vociferousness, through the wire fence with two visiting St Lucians: 'Yuh see Lara, allwe could call him Lara allyuh had to call him SIR!' To add emphasis to his point, a small red man launches himself at the fence until a partner twice his size bear hugs him away. The St Lucians, half away through their first bottle of Vat, grin and wave their flag.

Nuts Landing, resplendent in short cream jacket and tie, is making his rounds like a hyperactive waiter while the throng continues to pour in armed with heavy coolers, pots and boxes steaming with pelau and other Oval fare. Rum is being consumed below for that special cricket head, while on the top of the stands the heady aroma of marijuana floats by.

I doze amid desultory games of All Fours and 'ole talk till the ground staff emerge at 6.50 a.m. to remover the covers. The first sun of the day shines but soon the umbrellas are back up again and the old Spanish man in front of me hits a hard black and white to chase away the damp.

8.00 a.m.: Tension is mounting and the Pakistan team lope round the pitch to appreciative roars. The Oval posse swings into gear, bells ringing. The West Indies follow – Ambrose and Lara to standing ovations.

Two well-attired white gentlemen (panama hats, MCC hatbands, navy blue blazers – one in white flannels and bow tie, the other in grey flannels and club tie) consult sagely on the wicket. I surmise *Grey Flannels* is Geoff Boycott of stone-walling fame. He scuffs at the wicket, prodding with an expert toe, while the old Spanish man roundly curses him for arrogance that seems to have earned him international antipathy: 'Yuh hear he commentary in Jamaica? Is only a pack of s… he talkin. He feel he is de onliest man who does know bout cricket. Dey shoulda cut he arse!' Everything in good time, Spanish.

Bow Tie, it transpires, is no less than that jolly fine chap, Henry Blofeld, hailed to my left as 'the best commentator in the world.' I silently confess to enjoying this old-world turn of phrase.

9.00 a.m.: I decide to make a last spin and ease the concrete-bruised buttocks before the match gets started. Back at the top of Constantine I watch a street drama unfold. A riderless police horse is cavorting wildly in the road. With a fling of the head he breaks his halter to the delight of a small crowd gathered at the top of the steps. A stout mounted policeman dismounts and attempts to calm him. Loud jeers from above. The horse backs frenziedly, throwing off the policeman whose angry expletives reach us on the wind. A casual limer stretches out his hand to the horse, patting and then stroking its head till it calms. 'Now dat is horseman!' The small crowd exclaims approvingly and from its safe vantage turns to taunting the embarrassed policeman.

9.25 a.m.: En route to my place I pass the legendary *Jumbo* – pelter of nuts extraordinary. His fame and new-won affluence reflected not only in his colourful style and heavy gold chains but also the presence of two young helpers. Like a born star he strikes several poses for the benefit of the camera.

I purchase a piece of foam and am seated in time to hear that West Indies won the toss and are sending Pakistan in to bat. The first over is bowled in a blaze of sunshine.

10.00 a.m.: Six overs gone and I'm restless with confinement. Down on the cycle track I meet my partner, the teacher from Holy Name who has taken advantage of the 'Cricket Holiday.' Accepting his kind offer of liquid refreshment, I park up, while he keeps me abreast of the score, which for all my myopic squinting only resembles algebraic equations.

Soon I am off wandering again below the stands, savouring the smells of many lunches in the cooking. I bounce up an old police partner from the east with his silver trumpet slung around his waist. Authoritatively he orders me over. I decline. He approaches and, his large moustaches parting in a grin, upbraids me boisterously: 'Yuh see yuh, yuh does like tuh enjoy yuhself too much.' Having learnt long ago not to answer back to those in uniform, I raise my arms wordlessly and protest mildly that I'm working.

I slip back to the match in time to see Trinidadians, Ian Bishop and Phil Simmons, dispatch the first two batsmen. Now that is cricket.

11.30 a.m.: Rain is down and, for many, this is the opportunity for an early lunch. Flotillas of drunk spectators lurch by grabbing for roti or a refill.

On the cycle track, after the rain, I spy the familiar form of my friend the photographer, perched on a Carib case in front of his tripod, floppy Richie Richardson hat in place. 'Got any good shots?' I query professionally. 'If I haven't I'm gonna throw away the camera,' he grunts in equally professional tones.

To our left are the St Lucians who have draped their flag on the wire fence. They keep up a steady barrage of heckling: 'Don't touch that flag!' as it whips in our faces. Their bottle of Vat is all but empty, their heads pleasantly fired and we return their verbal sallies good humouredly. So engrossed are we in passing picong, we miss the next three wickets, though, by the time another falls, I am ready to leap off the track triumphantly throwing my planter's hat skyward.

Lunchtime: Assured the score is 194 for 7 after 45 overs, I wander beneath the stands light-headed. The previous night of excited dreams is beginning to take its toll. A diminutive girl (a sixth former also on a cricket holiday?) complains through her tooth brace about the vile behaviour of her neighbours in the stand: 'When my friends drink they know their limits. But those people come to make a public spectacle of themselves … Why pay money to come and see cricket, all you're doing is picking up man?' Ah yes, the Oval Lime: so diverse, so perverse.

I encounter an extremely polite and pale-faced Englishman, one Philip Pedley, who proudly informs me he's here on tour with the Oundle School Under 15 cricket team from Northants. 'Round them up,' I tell him in a rush of nostalgia, 'and I'll take their picture.' Soon, I am faced with a collection of equally polite English adolescents, a species I haven't encountered for some years. They have apparently doled out some good licks to local schoolboy teams (unlike their senior national side I muse) and are Bimward-bound. Amid some friendly Trini heckling Mr Pedley tells of the great time they've had and the friendly people. His only wish – that they could spend another week here. Agreeing, I advise him to return for Carnival when he can meet the donkey.

After lunch: I assume my customary spot at the top of the Republic Bank youth stand. Unlike previous occasions when forced to retire with heat stroke/sunburn I am armed with sunscreen. Sinking into my foam I relax to the pleasant sight of the West Indies as they stroke play with the Prince of Port of Spain apparently immoveable, steadily totting up the runs.

3.00 p.m.: The afternoon settles itself and to the right of the scoreboard a brass section strikes up. As alcoholic torpor sets in, a ragged Trini wave, all iridescent colour and loud guffaw, radiates the ground. The trumpetman urges the wavers on.

On the level below, a fat Indian is wining for everyone's entertainment, his hips swivelling to the steady rhythm of spoon on bottle. A young man with mauve bandana invites all to 'Pick a pan,' Mastana Bahar style, and then launches into some scurrilous extempo. The winer man conducts a complicated percussive movement before collapsing.

Back on top, a very sunburnt Englishman, whom I had seen drifting through the lunchtime throng, plants himself unsteadily by my side. I make friendly noises about the dangers of sunstroke and in a passing fit of generosity offer him some sunscreen. His Vat-infused, watery blue eyes attempt unsuccessfully to meet mine. (I hasten to add neither Vat-infused nor blue.) Taking me for some cheap hustler no doubt, he refuses my offer, says he has his own. Looking at the gaping patches of raw flesh on his legs I wonder why he doesn't use it.

Dismissing me, he turns his attention to more important matters, conjuring forth from his plastic bag a flask of Vat. My neighbour and I exchange knowing smiles and I hum the old Noel Coward tune, making slight amendments to the lyrics: 'Mad Dogs and Englishmen get drunk in the noonday sun.'

Back to the game. The elegant Hooper goes first ball lbw – 'like a dunce,' growls my neighbour from Arima. Now it's up to another Trinidadian duo to save the day. Little Gus strides to the wicket. Unfortunately, he doesn't remain long enough to make a difference.

4.50 pm: The lobster-red Englishman, having dozed fitfully through his 10-over stint, wakes and plunges for the iron staircase. Reports reach us his plunge took him all the way down to the ground and, peering over the edge, we see him sleeping at the bottom of the stand oblivious to the tension mounting all around him. 'He had a right to be so sunburnt de way he does sleep away,' growls grizzly from Arima.

With 14 runs for a win, the crowd is urging Lara on with every stroke, hoping for another century that this time eludes him, as the winning score comes first.

Resisting the temptation to join the pitch invaders, I amble across the Queen's Park turf as the sky begins to streak with violet, savouring the last moments of my Oval Lime. I won't lapse into tastelessness and tell you what I saw another Oval Limer up to in my partner's garden on the slow walk back into town.

Barbados, Where Life Is a Musical

Robert Edison Sandiford

Life in the Caribbean, to many outside the Caribbean (and a good many in it, too), is a carnival, a festival, a fete – African bacchanal! Trinidad has the steel pan and *the* Carnival. Jamaica stirs a wicked Calabash of words and reggae. In St Lucia and Dominica, the flavour is Creole. And in beautiful Barbados we have Crop Over's Kadooment. Visitors come to know the winding rotations of the island through this one-day street-party jump-up of increasingly massive proportions. This is so much the case that 'locals' often define themselves culturally in these terms. It's as if the rhythm of the annual Crop Over festival can't be distinguished from the everyday reality of their lives.

Yes and no – this is true, and yet not true. If anything, life in the Caribbean – in Barbados, at least – is a musical, a form I've grown rather ambivalent about over the years, particularly as a staid Canadian of sensible Barbadian stock.

There is this tendency to burst spontaneously into song – whether young or old, in public or private, male or female, when a tune one likes is played. For a stoically self-conscious people, fearful of even the slightest public embarrassment or perceived slight, Bajans absolutely free up when presented with their favourite hits.

I'm in a ZR van – a public transportation route taxi – and I'm heading into Bridgetown. Suddenly (after eight years of living in the island and countless visits prior to this, I'm still not expecting it) I hear the schoolboy beside me crank up like a low rumble before I hear the chanting from the ZR's brash radio. The ZRs almost always have music, almost always played loudly.

It used to be uncool for boys to sing in public places, outside the shower or bedroom, unless they were part of a band. Air guitar was as far as it went for the pretenders. Now here sits this schoolboy, who has, in fact, already started to lose his mother's features with the sprouting of some scraggly corn on his chin, mouthing the words to a song I don't know or can't comprehend by Buju Banton or Beenie Man, twisting his hair absently, like a sky-larking poet.

My Mom, a Bajan and a retired nurse, used to warn me that talking to yourself out loud was a sure sign of mental instability. 'Doing that would land you in Jenkins,' she said, always using the old name for what is now known as The Psychiatric Hospital. 'Particularly if you were arguing with yourself.' If this was true, then what was singing to yourself a sign of? Surely of something more than an overheated musical imagination.

Walk down Broad Street in Bridgetown, Barbados's capital city, any time of day or night, and you'll hear a 'local' singing audibly to himself: dub, gospel, 'mellow mood' music, so-called *oldie goldies*, or the latest calypso. More remarkable: these walking jukeboxes often know all the words to the song they're singing.

It's hard to stop someone from singing when they know all the words to the song. In a government office, I once entered stage left for an appointment, presenting myself to the robust receptionist. 'Good morning,' she began to answer. Chris de Burgh's 'Lady in Red' started to play. Our exchange became a reluctant recitative.

'*I've never seen you looking so lovely as you did tonight* ...You're here to see ...?'

'Mrs ...'

'*And when you turned to me and smiled, you took my breath a-way* ... Go straight down the hall, turn right, ask for...'

'Straight down the hall, turn right ...'

'*My Lady in reeeeeeeeeeed* ... *is dancing with me* ... *cheek to cheek* ...Yes.'

'Thank you.'

'You're welcome.'

She – we – never missed a beat. And this is where the whole musical thing becomes insidious. Before you know it, you're no longer an extra. You've got lines, a bit part – you've moved from the background to the foreground – singing along with the rest of the cast and crew, no longer mouthing to the voice in your head. You've joined the chorus, and you didn't even know you were part of the choir.

There are probably as many karaoke bars across the island of Barbados as there are rumshops. In fact, a number of bars and restaurants serve up songfests with their fried flying fish and shots of Mount Gay that are fiercely, laughably contested. Television shows have been made out of these events. A popular one, hosted by a one-time politician, has been *Carry Yuh Own Key*. Courts, one of the island's leading furniture stores, has had its own version of the popular American talent show *Star Search*. You can perform with any God-given gift, but most participants come to sing. Though crooning for cash, appliances and gift certificates, I doubt the size of the prize would make much difference in participant turnout. Everyone wants to be a star, a singing sensation: a Celine or Luther or Skeeter Davis. Or Harry Belafonte.

I've seen a man, full grown, hardback, ducking to the dub, beating out the bass, slapping out the beat on his thighs, his locks wild, getting into that ghetto jungle rhythm being strummed on a Spanish guitar. And that's the thing: all this public performance goes beyond humming, foot-stomping or pretend-playing. What gets you is that it's completely unselfconscious, unpractised, unstudied. It could be another form of that fabled Bajan pride, which has been interpreted as arrogance – *I may not be able to sing, but I like this song, and you can't stop me from singing it, right here, right now* – but people burst into song, fearless and foolish, as if on New York's Broadway or in London's West End. But there is no fear of the smiling, singing native here, of that minstrelly caricature who taps and tumbles for a living. Because you could be in the most public of places, at a checkout line in a Bridgetown shop. There's piped-in music from the public address system, or maybe somebody just has on a radio under the counter. A song comes on – it's Lil' Rick's 2002 Crop Over calypso hit 'Doan Tell Muh So.'

And everybody starts to sing: men, women and children, including the cashier, who stops everything she's doing to turn up the radio, pump up the volume. Voices rise, like a rumble, a gathering storm, with thunderous force and conviction: *Oh, no, where have we gone wrong …?* All thoughts of whatever else is happening in the world around you are briefly forgotten. The song is now more important than any service, any conversation, any items you've come to purchase. The song, whether you want it to or not, *becomes* the transaction, the desired exchange, the very goods themselves.

Shakespeare Mas'

Rob Leyshon

*'How many ages hence
Shall this our lofty scene be acted over,
In states unborn and accents yet unknown.'*

I should never have left Grenada in this weather. I should have taken the tiny plane. What the hell was I thinking?

I was thinking of saving my wretched skin, that's what.

Once before I'd taken the shuddering, boiling-hot six-seater. Bear in mind we're talking about a plane so tiny that all your luggage has to be piled on your lap, so tiny that you're virtually riding pillion with the pilot, close enough to see the sweat-stains under his armpits, the pimples on his neck. I'd spent the entire flight with my eyes and teeth clenched in a dreadful grimace, certain that if I stopped concentrating for even a single second the little engines would cut out followed by a terrible moment of silence before the screeching plunge into oblivion.

When, at last, we somehow managed to land and I'd grovelled on the tarmac and sobbed out my gratitude to the travel-gods for allowing me to live, I made a vow: Never again. *Never* again. Next time I'd go by water.

So that's why I'm here on the deck of the *Osprey*, the ferry to Carriacou, in the middle of a shrieking gale. We're lurching through the swell, plunging into trough after trough. But strangely enough, this time I *want* to die. I want to be put out of my misery. The sea's mountainous, a dirty grey, choppy mess streaked with foam, the sky's an unbroken sheet of stinking pitch and, on the seat opposite me, sprawls a skinny guy who's swigging from a bottle of Jack Iron. We're the only passengers up here on the drenched deck. He peers over at me, grins and raises a thumb. His face is pinched, whiskery, like an old rat's. I scowl back. I'm in absolutely no mood to be chummy. He bawls something at me, jerks the same bony thumb towards the side of the boat, laughs and winks clownishly, guzzles some more rum, then emits a big fat belch into the howling wind. It occurs to me that, if I could move, I'd like to get up and tip him overboard. But the storm is up, all is on the hazard, and it's impossible to stand on this wildly-bucking bronco. The only thing about me that can move in this world of incessant motion is my gorge, which I begin to feel heaving yet again into my mouth. O Cassius, I am sick ...

* * *

'This guy ... he go into the room before the Mas' ... he shy, he don't say much ... but the moment he put on his face ... I tell you, he come out a tiger, a lion, a god! A *god*, man!'

The words are Winston Fleary's, the night I first ran into him in St George's. I was drinking in the Carenage Bar, my favourite hangout when I'm in the Grenadian capital. It's a typical seaport dive, full of sailors and drug-dealers and artists and whores and pimps and politicians and various other criminals – the perfect place to kill a few hours in other words, but very hot and rowdy, and I'd come outside for a breath of fresh air. On the bench next to me was an old fellow reading a book – a book that turned out to be *Julius Caesar*. So we got to talking and, over the next few hours by the glittering waterfront, I sat spellbound while Fleary gave me a crash-course on the Carriacou Shakespeare Mas': its history, its form, its language, its cultural significance – every blasted thing, down to the last astonishing detail.

Yet it was the graphic image of the beast-god which really gripped me: of the quiet man putting on a mask, summoning a denizen of the spirit-world and instantly transforming into something quite literally awful. It was an image beyond metaphor; it was metaphor sliding close to the brink of metamorphosis, towards full incarnation. Fleary's words had conjured up some kind of potent reworking of an *egungun* ancestral rite, a Caribbean fusion of Shango and Shakespeare. I was enthralled to the point of rapture, like a bug-eyed fanatic discovering a new cult.

But that was seven or more years ago. What about this morning: is this a beast-like transfiguration I see before me, stalking through the buzzing crowd at Brunswick crossroads? Is this the embodied *orisha* I'd envisioned, a lion or tiger of wrath?

No. It's Donkey.

Mr Alfred Duncan: a mild-mannered 40 year-old municipal groundsman, loving father to a teenage daughter, pillar of his local church, known to everyone in Carriacou as 'Donkey.' For over a decade he's been the undisputed Shakespeare Mas' champion (or *king*), not only of his home village of Brunswick but of the whole of Carriacou, which means that Alfred 'Donkey' Duncan is a truly formidable character: a donkey of wrath, indeed. And the *king*'s here to do battle for his crown once again.

He comes to a halt and the crowd falls silent. In his full Mas' regalia he cuts a striking figure, and is quite unrecognisable as the tender-hearted Mr Duncan.

The first thing you notice is his mask (or *face*). Constructed out of screen-wire, painted pinkish-white, with the features roughly drawn in black ink, it's a big, crude-looking object: the eyes are misshapen blank circles, the nose and mouth mere vertical and horizontal slashes. You might think this crudeness would be comical, but it's not: it's ugly and menacing – deliberately so, of course. Because this is a *face* designed to intimidate.

It's designed to protect, too, like a duelling mask. One lash from his opponent's whip (or *bull*) could slice Donkey's flesh to shreds, a fact which also explains his need for a cape, or *crown*. This is a long, painted swathe of heavy material (a cement-bag, actually) rising up from the top of his head and draped down over his shoulders and back.

Below this he's wearing a dazzlingly bright, loose-fitting shirt (or *chemise*) made up of overlapping triangular segments of red and black fabric, which goes over an old-fashioned white cotton petticoat, the kind his granny might (and for all I know did) wear. This, in turn, goes over some heavy-duty black breeches which are tucked into long red stockings. On his feet – a bizarre anachronism – are a pair of very stylish brand-name running shoes. With a *bull* in his gloved right hand and a small bell in his left, his battle gear is complete.

So there he stands, King Donkey at the crossroads, awaiting his first challenger. His body is utterly still, but his masked head, grotesquely enlarged by the cresting *crown*, moves slowly from side to side. The effect is chilling – like a snake, a hooded cobra maybe, reared-up and poised to strike. The empty eye-sockets of his *face* stare at us coldly.

The crowd stirs. Something is happening behind us. I spin round. You can almost smell the wave of excitement thrilling through the crush of bodies.

'Lennox, what's going on? I can't see.'

Lennox Caliste towers over everyone and can see everything. He looks down at me and grins wolfishly, smacking his baseball bat, his peacemaker's *bois*, into the meaty palm of his hand.

'Six Roads come. Clash start!'

But now I can hear it for myself: a violent shouting and stamping, getting louder by the second. The crowd starts to push and jostle, craning their necks to get a better look. I feel an elbow jabbing me in the kidneys, and I'm about to give a shove back when suddenly the crowd gives way directly before me, and at last we can all see. Coming up fast, surrounded by his posse of screaming supporters or *backers*, is the *king* of Six Roads.

He's about the same height as Donkey, but of much heavier build, a big shambling bear of a man. Apart from a few minor variations in colouring – some splashes of green on his *chemise*, red rather than black insulating tape wrapped around his *bull* – his gear is identical. But it's his mask I can't take my eyes off as he sweeps by, just a few feet in front of me. More detailed and more skilfully drawn than Donkey's, it's a genuinely terrifying thing. With its gaping mouth crammed with great yellow teeth and its dead eyes, it's a *face* from the world of nightmare.

As the two warriors close in on each other we move up behind, forming a ragged ring, a stick-lickers' *gayelle*, hemming them in. I glance swiftly around me, and notice three things. First, everyone is carrying some kind of potential weapon: a stick, a stone, a bottle. Second, everyone over 60 seems to be wearing a baseball cap. Third, everyone – young or old, male or female, from the little wrinkled white-haired lady opposite to the dude in cornrows and cargo-pants standing next to me – shares precisely the same expression. You see it in their eyes, and I'm positive they can see it in mine too: the fierce eager gleam of anticipated violence. It's not a pretty sight, but then we're not a pretty crowd. In fact we're not a crowd at all anymore; we've become a mob. Forget Hollywood. Our Shakespeare's not in love, he's at *war*. This is *calinda*! The warriors want blood, and so do we.

Good words are better than bad blows, says the noble Brutus. But in the Shakespeare Mas' we want both: good words *and* bad blows. We want to hear the words soaring and see the blows flying, we want our man, our *chantuelle*, to crush his opponent, to chastise him with lashes and kill him with words, to fight for the honour of our village, of Brunswick or Six Roads, for the honour of our clan, the honour of our blood.

The Six Roads challenger steps forward. Donkey remains absolutely motionless. The challenger rings his bell and a hush falls. The *clash* has begun. First, the formal exchange of courtesies.

The Six Roads man is the first to speak. His voice is strong, though muffled by his *face*.

'Will you relate to me the speech about Caesar's will?'

Donkey lets the words hang in the air. Then, at last, he makes a move, very slowly shifting his weight on to his back foot and tilting his body and *face* backwards while raising his *bull* in warning. It's the classic defence posture.

Donkey rings his bell before he starts to speak.

It's always a shock for me to hear Donkey's voice again, because it's a hesitant, shaky, indeed barely audible mutter. It sounds nothing remotely like what you'd imagine a reigning Mas' *king*'s voice to sound like. If you didn't know better, you'd think it was the voice of a man scared out of his wits. Everyone here, however – including the challenger – knows the real reason for Donkey's apparently timid voice. Not fear, obviously, and not *clash* strategy either (though I'd once suspected it to be a kind of oral feint). No, it's something altogether more remarkable.

But now the *king* of Six Roads launches into his first speech. He's chosen wisely, for this is merely a warm-up, a short speech to loosen his tongue.

> 'Here **is** the will, and under Caesar's seal.
> To **ev**ery Roman citizen he gives,
> To **ev**ery several man, seventy-five drachmas ...'

It's a good start. His delivery's confident and fluent, and his *backers* urge him on.

> 'Brave!'
> 'Tell him!'
> 'That's right!'

He moves on, seamlessly, to Antony's next speech.

> 'More**over**, he hath left you all his walks,
> His **pri**vate arbours, and new-planted orchards,

On ***this*** side Tiber; he hath left them you,
And ***to*** your heirs for ever: common pleasures,
To ***walk*** abroad and recreate yourselves.
Here ***was*** a Caesar! When comes such another?'

A roar goes up from the Six Roads crew. Their man's spoken flawlessly, word-perfect and in the approved Mas' style. That is, he's bellowed out the words at the top of his voice, placing heavy stress on the second syllable of each line – a kind of vocal stamp – along with an actual stamp of his right foot. I catch sight of Fleary. He sees me too and raises his hand. He'll have been listening as intently as Donkey to the challenger's speech, but his face is inscrutable as always, so what he thinks of it I can't tell. Not bad for a Six Roads man, perhaps.

Now it's Donkey's turn. Six Roads man steps forward. He rings his bell, and announces his challenge.

'Will you relate to me Cassius' speech about Caesar and he legs?'

The Six Roads man rings his bell again. We press forward. We know what's coming. Without warning, Donkey springs forward, his *crown* flaring out behind him like a lion's mane. He's right up in the challenger's *face*, almost head-butting it. Before our eyes he seems to have grown, looming like a storm-cloud over the challenger. His whole body's tensed, coiled, charged with a predator's ferocity. He raises his *bull*.

'WHY, ***MAN***, HE DOTH BE***STRIDE*** THE NARROW ***WORLD***
LIKE ***A*** COLOSSUS, ***AND*** WE PETTY ***MEN***
WALK ***UNDER*** HIS HUGE ***LEGS***, AND PEEP A***BOUT***
TO ***FIND*** OURSELVES DIS***HON***OURABLE ***GRAVES***.'

Suddenly, it's pandemonium all around me. We're screaming, jumping, clashing sticks against cans, stones against bottles. We can't help it, because the change in Donkey's voice is extraordinary. The shy mumble has vanished and become the voice of a giant, of a colossus indeed, rich and deep and rolling, gushing up from the depths of his stomach, pouring out of his mouth in an unstoppable flood.

'Words, man, words!'

'Power!'

'Hail Caesar!'

And, through the din, the words keep coming, relentless, each of the triple-inflections crashing like a bludgeon into the *face* of the challenger. I see Miller and Walston hooting and tossing up their caps high into the air, Lennox is pounding the earth rhythmically with his baseball bat; even Winston is nodding and smiling, his eyes shining.

At last the thunderous speech comes to an end. Donkey steps back, as gracefully as a *kabuki* dancer-warrior. Now it's the turn of the man from Six Roads again, this time a speech by Brutus from near the end of the play (or *book* as everyone here calls it). Then Donkey recites again, and then the challenger, and each time he speaks accurately, but you can tell he's beginning to struggle; much of the stuffing has clearly been knocked out of him by Donkey's terrific onslaught. And so it goes on, for an hour or more, this battle at the crossroads under a scorching sun, back and forth, attack and defence, challenge and response, with the challenger gradually running out of steam and out of speeches, while Donkey, who knows the *book* by heart, seems only to grow in power and authority with every speech, with every line, with every word.

But the mob is getting restless. We want the *king* to kill off the challenger. Even the Six Roads *backers* want it. We've had enough words. It's time for blows, for bacchanal. And this is how it happens.

The challenger is half-way through the most famous speech in the play, Antony's first oration in the market-place. Though it's long at 35 lines, it's also relatively easy to memorise. For this reason it tends to be the speech a Mas' man uses as a kind of lifebelt when he's flagging, something safe to clutch on to. The trouble is, we all know that's what it is: a sign of vulnerability, a distress signal. And as the most familiar speech to everyone here, it's certain that any mistake the player makes will be pounced on instantly.

He's into the last third of the speech. His voice is hoarse now, his breathing heavy, his delivery monotonous and ragged. All the assured stresses and stamps of earlier have vanished. He's clearly trying to focus all his dwindling energies on remembering the words, but the pauses between the line-breaks are getting longer and longer. He's losing it, and the mob smells blood. We close in, crowding him, mocking him. And directly in front of him stands Donkey, cool and composed, biding his time, just a whip's length away.

At last, inevitably, the challenger stumbles.

> 'Yet Brutus says he was ambitious,
> And Brutus is an honourable man.
> You all did see that on the ...'

He tries again.

> 'You all did see that on the ...'

He shakes his big head wearily, a bear in the pit, at the end of his tether. His hideous *face* has somehow been drained of all its horror and now looks merely laughable, a child's fright-mask. Donkey raises his bull. The mob quietens.

'*Lupercal.*'

His voice isn't loud. It's cold and measured and deadly, each syllable like the slicing of a ritual-knife. *Lu-per-cal*. The challenger waits for the final stroke. Attached to the front of his *chemise* is a piece of fabric in the shape of a black heart. Donkey taps the heart lightly with the tip of his *bull*. It's a curiously playful gesture after all the passion that's just been spent, the ceremonial *coup* of the victor. Donkey's about to turn away when the Six Roads man (to the great joy of those of us panting for licks) does something both unceremonial and utterly reckless.

The front of Donkey's *chemise* is covered with glittering mirrors made of small patches of silver-foil. These are primarily adornments, but their vaguely metallic look hints at something else too; a stylised representation of a piece of armour, like a Roman centurion's breastplate. As Donkey is turning, the challenger flicks out his *bull* and catches one of the mirrors. The blow is clearly petulant rather than bellicose, but the mob instantly explodes. And so does Donkey.

Swivelling on his hip, he brings his *bull* smashing down on to the challenger's head, nearly knocking him to the ground. The challenger gives a grunt of pain and tries to back off but he's pushed back by the screaming mob straight into Donkey's tremendous back-hand slash. The challenger drops to his knees, cowering under his *crown*, but if he thinks that's going to save him he's sorely mistaken, because Donkey has only just started his chastisement.

'IF *YOU* HAVE *TEARS*, PRE*PARE* TO *SHED* THEM *NOW*!'

It's perfect. Kept in reserve till now, till the very end, like a virtuoso holding back his most brilliant piece for the encore: Antony's speech over Caesar's corpse, thundered out by King Donkey over the remains of his challenger. Incredibly, he seems to have been able to turn up the volume on his voice-box yet one more notch. The bottled-up furies of the last few hours are unlocked and the glorious drumbeat of the pentameter comes pumping out at full throttle, each of the five crunching iambs punctuated by a vicious lash of the *bull* and a bloodcurdling howl from the mob.

'O, *WHAT* A *FALL* WAS *THERE*, MY *COUNT*RYMEN!'
'*LASH* HIM!'
'*LICK* HIM!'
'*BEAT* HIM!'
'*KILL* HIM!'
'*TEAR* HIM!'

'O, *NOW* YOU *WEEP*, AND *I* PER*CEIVE* YOU *FEEL*!'
'*BUS'* HIM!'
'*RIP* HIM!'
'*TEAR* HIM!'
'*TEAR* HIM!'
'*TEAR* HIM!'

And with the blood thumping in my head, thrillingly abandoned now to the will of the mob, I howl too, in an atavistic delirium, and I laugh as I howl, like a lunatic, until at last Lennox steps in as peacemaker and moves to pull Donkey off his prey – Donkey Duncan the Mas' *king* who speaks with the voice of an avenging angel; the *king* who at all other times apart from the Mas' suffers from a crippling stammer, a binding spell on his tongue that only Shakespeare's words can loosen; the Mas' *king* who at this moment is truly our champion, our beast-god, still trying with all his might to do what we all yearn to do as we howl and laugh, what only the mighty presence of Lennox and his baseball bat prevents us from doing: rend the challenger with words and whip, hew him as a carcass fit for hounds, carve him as a dish fit for the gods. *Bacchanal*! *Tear him! Tear him! Tear him to shreds! Tear him for his bad verses*!

On d' beat

Philip Nanton

... lef ri lef ri ... d' government boots ... d' government boots ... this is the radio programme of your national police force hand in hand let's build our land ... it's inspector mcconnel bringing you on d' beat and i have a whole mouthful for you ... the police is of course your friend and we sharing information with you the public ... today we zero in on prevention with my good friend inspector james head of fire but before we goes to inspector james who i am sure you all know well from his other exploits tell them something about yourself inspector everybody knows who you is quite well in that department don't be shy i'm sure they know inspector james get pick for islands many times and come a selector now felicitous seasons greetings to you inspector mcconnel and a pleasant good morning to you too and to all the listeners out there this morning but before we talk with inspector james about fire and such what went on this weekend and what's happening around and about our beautiful island ... lef ri lef ri ... hand in hand to build a better land ... a white man visiting our blessed island just as he was leaving a night club in the capital at two forty-tree a.m. saturday gone two young boys push a revolver in he face as he reach his car door they stole $782 e c from the man it behoves me to say that a couple of good citizens came to the aid of the police and so with their help we identified and apprehended the two vagabonds as they call them and they were caught and arrested in a matter of hours in fact it took one and tree quarters of an hour to be precise as to the time it took and at the bottom end of town we find the revolver too we must get these firearms out of the hands of youngsters and vagabonds who will use them indiscriminately i'm sure most of the information we give is useful a next thing now was a tragic accident on the brighton road where the driver of car p 986 capsize over the bank at anderson's corner and was found in the wee hours wandering by the roadside in a dazed and confused manner his passenger was in a bad way and was rushed to hospital and sadly died a tragic accident and here I must offer my cond'lences to the passenger family may god rest his soul what a thing caused by rushing thither and hither i had cause to mention this before about drink and drive and check your brakes a next thing again something that is happening every year at this time of year it have a lot of smart boys tempting people all over town with the tree card game i telling everybody straight don't come to town and get involve in no tree card game when you involve yourself in this tree card game don't come and cry to the police especially you women stay way from it if you come to the police about this game we will arrest you because you not suppose to play that game it is against the law so put your money away as it will come in useful in two thousand and tree on the twenty fuss look out for the police band at layou on the twenty second it at the clinic four p m sharp then at the governor general house for kiddies party at five thirty and on the twenty third oh the twenty third is in-house business heh heh heh so anyway it's a whole mouthful today and the police is of course your friend ... lef ri lef ri ... hand in hand let's build de land and before we go to inspector james for a word on fire i must say congrats to inspector james who was just a sergeant till recently and he now elevate to inspector and i must say congrats also to sergeant belingey and sergeant prescod who also now elevate to inspector good let's look at fire as its Christmas we talking safety measures to safeguard your home for now for the season and for the future so inspector james what has it been like for fires this year this year was good for fires inspector mcconnel i mean to say last year we had one hundred and fifty seven fires to december nine inst compare to one hundred and tree this year to date which is a sixty five percentage point reported decrease house fires thirty eight last year this time fourteen bush fires last year one hundred and tree this year thirty six that is very commendable inspector james it is indeed very heartening inspector macconnel of course we must thank god and nature to have spared us but i guess that you are a very happy man inspector james let me stop you there one moment inspector james a caller is on the line ... hello ... hello caller ... yes hello this is on d' beat working hand in hand ... what ... no ... no he's not ... i tell you he's not there ... ok that caller did not want on d' beat so what cause the bush fire well people willy-nilly setting fire to bush and house fire what responsible for that well with more wall house it have less fire but often you find is really carelessness what cause it so we in fire department want to share some tips many start in the kitchen is a place everyone frequent where appliances of all sort and type could catch one of the things occur now a days in the kitchen is the ham and next thing you know children expose to hot burnings the neighbour call you and you forget the pan on the fire sometimes in the kitchen it have paint oil insexticides which burn easily so don't leave things willy-nilly and go and talk to your neighbour because children can push objects off the stove and sometimes electricals cause shack persons who drink and smoke should be extra careful at this time of year definitely inspector james we in the bedroom now what happen here heh heh heh well one thing that happen there at this time of year is people who have left our shores come back home and they not sitting down like long time the men especially they on the job night and day with they electric drills and bits fixing fairy lights christmas tree lights lights here and there all round the house and everywhere but they have to watch they step because they leave it on all night as they want to see the light flashing when they asleep so they have to get an electrician to fix it up in case it short ... lef ri lef ri ... the government boots the government boots ...

How I Got My Vodou Visa

Simon Lee

It was the sound of the drums that brought me here.

I met Haiti's leading 'Vodou Beat' band, Boukman Eksperyans, on tour in Trinidad. After an afternoon listening to the Boukman drummers trade cataclysmic rhythms with Trinidadian counterparts from the Shango sect, which shares common West African roots with vodou, I had no choice but to respond to Haiti's summons from across the Caribbean.

'Haiti is 80 per cent Roman Catholic and 100 per cent vodou.' I am sitting in a modest house in the Impasse Coumbite on a hill above downtown Port-au-Prince, sharing a corner with a battery of wooden drums, the goatskins held taut with wooden pegs. My host is Aboudja Derenoncourt, ABC's resident Haitian cameraman, master drummer and Vodou Emperor, or high-ranking priest. 'Vodou,' he continues 'is not just a religion, it's a way of life.' Aboudja confirms what I've long suspected – that vodou is fundamental to any real understanding of Haiti. The term encompasses not only the religion with its rituals of sacrifice, song, dance and drumming, but also a philosophy, a healing system and various forms of artistic expression.

The practice of worshipping ancestors and spirits who mediate between natural, supernatural and human worlds, originates among the Fon, Yoruba and Ewe peoples in an area which stretches along the

Bight of Benin, from present day Ghana in the west, to Nigeria and Togo in the east. The word *vodou* comes from the Fon word for god: *vodu*. The Congo word for spirits, *loa*, has survived in Haiti as *lwa*, referring to the vodou pantheon, also known as 'mysteres,' (mysteries), 'anges' (angels) or saints, according to the region.

Animal sacrifice (bulls, sheep and chicken) was traditionally made to the spirits to invoke their help. Priests guided initiates in their dealings with the spirits, who delivered their messages by possessing or 'riding' an initiate, hence the term 'horse.' In Africa, spirits belonged to a particular place, but once transplanted to Haiti, it was the spirits of the Kingdom of Dahomey (today's Republic of Benin) which emerged as dominant in the collective process of syncretisation which created vodou. In the harsh conditions of the French slave colony of Saint Domingue, a new 'nation' of spirits or *lwas* was called into being, to join the African 'nations' of Rada and Congo spirits. The meeting of runaway slaves and oppressed Taino Indians gave birth to the Petro *lwas*, a group of spirits characterised by their aggression. They were conceived to express the rage of slavery and to lead the revolt against it. It was a Petro ceremony at Bois Caiman, on August 14, 1791, presided over by Boukman, the Jamaican born *houngan* or vodou priest, which marked the beginning of the slave revolt against France.

This insurrection, infused with the spiritual power of vodou, culminated, in 1804, in the defeat of Napoleon's forces and the first ever declaration of independence of a former slave colony. But Haiti's successful revolt sent tremors throughout the Caribbean colonies and the Southern slave-owning states, which retaliated by isolating and stigmatising the newly-independent country. This process was helped by a series of inept and corrupt political administrations, while vodou itself, divorced from the underlying philosophy and sensationalised by exotic travel writers or Hollywood B movies, was stereotyped as black magic

I go in search of Edgar Jean-Louis, an old sequin artist, who, since the 1970s, has been painstakingly creating *dwapo vodou*, the intricate flags of the *lwas* used in the opening ritual of vodou ceremonies. I track him down to the Rue des Cesars, near the church of Our Lady of Perpetual Succour, amid the mud and decaying garbage of Bel Air. A tall man of great dignity, he ushers me up to his workshop, where two splendid untreated mango wood coffins are ranged behind his trestle work table. Edgar is also in the funeral business, so it's no surprise to find him working on a flag of Baron La Croix, the guardian of cemeteries. Over the design, which he has drawn freehand on a toile base, he is sewing a background layer of sequins, after which he'll sew the glass beads on top. The completed three foot-square flag will be mounted on a satin background. The thousands of glass beads and sequins of the *dwapo* are all hand sewn to create the kinetically sparkling 'vevers' or designs, which represent the various *lwas*.

Edgar says the designs are brought to him by his guiding spirits: 'The flags are a mystery. It was St Jacques Majeur and Erzulie who gave me the mystery of the flags.' He explains how each *lwa* is associated with a colour: Simbi, the spirit of fresh water, with green; Ogou, the war spirit, with red; white for Dambala, the life force spirit. As we talk, Edgar's son Jocelyn sits absorbed in his task of converting a print of the Virgin Mary into her vodou counterpart, Erzulie, goddess of love.

The Code Noir, introduced by the French to regulate slavery in 1685, stipulated that slaves be baptised Roman Catholic and all other religions banned. Faced with a choice between the bible and the whip, the slaves opted for baptism. But the spirits simply re-emerged in new guises as they syncretised with the Catholic saints: St Joseph represents Loko, spirit of healing; St Patrick, known for banishing the snakes from Ireland, became Dambala, whose sign is the serpent, and St John the Baptist was assimilated with Chongo, spirit of luck.

A few nights later, I'm at the Oloffson Hotel, Port-au-Prince's and possibly the Caribbean's most famous hotel. Immortalised in Graham Greene's novel *The Comedians* as the Hotel Trianon, this fantastic gothic gingerbead folly also inspired cartoonist Charles Adams' eerie imagination. I'm here with the haute bourgeoisie – *gwos manges* in Haitian creole – who've descended from their high-walled hilltop mansions. International aid workers, writers, artists and journalists have assembled to hear Ram, the Vodou Beat or Mizik Rasin (Roots Music) band, formed by Haitian-American Richard Morse, who also runs the hotel. Mizik Rasin developed in the late Seventies and Eighties when young musicians studied traditional vodou music and began blending vodou songs and rhythms with contemporary transnational music – funk, rock, reggae – to produce a compelling new sound. 'The Rasin bands are pretty much garage bands,' jokes Richard, 'but I've been hanging with ceremonial drummers.' Sure enough, when Ram blast into action they are powered by the drums. Soon the lobby and the black and white Escher tiled verandah are awash with dancers. As momentum builds, whisky and Barbancourt rum bottles are abandoned on the tables as people clamber onto chairs for a glimpse of the band, driven by the lead vocals and dancing of Richard's beautiful wife, Lunise.

If the Ram concert was popular vodou culture for the elite, the ceremony I attend for Erzulie Dantour two nights later, is strictly roots. My friend Michel has arranged to pick me up outside the Holiday Inn, on the edge of the sprawling Champ de Mars in the centre of Port-au-Prince. When I arrive there's a sea of people stretching from the roadside to where the trees and darkness swallow them. Brightly coloured Rara flags wave above the heads of the crowd. On this January night in the run up to carnival, the Misik Rasin bands are giving a free concert for what seems like the whole of Port-au-Prince. Miraculously, Michel emerges from the melée and we head for the outlying district of Carrefour and the peristyle of the Societe Nouvelle.

The sky blue walls of the temple are adorned with paintings of the saints; tinsel and paper Christmas decorations hang from the green, yellow, red and white rafters. The *po-mitan* – the all important centre pole down which the spirits descend to earth – is constructed of three drums, red, white and green, one on top of the other. We take our seats close to the burgundy damask-covered altar, presided over by a black doll, representing Erzulie Dantour, whose day we're here to celebrate. She's obviously a spirit with refined tastes, as the offerings of champagne, cognac, wine, rum, cinzano, brandy, vermouth, creme de cacao, cigars and bottles of perfume which crowd the altar attest. Her sweet tooth is catered for with plates of marshmallows and petit fours and several heavily-iced cakes.

A relaxed atmosphere prevails among the predominantly working class celebrants, who sit chatting and smoking, awaiting the start of the ceremony. Behind me, two men in African dress suck abstractedly on lollipops. After some tentative rolls, the drums at the far end of the peristyle pick up speed and the invocation to Legba, guardian of the gate between the spirit world and this one, can be heard. Two *hounsis* (initiates) circle the *po-mitan*, one with an *asson*, (sacred rattle) in one hand and a sequin covered libation bottle in the other; the second carrying a candle. The female *hounsis* who now crowd the floor begin a series of complex call and response songs, each song sung and danced to its own rhythm.

After midnight, the *hounsis* exchange their everyday clothes for ceremonial dress, national colours of red and blue with some white. When they're joined by the male *hounsis*, the ceremony becomes more colourful and intense. The singing, dancing and drumming never cease, only pausing momentarily in the cycle before plunging onwards. The atmosphere, though charged, remains relaxed among the observers, who imbibe small shots of herb-infused rum. Even the *houngan* takes time out to sit and smoke a cigarette before returning to the thick of the ceremony.

Then, at 2 a.m., a girl in the audience goes into spasms; a female *hounsi* writhes in the dust; another apparently glides across the floor at hip level, one leg stretched out in front. Erzulie Dantour is riding the devotees. It seems possession is contagious and many *hounsis*, eyeballs rolled back, collapse in the laps of the spectators. Erzulie descends on the *houngan*, who is swiftly supported by two worshippers who bind his head with a blue bandana. The drums power on relentlessly. I can still hear them echoing as we drive off into the predawn.

My first experience of vodou, I realise, is that of an outside observer, but three months later I'm lucky to be able to take up Aboudja's invitation to attend Haiti's oldest vodou ceremony – the six days and nights celebration of the Dahomey rites at Souvenance. I arrive in Port-au-Prince on Good Friday. Before the sun rises over the city next morning, we're bouncing through potholes on the road north to Gonaives, in Aboudja's four-wheel drive landcruiser. In the lush Artibonite Valley small boys bathe naked in the irrigation ditches.

After St Marc, it's sometimes easier driving on the shoulder and certainly safer, as trucks, trays packed with passengers, head straight for us. We pass a bus upended in the ditch as we press on through the dusty streets of Gonaives, where the triumphant ex-slaves declared their independence in 1804. Above the plain of Gonaives rise the bare stripped hills. When the wind blows it's difficult to see further than your outstretched hand through the swirling dust. (In 2004, the erosion led to disastrous flooding and thousands were made homeless.)

Finally, we reach the Lakou Sovenans. At first sight, the vodou compound resembles an African village with its mud-walled, millet-thatched huts, dominated by the large temple, Souvenance Mystique, in the centre. Aboudja explains that different locations in the compound represent towns in the ancient Kingdom of Dahomey. Although the names of the towns have now been forgotten, the ceremonies the towns held for separate *lwas* are still celebrated. Here in Souvenance, the *lwas* and their initiates are divided into two camps, Hunters and Warriors, a division some think goes back to the days of the Franco-Haitian war. Each camp has its own songs and dances.

A small walled enclosure opposite the peristile is the park of Ayison, a *lwa* who lives alone, neither hunter nor warrior but belonging to both camps. Fernand Bien Amie, the Serviteur or high priest responsible for conducting the ceremonies, tells me that, 'Ayison is a symbol of freedom, who represents the universe,' and that, 'in any ceremony, after calling Legba, you have to call Ayison.'

A massive tamarind tree on the edge of the open space in front of the peristile is dedicated to Ogou the warrior spirit. A small pond next to it is reserved for the spirit Zammadonn, while a larger pool behind the peristile is for Atchasou, who is associated with Damballa. I take a rest in the mud hut I've been assigned. The millet pallet is surprisingly comfortable. Returning from a stroll through the compound later, I find a black pig rooting underneath it who obviously thinks it's his dinner.

By nightfall, the *hounsis* have gathered in the peristile in their ceremonial white, which Aboudja tells me is worn to summon power for the ceremonies. They've been chanting all afternoon and some are already in a trance. Welcoming songs are sung in Fon. Then a procession sets off for the entrance to the Lakou, following the Serviteur who stands head and shoulders above everyone. He walks with a slow bouncing gait, carrying a candle in one hand and a large enamel libation mug in the other. The *hounsis* begin to chant: 'Papa Legba open the gate for us.'

The Serviteur moves in slow step out into the dusty track leading to the Lakou, pouring a libation to Legba in the dirt. Re-entering the compound he pours a libation before the 'admirals of the drums,' the master drummers whose inconceivabe energy will keep the *hounsis* singing and dancing for the next five nights. The ceremony has now begun and in the peristile, the *hounsis* dance till long after midnight.

By five in the morning they are back in an inner room, to emerge after dawn, their white vestments splashed with sacrificial goats' blood, ready for a day of sacrifices to the *lwas* of the compound. After the ceremony for Ayison, a large black bull is led through the crowd to be secured by the horns to Ogou's tamarind tree, whose trunk is wrapped in a blue and red flag bearing the legend 'fraternity.' A machete placed on the bull's neck is pounded in for the coup de grace and while glasses of sacrificial blood are given to the ritual slaughterers, the *hounsis* circle the tree, dipping their cutlasses in the blood. As the ceremony moves on to honour Zamadonn, the bull is skinned.

By dusk the sacrifices to Ayison, Ogou, Zamadonn, Atchasou and Damballah are complete and the *hounsis* have exchanged their white vestments for a riot of individual colour. While the majority of the *hounsis* are local peasants, the spectators represent a broad cross section of Haitian society. There are writers, artists and musicians (I spot a couple of musicians from Boukman Eksperyans) and many have made the pilgrimage from the US for the ceremony.

The crowd in the compound has been growing all day and several thousand are packed tight to see the Serviteur with his satin sash of national colours: blue and red, fringed with gold, flanked by the Haitian flag and the pale blue flag of the Societe Belle Etoile. The Souvenance congregation lead a procession round the tamarind tree of Ogou, the warrior spirit. In the failing daylight the colours are intense. The ceremony is a fusion of elements propelled by the drums, sustained by the call and response songs. Many *hounsis* and spectators alike have been possessed by the different *lwas*, yet, in this context of devotion and joyous celebration, possession is not in the least intimidating.

Although none of the *lwas* choose to ride me as their horse, I do get caught in the spirit of possession which now rules the Lakou. Since my arrival I keep bumping into a petite, fiery *hounsi* from Gonaives, whose eye unfailingly catches mine, even in the thick of the impassioned peristyle communal dances. Tonight, as she steps shining with sweat from the temple, she takes my hand in hers and moments later we're on the millet mat in her hut, exploring and merging with each other to the rhythms of the drums, which thunder through the earth and our bodies. Much later, when the realisation surfaces that initiates aren't supposed to have sex during ceremonies, she reassures me we have the spirits' blessing. After a long period of self-imposed abstinence, she's been praying to the presiding spirit of the compound to send her a *ti-gason* and apparently I am the answer to her prayers.

When the serviteur knocks on her door in the morning, I scramble to hide under the mat, envisioning my vodou visa being cancelled on the spot and being drummed out of the compound. But the serviteur is magnanimous, following his morning greeting with an invitation to return for next year's ceremony. Whatever rhythm it was that brought me and the *hounsi* together in our celebratory dance (I like to think it was Erzulie Freda's, goddess of love, whose magenta ceremonial scarf I'd travelled with), the drum is vodou's seminal instrument. In the Rada rites of Souvenance there are three: the *manman* (mother) played with one hand and a hammer shaped stick called *agida*; the *segon*, played with a straight stick and a half moon shaped stick (*abara*), plays intricate dialogues with the *manman's* low register which leads and choreographs the dance; the smallest drum, the *boula* or *katabou*, played with two straight sticks, plays a regular pattern coinciding with the strokes of a bell. Rattles (*ason*) are used by the *oungans* and *mambos* (priests and priestesses).

Of all the amazing Souvenance ceremonies, perhaps the Tuesday night Asoto ceremony, commemorating the drums brought from Dahomey, is the most striking. Two chest-high Asoto drums, wrapped in red cloth, are brought to the centre of the peristile, forming the centrepiece for a ritual of homage which swiftly develops into a series of highly specialised formation dances, performed by several hundred *hounsis*, many of whom are possessed. The peristile reverberates not only to the crashing thunder of the drums but the hollow thud of many feet pounding in unison on the mud floor. The colours of the dancers' scarves make kinetic patterns as they move, plain scarves in the colours of the *lwas*: red, turquoise, yellow, green and purple, and many others decorated with polka dots and paisley or floral motifs.

A woman in burning orange spreadeagles her arms and goes whirling round a circle which has formed to watch two men face off. Their heads go down; one foot is kicked forward and then flicked back before the feet cross momentarily in the front. A leg is lifted till the knee is perpendicular to the ground before being swung back in a flashing arc. Tonight, two women get to take a place in front of the *katabou* drum, supplying the regular beat for the dancers. Singing and drumming are essential elements of devotion, 'holy work,' and if one function of the vodou ceremony is to provide a beautiful entertainment for the spirits, with food, drink, song and dance, the ceremonies are highly successful.

By the time Friday morning comes, and, along with the rest of the Belle Etoile congregation, I've received the Serviteur's blessing, I'm exhausted. At the same time, I'm infinitely enriched. As we bump back south toward Port-au-Prince, I give serious thought to Aboudja's invitation to the 15 day and night ceremony held at Soukri Danach for the Congo *lwas*. As the presiding Emperor there, he assures me, 'It's a real party.'

I Mus' Play Mas

Kim Robinson

I sit on the plane heading south from Kingston to Port of Spain for Trinidad Carnival. I am travelling alone. The friend who should have accompanied me had to cancel at the last minute. It does not matter. I am on my way to Carnival. That is all that matters.

For me this annual trek to Carnival is – dare I say it – something of a personal pilgrimage. Carnival is my main stress reliever. Carnival – with all its insanity – is what keeps me sane.

'It keeps me balanced,' I hear another Jamaican saying as we stand in the Immigration line at Piarco Airport. He is explaining to a friend why he has found a way of coming to Carnival nearly every year since 1978. He is the high-powered CEO of one of our largest private sector companies, so this must take some doing.

It takes some doing for me too. I try to remember how many times I have been to Carnival. I know my first was in 1981, and I know that I haven't been able to make it every year since then, but I also know that it has had to be something pretty serious to stop me: high-risk pregnancy or childbirth, for example. Illness? No, that stopped me once and I won't make that mistake again. No money? A way will always be found.

What is it about Carnival that is so addictive? Part of the answer hits me as I step out of Customs and am greeted by my Trinidadian friends.

Immediately, the jokes are flying Trini style, I am laughing, and within minutes, guess what, I am making jokes too. It's a me that I haven't seen ... well, not since my last Carnival.

The jokes continue to fly as we drive into the city. As my friends stop to pick up tickets for tonight's fete, a car swings in front of us. It is Brian Lara, world record-breaking batsman, a friend of my friends. Next thing I know, we are liming with Lara at his mansion overlooking the Savannah. In between innumerable cell phone conversations, he tells us some of his plans for his big fete on Carnival Sunday. He has organised the pilau and the roti and the curry and the bake and shark. He has booked Machel. He has printed 1,000 tickets. My friends immediately put in their order. We need four. No, make that 10. No, make that 20. Urgent calls are placed. 'You want tickets? Tell me now, I up by Lara, I could get them for you, they going fast!'

I love my crazy Trini friends. I love Trinidad.

People love Carnival for different reasons. My friend the CEO, for example, comes primarily for pan. 'A hundred people surrounding you, all playing – it's like bathing in music.' Others come for the calypso tents, the spectacular shows: Costume King and Queen finals, Dimanche Gras, watching the mas bands from the stands in the Savannah on Carnival Tuesday.

I come to fete, and I come to play mas.

The fetes come fast and furious. Wednesday night: the Oval; Thursday night: Anchorage; Friday night: Ambassador; Saturday evening: Penny Commissiong; Sunday evening: Lara. The time in between fetes is spent liming – and laughing. As I proceed from day to day, or rather from night to night, my absorption of the Carnival mood and Carnival madness is slow and steady. The first two nights are good, great, even, but no, not *stupendously* great, I tell myself, the music isn't quite as good as last year, or maybe I'm getting old ... I don't *have* to come back next year, next year I'll give the break to my family instead of myself.

But, by Day Three, the music is in my blood and I find that my feet are constantly tapping from when I get out of bed till I go back to it the next day; and by Day Five, Lara's fete, I am floating under the spell of Machel in my own exquisite world of ecstasy.

Then (too soon, too soon, because it means the end is near) we have reached Days Six and Seven: time to play mas.

I am 'playing Poison,' i.e. playing mas with Poison, a large band (some 2,500–3,000 players) one of the three most popular bands. Poison is known as the good-time party band – the opposite end of the spectrum from the high art of Minshall. This year Minshall's players are wearing black or white overalls: at the climax of the mas the two groups will meet up and spray each other with black or white paint. The theme: 'All ah we is one.' Nice theme – 'deep, deep,' as my Trini friend acknowledges; and everyone should experience playing with Minshall at least once. I played Minshall's 'River' in 1983 and it was unforgettable: a sea of white, highlighted by brown skins. I will play Minshall again. But this year I don't want deep. I want *pretty* (read mindless, superficial) mas.

And Poison is certainly pretty. The costumes in the 15 plus sections, an incredible array of vivid colours, are all dazzlingly beautiful – and dazzlingly skimpy. I don my silver and gold sequinned, bejewelled bikini costume with its plumed, jewelled headdress and look at myself in the mirror: well, not as good as last year, but it could be worse. In fact, the bottom line, as I knew even as I spent the last few months trying to reduce my own bottom lines in preparing for this moment – extra abs, extra twists, extra leg raises – is that those extra inches really don't matter.

Because I will be on the road playing mas in a mass of women – there are always very few men – and the women will be of all shapes and sizes: some slim, some fat, some firm, some flabby, some with big breasts, some with no breasts, some with big behinds, some with no behinds, some with big bellies, some with flat bellies, some nubile, some middle-aged, some old. In this mass of female flesh – some black, some white, some red, some yellow, all quivering and rippling – how I, or any one person looks, will not matter. In my outrageously skimpy costume, in my state of near-nakedness, I will be anonymous.

The music starts. The band moves off; and a surge of women, punctuated by a few male bodies, flows down the streets of Woodbrook. The mas has started.

The day progresses. The sun beats down. I lose my friends. It does not matter. The music carries us – chipping en masse behind the music trucks till 8 p.m. on Carnival Monday, and back at 7 a.m. the following day.

At midday on Carnival Tuesday our band is in a long line of bands waiting to get onstage at the Savannah – we have been waiting in one spot for four hours, 3,000 revellers in blazing colours, standing in the burning sun. We are feeling no pain. We are as sun-drunk as we are liquor-drunk, and the music is getting sweeter and sweeter. A music truck pulls up alongside us; two shirtless men – young, beautiful, well pec'd, well ab'd – are standing on the top singing and moving their waists in a way only Trinis can. I hear Machel's 'United Nations,' and my hips start to undulate in my version of a chutney-soca-dancehall wine.

The two women beside me give me approving nods. 'Where's our section?' one asks. Our costumes identify us as being in the same section within the band and we need to find it before we cross the stage. It is nowhere in sight – in fact in my two days on the road I have never seen it – but with a band the size of ours that is no cause for alarm: it will find us eventually.

In any case, I know that the question itself means little, that it is the gesture, the connection, the acknowledgement of sisterhood that matters. I shrug and smile at her, taking a swig of my ice-cold Carib beer bought for me by a friendly Canadian stranger who has since disappeared. She smiles back. Then she gets absorbed in the music and performs her pure Trini wine. She is performing not for her friend, not for fellow mas players like myself, not for the onlookers who line the street. She is performing for herself.

This is what it is all about, then, amidst all the spectacle, the grandeur, the colour, the art, the music: a celebration of womanhood, a celebration of sisterhood, a celebration of female independence, a celebration of female liberation, a celebration of female sexuality, a celebration of the female body with all its imperfections.

> Yes, I ready to get on bad
> Yes, I ready to mash up the yard

Or, as another female calypsonian puts it:

> De iron have me so basodee...
> De winin' will never stop
> Inside o' de mas....

And as the winin' continues, I am energised, rejuvenated.

RETROSPECTIVES

What Sweet Goat Mout Today Does Burn He Bam-Bam Tomorrow: Selling the Bahamas

Ian Bethell Bennett

The Bahamian islands have been described as places that time forgot. How I wish this were true. I think back to growing up on those little two by four islands and wonder where the time was that forgot them. Some of my favourite places have been catapulted into the 21st century without so much as an apology. But we all want progress, even if it comes at the cost of losing what we love.

When I was a child in the Bahamas things weren't easy. The water would go daily, the electricity too, and often the telephone. Life has come a long way since then. We even get high-quality fruit and vegetables now, unlike the fluffy apples that seemed to have sat around some other place for months before arriving as if by chance in our food shops. All of this was in the city, where we couldn't walk the streets by ourselves for fear of traffic, bad people or some other evil. All of this was inexplicable to me as the tramps were well known by everyone, and everybody knew how they became the way they were. Nonetheless, the city was a life of children cannot do … So, when it was time to go to the islands – as we did practically every holiday – it was exciting. We would set out in our little 19 foot boat for Eleuthera, the Exuma Cays, or my favourite, Harbour Island. I have maintained a relationship with that island all my life.

Harbour Island, or Briland as it's also known, was paradise for a young, spirited child who wanted nothing more than to run and play and chase lizards or chickens or whatever else was running – we tended not to mess around with the goats too much. We would arrive in Harbour Island and we would be set free. We children could run wherever we wanted, swim, fish, play to our heart's content. In those days there were perhaps two cars on the island, so the dangers were minimal. Everyone knew everyone, and everyone watched everyone else's children. Of course, that meant that we could get beaten by anyone older if we were naughty. Harbour Island had its drawbacks too, but they were minor. No electricity meant that bedtime came early, but by then we were usually so tired that it didn't really matter. No television, no street lights that I can remember. But life was bliss. And so it went for years. The adventures on Harbour Island were hair-curling, but the main effect on me as a child was that my hair would be bright red from the sun by the time we left.

Slowly, Harbour Island started to change. More people started coming, more different children, but it was still paradise. You still had to speak to everyone whom you might run into in the streets. Neglecting to speak to someone we passed meant punishment. That hasn't changed, even today.

Soon I was off to university and Harbour Island was far away. I lost touch with it for a while. My nightmare was always that I would land in the middle of Harbour Island and not know how to find my way around. After university, trips resumed, only now it was different. I was different. We were all different. All of a sudden nightlife was important, and while it wasn't Nassau, Harbour Island gave Nassau some stiff competition. Nights would be spent at Gusty's, a bar on a hillside with sand on the floor and a great view. In those days, we would walk through the Tip to get there quickly, or commandeer someone's golf cart. Today the Tip is gone and the huge foul snakes that would hangout around it are gone too. But Gusty's remains. Then there was the WICOM, in the heart of the Ghetto; well, Harbour Island style. Valentine's bar was one of the early afternoon favourites. Sadly, it too met its demise in one of the hurricanes, destroyed by a fire.

Back then, mainland Eleuthera seemed large and 'far away' but now it's as much a part of my Harbour Island time as is Harbour Island. It's now easy to get to Briland. Before, we had to search out someone with a boat or beg to get the money to go up on the old rickety mail boat that made the return trip once a week, usually leaving Nassau on a Thursday morning, arriving in Harbour Island four, five or six hours later, sometimes even seven depending on if it stopped first in Spanish Wells on the way and, if so, how much freight it had to offload. We would return early Sunday morning, hungover or not having gone to bed. In those days we skipped sleep for bar-hopping, beaching, skinny dipping and watching the sun rise, particularly if there were more of us staying in a room in Tingum Village than there was bed space for. In the old days, Spanish Wells was somewhat off our path as the locals were not very open to outsiders. A closely-knit, white fishing community, they did not take particularly kindly to having non-locals, particularly non-whites, come to their island. That too has changed. While it is still better to leave before nightfall, they are more welcoming than before. Neighbouring Russell Island, now joined to Spanish Wells by a bridge, is home to a large Haitian-Bahamian community. It's rumoured they were not allowed to settle on Spanish Wells. Bahamians joke that Spanish Wells – Scallians – are all related and run any black people off the island before sunset. True or not, it is a beautiful island to visit. But there are no bars. They don't drink on Spanish Wells, being a very Christian society. Rather, they go to the other islands or the mainland to drink.

Nowadays, there are several ways of getting to Harbour Island. The Bahamas Fast Ferry goes up daily in the morning and returns in the afternoon. It goes first to Spanish Wells and then around the Devil's Backbone – as the reef off Riddly Head Beach is known – famous for Preacher's Cave, where the Eleutheran Adventurers lived. It is spectacular, the translucent blue water gently rolling onto deserted pink sandy beaches with incredible rock formations that dip into the water and amazing reefs and even dolphins. Secluded coves provide for even more private bathing and relaxing, but there's no one else there anyway. The mail boat still goes up weekly, while Bahamas Air flies into North Eleuthera Airport two or three times daily, along with a number of charter companies.

In the last 10 years, Harbour Island has become a playground for the rich and famous, and the home of a number of boutique hotels and gourmet restaurants. Now, instead of chasing lizards, I go there for the food: The Landing for Sunday brunch; Sip Sip, overlooking a pink sand beach for asparagus with roasted peppers and goat's cheese or a local venue like Angela Starfish restaurant. Nothing beats going down to Bay Street in the morning after a long night and having a good spicy conch salad from Queen Conch. In the old days, we took all our own provisions with us on the mail boat on Thursday and always by Saturday we would have run out of beer.

The island is still easy to get around on foot on the oddly cut roads in the downtown section, where the houses are close together and the gardens strangely shaped due to some interesting surveying. But we found out that having a dinner at home until six in the morning could still disturb the neighbours, even when we thought we were being quiet.

We would hop in a water taxi across to the Three Island dock on mainland Eleuthera, hire a car and drive around to places like the Glass Windows Bridge, where the land is so narrow that the calm sea almost meets the rough ocean, only separated by the thinnest strip of rock and the bridge, which often gets washed out in heavy seas. There's a beach just outside Gregory Town where the surf is usually kicking and there are caves. Further south, there's Governor's Harbour with an Italian hotel and restaurant – Coco Di Mama, perched above a calm cove beach – or even further, Cape Eleuthera, at the southern tip of the island, once the home of a very exclusive development and marina that fell on hard times in the Eighties.

Nature is so relaxed that when my sister and I were exploring some of the ruins the other day, a chicken snake didn't even seem fussed that we there. He actually decided to come and take a closer look. Our local potcake, Lucy, did not even notice the snake. She walked over it at least twice running around sniffing other things that caught her attention. I don't know which one was less fussed, her or the snake. We, however, decided that it was better to leave the snake to his environment. Lucy wasn't too happy about leaving.

Eleuthera is a long island and it takes a few hours to drive from north to south. We, on our jaunts, would often stop in various settlements and have lunch or a snack or just a soda – or, for those not driving, a beer. I now have an added reason to go there. A few years ago my sister moved to Rock Sound to teach, fell in love, got married and stayed.

Every settlement on the island has what they call a 'homecoming.' Sometimes these will include sailing races and the like, but usually it's all about socialising, drinking gallons of Kalik beer, or gin and coconut water, and eating conch fritters, cracked conch, or peppery conch salad, not to mention all the sweets the local people bring out for sale – coconut tarts and pies, benny cakes and fudge.

The recession has affected many of the businesses and a hurricane in 1999 closed down some of the resorts but there are still enough little places open to have a great time. Club Med in Governor's Harbour closed soon after the 1999 hurricane and has not reopened, but the beach in front of it is spectacular and usually empty. It's long and begging to be walked on and explored. The Italian all-inclusive Venta Club also closed, but developers seem to be poised to move back into the island.

I weathered the 1999 Hurricane Floyd in Harbour Island. It seemed rather tame until after the eye had passed over, when we all went outside to see what had happened, and then the winds picked up again and took off the roof of the house we were sheltering in. We sat and waited for the storm to finish, with a bottle of red wine and some crackers for company, once water, electricity and telephone had all gone off.

Briland's basic beauty and charm are still intact despite million-dollar mansions. I still run away from the city and along the pink sand beach, chill out in the Blue Bar, get happy with Sip Sip's Mango Margarita, slurp down a dilly daiquiri from the stand opposite Arthur's Bakery, or get a hangover on Friday, Saturday and Sunday mornings after hanging out playing pool at Gusty's, shaking the night away at the Sea Grapes or hanging loose in one of the more relaxed, low-key bars. Or simply sit outside having a barbecue with friends on the veranda overlooking the ocean and listening as wave after wave crashes on the shore.

I may no longer be the six or eight year-old running wild on Briland, or the 19 year-old drinking until dawn and skinny dipping as the sun crests, but I still yearn to go back to Eleuthera. I live on Puerto Rico, but Harbour Island still calls me home. There may be more cars than there were 20 years ago, but the news of what I did last night still circulates faster than I can walk from one end of the three and a-half-mile-long island to the other. There may be a little more crime than years ago, but everyone knows who's done it by morning.

However, I may soon find myself unable to afford these simple pleasures, as locals sell land and homes to 'outsiders,' not realising that they will never again be able to afford to buy back into the island. Prices rise and, on a small island, property runs out quickly. Old houses are flattened and new ones are erected in their place. The landscape has changed. The once sleepy island where we all ran around, welcomed by everyone, knowing everyone, has become a place where servants look after houses in the off-season and people are aloof. As movie stars move in because it's so quaint and naturally beautiful, all that was once special about it vanishes. It is hard to find an indigenous Brilander who owns land, does not work as a house-keeper and can still afford the rising cost-of-living.

There are as yet no multi-storey, thousand-room resorts but 'controlled' or sustainable development is an oxymoron here. We can probably celebrate the small victory of small-scale developments. But what happens when suddenly the rich and famous look around them, and find themselves looking at each other rather than the natural beauty they moved there for? Will they abandon ship for a new, 'unspoilt' spot? And what happens to us, the people who once inhabited this under-developed paradise? That place we once knew is gone forever. We have become exotics in our own homes, pushed further into the margins of land-ownership and citizenship. Our little piece of the rock becomes someone else's vacation home.

I am saddened by this re-mapping of Harbour Island and that my children will never know it the way I knew it. It seems absurd to lock ourselves out of our own country in favour of short-term economic prosperity. As the old saying goes, 'what sweet goat mout today, does burn he bam-bam tomorrow.' We are being sweetened by the prospects of riches and have sold paradise for a new spot on the plantation.

Eating Jamaica

Opal Palmer Adisa

Growing up thin in a society that praises meat on one's bones made life rather trying for a girl-child such as I was, for whom food was mostly inconvenient. The most vivid image of myself as a child is sitting alone at the dinner table after it has been cleared except for my plate. Head propped in hands, I sit wriggling, watching the evening turn to night and praying that a duppy will materialise and eat the food piled on my plate. But I was never so fortunate. Even the dogs knew better than to eat my food and unleash my mother's anger. My mother took her duty seriously, and I was a source of embarrassment, since no matter how much she fed me I remained thin, causing strangers to call me 'weeny,' no bigger than a comma. Nonetheless, my mother, who took both the preparation and presentation of meals seriously, persevered, presenting me with three meals daily.

The ritual began in the morning with a large bowl of porridge. This I could ingest if it was oatmeal or cornmeal, but a great big lump always grew in my throat whenever it was banana or rice porridge. Accompanying the bowl of porridge were toast, hot cocoa or warm Milo and an orange or some other seasonal fruit. That was the Monday through Friday morning menu, to awaken the brain and make it ready for learning.

At weekends there was more variety, but on Saturdays we often had the absolute worst: sautéed liver and kidney, 'essential nourishment for the body.' This disgusting opener was often accompanied by boiled green bananas, plantains which I loved, lots of onions which I detested, hard-dough bread and something warm, to help you 'belch de air off you chest.' The only reason I was able to swallow and keep down such a breakfast was because my mother would make one of her famous concoctions of blended juices with spices, and maybe a dash of port wine or Horlicks to add richness. This tall, cold drink was very sweet and delicious and I relished it as long as I wasn't privy to all the ingredients – in particular, raw eggs.

Sunday breakfast was either ackee and salt-fish, with Johnny cakes, fried plantain, steaming, hot, very sweet cocoa (the chocolate fresh from my mother's village, grated and boiled, always with an oily film on top); or callaloo and salt-fish, green bananas and dumplings and another of my mother's blended concoctions to wash it all down. On rare occasions there was susumba; bitter and green, susumba was perfect to play marbles with but certainly not to eat. Sometimes we had my mother's famous sardine omelettes sprinkled with pickled pepper sauce. I especially liked mackerel-run-down with soft-boiled green bananas and dumplings. My absolute favourite breakfast was leftover stew-peas and rice, but that was a rare treat.

The first meal of the day was followed by an equally solid noonday meal. During the week there was only so much my mother could pack in my lunch bag, but she managed. My friends at school enjoyed my lunches. When the bell rang, they fought to see what treat my mother had fixed. They were often ecstatic: half a roasted pigeon with hard-dough bread, juice, fruit and cookies. I truly envied those children whose mothers didn't pack them lunches, but handed them a few coins to buy the school lunch staples: patties and coco-bread with chocolate milk or juice; bun and cheese and milk; banana chips, cheese sandwich, fudges and plantain tart. I always had enough lunch to share with at least two friends and still be full. Usually, after we had gone through my lunch, my friends and I visited the woman who sold sweets and other snacks by the school gate. We bought asham – pounded corn with brown sugar – tamarind balls, coconut-drops, paradise plums, Bustamante – a very hard candy made with coconut, ginger and molasses – or whatever fruit was in season. Those were my kinds of food. Sometimes, on the way home from school, Harrison, the school-bus driver, would stop so we could get icicles or fudges or some other delicacy. As a result, I was almost never hungry or ready for dinner, but the table would be set: knife, fork, spoon, napkin, glass, plate, each in its place and the food cooked to perfection and arranged creatively on the table.

Monday through Friday dinner was always punctually at 5.30 p.m. With washed hands, we sat for our meal. We had to abide by the table rules: 1) Sit up straight in your chair. 2) Use your knife and fork. 3) No elbows on the table. 4) Chew food thoroughly. 5) No smacking or gobbling. 6) Don't put knife in your mouth. 7) No singing at the table. 8) No water or juice until plate is clean. 9) No talking with food in your mouth. 10) Eat what's on your plate, don't put what you don't want on someone else's plate.

The weekday meals varied, but remained constant in that there was always too much. We never had left-overs, except as lunch the next day. Meals were cooked daily. Escoveitched fish, usually snapper or kingfish, head and all, decorated with a generous helpings of sautéd onions, pepper and carrots; ox-tail with broad beans and rice; meatballs and spaghetti and rice; curried goat; smothered chicken or stew-beef. I could always count on a freshly cooked, aromatic dinner daily, complete with vegetables, a feast much more than was reasonable for the size of our family. The starving children of the world would be dragged to our dinner table to make me feel guilty for not eating. I offered to send them my share, which upset my mother. Didn't I know how fortunate I was? Didn't I want to be strong so that the hurricane winds wouldn't blow me away? My mother was patient and accommodating. When I told her I didn't like meat because it was too hard to chew she offered to chew it for me, and would cut my meat into the smallest chewable pieces. She often fed me although I was capable of feeding myself. She also tried bribing: 'You can stay outside longer and play with your friends if you just eat six fork-full.' Or she cited health, claiming that this vegetable or that meat would make me have glowing skin, strong teeth, in general enhance my body and make me more beautiful. But how much more beautiful could I get? She tried to scare me by saying that a wind would blow me as far away as China and they would never find me, but I stood my ground, rejoining that I was big inside. In short, mealtimes were an exercise in resistance. I eventually won, at the price of endless hours sitting alone at the table. I came to know all the grooves and spots on that mahogany table. I missed out on after-dinner playtime with friends and worst of all, I didn't get any dessert! It didn't make sense that my mother would deny me the foods that I loved, while insisting that I eat those things that I detested.

This, however, was not the end of my mealtime ordeal. There was a light supper just before bed, thankfully only warm Milo or Horlicks with either biscuits or crackers and cheese. Then the weekend began. The entire house would be perfumed with my mother's baking and I would be full from the smell alone.

On Saturday we had a one-pot meal, eaten in the early afternoon. It didn't matter if I begged my mother for us to visit friends or relatives, hoping for a change at someone else's house. Everyone I knew had soup on Saturday, mostly yellow soup or chicken soup, peppery and consumed very hot so that by the time you were through, you felt as if you'd been in a steam room fully clothed. Initially, I didn't like soup. It was too hot for the weather, and it always left me feeling bloated and sluggish. My mother loved soup and, like most Jamaican women, swore that soup was good in a hot climate as it opened up one's pores and allowed one to sweat. So Saturday was soup day. Not thin American soup – flavoured water as Jamaicans call it, or soup's distant cousin. In Jamaica we make soup puppa – a complete meal.

Take for instance thick, delicious yellow soup, made with either salt-beef or chicken feet with fibrous African yams and pumpkin which give it its colour, chocho, carrot, turnips and coco with lots of seasoning; more 'hot spicy' than 'mild spicy' and as we say, 'Is whole heap of sumting dash together.' It wasn't my favourite, but I could manage because there's no soup without dumplings and I love dumplings, especially the little roly-poly ones. Some Saturdays, after I finished my soup, I would be so exhausted from sweating and the labour of my jaws to bite and chew those hard foods, I would go and lean under my special tree and doze like Anansi.

My favourite soup was and still remains, pepper-pot made with pig's tail and salt-beef, callaloo, okra, a whole scotch-bonnet pepper, yams, lots of dumplings, coco, chocho, turnip, sometimes green bread-fruit – a wide variety of foods smothered together, so good I couldn't get enough. It was a meal that lasted you all day.

But then there would be Saturday supper. For the greater part of the day my house was perfumed with my mother's baking. She can 'burn,' as the saying goes, and always made breads, cookies, all kinds of pastries and pies, like sweet-potato pudding with the scandal on the top – my name for the soft, oily crust that I would insist my mother skim off – coconut frosted cake; pineapple upside-down cake; banana cake, scones, pones and whatnots. The house would smell so good it was edible. My sister and I licked the mixing bowl clean.

Then there were the drinks and wines my mother made, which neighbours and friends would come to sample. But the fruit juices and ice creams were my passion. Long before stores sold these flavours, my mother made mango, sweet-sop, guava, papya, even tamarind ice-creams for family and friends. She experimented with everything, and anything that could be eaten was blended, mixed and combined, resulting in the most tantalising tastes. She always cooked enough to feed an army. Growing up, I believed there was a never-ending supply of food, and my mother was its keeper. My brothers would invite their entire soccer team to dinner and everyone would be full.

Sundays were special. My mother would select a chicken from the coop, wring its neck and pluck its feathers. The neck and wing were my mother's and my favorite parts of the fowl; my sister and the men folk argued over the legs. Sunday was also the day for rice and peas, the sweet coconut-milk flavour of which I truly loved. Since I didn't like red beans, until I was sixteen my mother diligently picked out every one from the rice, just so I would eat. Along with rice and peas, chicken, roast beef and carrot-beet juice, there was salad, usually shredded cabbage, tomatoes, cucumber and slices of avocado, topped with homemade dressing, and potato salad made with diced hardboiled eggs and peas and carrot. Dessert would be a dream I could never get enough of. While I was never forced to eat all my dinner on Sunday or left to sit at the table, I did have to have my carrot juice and a fair amount of my food in order to get dessert.

When I was growing up most Jamaicans had the same meal on Sunday: roast beef, baked ham, curried goat and sometimes fish, although fish was usually reserved for Fridays. Sometimes too, there would be macaroni cheese and baked potatoes, boiled yam, plantain, pumpkin, but always there would be rice and gravy, in which the food swam. The idea of having everything separate on one's plate and eating a little of this and a little of that without mixing it all together is a notion of eating that I still find disconcerting. Many Jamaicans, like me, believe that foods have to be combined, mixed together to be truly enjoyed. Preparing and presenting food was an artistic pursuit with my mother. The centrepiece of flowers was as integral a part of the presentation as was the marinating and cooking, which foods were served on which plates, how they were arranged on the table, the solemnity with which we approached the table, permissible subjects to discuss while eating, the pace at which we ate – the whole decorum was an art and ritual. My mother made eating an act of love which I am incapable of forsaking with my own children.

Spirits Before My Face

Marina Warner

My father went to Carnival in Trinidad sometime in the Sixties and had such a good time he had a heart attack on the plane coming back. At least that was the family story. He showed us the Carnival programme he'd marked up with exclamation marks and triple stars and underlinings everywhere, as well as photographs and news clippings about the visit and we listened in while he described to his friends the tremendous times he'd had. He recovered quickly, and it was all worth it; he had loved all the excitement, the company, the new relations he had not known before, including our cousin Suzy to whom he had lost his heart. He was a vehement man, both in matters of love and anger, and given to crushes. My mother, my sister and I looked at the snapshots with our usual weary scepticism: we found it hard to share the enthusiasm he felt on such occasions. But boredom vanished when Suzy, whom he fondly pointed out in the group, turned out to be black. That was something wholly unexpected from my angle of view; it opened a new, utterly fascinating retrospective on the Warner family history.

When I travelled in the Caribbean in 1992 and 1996, I kept meeting Warners: it's a common name in that part of the world. My father, Esmond, was the eldest son of the Trinidad-born cricketer Sir Pelham 'Plum' Warner– hence the news items about my father's visit – and Plum was one of 18 children. Plum was born in 1873, into a family that had been in the West Indies since the early days of colonial settlement: Thomas Warner, who landed in St Kitts in 1623 and claimed it along with Nevis for the English crown, was a direct forebear. Since then, the family had been scattered between St Kitts, Nevis, Antigua, Grenada, as well as Trinidad, for centuries. My grandfather was already a frail, slight old man when I knew him, and I never asked him if he was a West Indian or an Englishman. We wouldn't have thought in those terms then, for many reasons. He was very fond and proud of his youth in Trinidad, but he really only had one topic of conversation: he lived for cricket. In 1945, when my mother, very young and southern Italian, arrived for the first time in England on one of the first passenger flights to land at Heathrow after the war, and was taken to meet her new father-in-law, he immediately began the urgent business of teaching her how to play the game. He showed her how to bat, in the sitting room, on the Persian rug, in the South Kensington mansion block flat where he then lived, which, when I came to know it around five years later, smelled of Quality Street assorted toffees and the cabbagey stews of Fifties' London.

In the French islands of the archipelago and in the former Spanish territories, families like the Warners are Creoles, seeing themselves as part of a local, complex, multifarious culture. But a peculiarity of the British is that they never adopted that term in their empire: home remained England. In their imagination, they saw themselves as belonging nowhere else. Nevertheless, for all his mien of the perfect English gentleman, Plum was born in Port of Spain to a mother called Rosa Cadiz. He was first educated in Barbados and then later sent to Rugby and Oxford, before returning to the West Indies where he soon became captain of the team. His attachment to his childhood home, its people and its history, comes through strongly in his many and various memoirs. In the opening of *My Cricketing Life*, for example, Plum describes how he first learned to play cricket indoors, 'batting on a marble gallery to the bowling of a black boy, who rejoiced in the name of Killebree.' This sentence, with all its unconscious attitudes, has trodden my imagination with burning feet, and inspired the character of the patriarch Anthony Everard in my novel *Indigo*. That house burned down a long time ago, but in 1996 I was shown 'the Hall' in Port of Spain where the family lived later, now a school. What I saw over the fence through luxuriant light-flecked foliage and the tall tangle of tropical trees was a quiet, shuttered, cream-painted traditional colonial house with a broad veranda, on a scale few domestic houses anywhere are built today.

When my sister Laura and I were children, Plum was a distant, heroic figure who lived and breathed the mysterious essence of cricket. His keen brown eyes were legendary (we were told he never needed glasses), while his prolific fluency as the game's historian also inspired awe (he had written more than 20 books about cricket). Even now, as Plum Warner's eldest grandchild, I find strong men still scrutinise my face for a glimpse of the great man. Famous playwrights, city brokers, literary biographers, professors of Latin, will engage me in discussion – over 40 years since Plum's death and a century since he was playing cricket – on his prowess, his decisions, and the difficult episodes of his career, as if it were all still happening now and remained a matter of some urgency. When I met Professor Hilary Beckles in Barbados, leading cricket authority and author of *The Development of West Indies Cricket*, he too greeted me warmly because, he said, my grandfather had played an important part in desegregating the West Indies team when he took black players to England. (I have to say that I wasn't only proud, but also relieved, to hear this.) This was at the start of his career, before he changed teams and became the England captain. Another family legend relates how, when he first returned to the West Indies in that role, his brother Aucher was then captaining the West Indies, so that the two brothers had faced each other on the pitch.

Soon after those first lessons in the South Kensington flat, my mother was to be introduced to the King at a garden party. She made herself a beautiful and dramatic black and white dress in the 'New Look' fashion, trimmed a magnificent picture hat for the occasion, and was photographed walking in with Plum. Later, when I looked at the photograph published in *The Illustrated London News*, it seemed that the sphere of cricket and the power of England existed in some deep relation to each other and made Plum at the MCC the King's sporting counterpart. An aura of patriotic nostalgia for a grand historical narrative about power, patronage, and nation hung around Plum's slight courteous figure, and though it's a bit absurd to think this, I might as well own up to it now. In my novel *Indigo* I tried to capture this nexus of national mythology through the character of Sir Anthony Everard, though my fictional figures are much more tyrannical and worldly than Plum was.

When my father went to Trinidad that first time in his life, he was on a mission on behalf of the family to sell a plot of land in Port of Spain. Plum's numerous brothers and sisters had produced many progeny in their turn, including my father, and 'Erthig,' as the property was called, passed to them all. It had been developed in the 19th century as housing for the servants of the big houses nearby, on the edge of the Savannah. The numbers of beneficiaries meant complications and costs in administering and distributing the revenue from the rents – and this was no longer desirable housing in a good area. When I was young, I overheard talk about quarrels, flurries of correspondence between siblings, their impoverished spinster cousins and yet more distant relatives. Suspicions grew that some skulduggery was going on, that those handling the funds were not straight dealing. The decision was taken to sell it off and divide the money equally. My father was dispatched to do so.

On my own first visit to the island, I walked around the small, pretty grid of streets where the houses have painted clapboard walls, wooden porches, fretwork eaves and columns and picket fences. Some were rather tumbledown and their yards higgledy-piggledy, the woodwork splintered and rotten; others were coming up in the world, restored to old-world 'gingerbread' charm. It was very strange to think that my father had once owned a little bit of it.

When I was young I didn't know about the family's involvement in all the stages of colonial history. But in the Eighties I was thinking about these things, and writing my novel *Indigo*, a reworking of *The Tempest* as a drama of encounter and destruction and its repercussions in the post-imperial world. Tracing the presence of the Warners' past in Trinidad gave me a vertiginous sense of the uncanny. The names of the streets were family names (Cadiz, Warner, Aucher, though this last has been emended to the more plausible Archer). This was a history I belonged in; I had been here before, though not in this time and in this body. Here was the final chapter of the story of my grandfather and father: absentee landlords to poor families. It had come to these streets, to low-grade housing and tenants who sent their rent money to England to maiden aunts in Surrey and others among my relations.

I wanted this not to be the final instalment, the end of the story. In the next generation, I wanted to try and twist another thread into the carpet and make my own reckoning with this past. Edward Said raised a furore when he discussed Jane Austen within the economic and political realities of imperial trade; but he saw keenly past the surface of her stories, because that unconsciousness displayed by the Bertrams in *Mansfield Park* forms the ground against which the figures of history move. My family in England wasn't grand landed gentry, but my father identified very strongly with that class: it was his own family romance.

There was a moment during my research for *Indigo* that made me understand what it means when the Bible says, 'Then a spirit passed before my face; the hair of my flesh stood up.' (Job 4:15). Jamaica Kincaid had a new story in the *New Yorker*, and I was reading it hungrily, as her book *At the Bottom of the River*, singing out in fierce, bright anger, was one of my inspirations. I came to a sentence about the heroine Lucy hating her surname, 'Warner,' because it was the name of the family who'd enslaved her ancestors. A spirit brushed past me, the floor of the kitchen where I was standing felt as if it were was slipping away under me and the magazine fell from my hand. The past came rushing up, so close, speaking out – of course, I told myself, she just needed a name to set off her heroine's anger, and she lit on this one; my family had been there, in Antigua, and some of them are lying in the churchyard in St John under stone tombs.

By coincidence, I met Jamaica Kincaid soon afterwards in London and have continued to see her over the years. We watched together Stuart Hall's television series on the Caribbean. I never asked her about the story. Later, when the book – her novel *Lucy* – came out, containing the excerpt that was in the *New Yorker*, her heroine's surname was different. I breathed out a little more easily, and the floor came back to something like its level state.

Santa with a Suntan: A Jamaican Christmas

Anthony C. Winkler

When I was a child growing up in Kingston, nothing disturbed my peace of mind more than the onslaught of the Christmas season. And, as I learned more about the world around me, my sense of anxiety and wonder about who I was and where I lived grew seasonally worse as every new year inched its way through the calendar into the terminus of December.

I was a serious, idealistic child with a dopey sense of rectitude about my world and a hunger to understand its rules and see them obeyed. Throughout most of the year I was firm, even smug, about my beliefs.

Christmas, however, had a distressing tendency to turn my world topsy-turvy. Jamaica is so close to the US that, all throughout the year, our hulking continental neighbour dusted us with a mushroom cloud of idealistic images about American life. The problem was that at Christmas, these images and the reality of my Jamaican life simply didn't match.

The crux was that we had no snow. We had never had snow. We would never have snow.

It was no small absence. Snow is as essential to the North American Christmas myth of Santa Claus as Sherwood Forest is to the fable of Robin Hood or the iceberg is to the saga of the *Titanic*. We couldn't help but miss the snow when there was a blizzard of exotic imagery about sleigh rides and reindeer in nearly every Christmas carol played on the radio. Most Jamaicans had never seen a sleigh or reindeer, except on Christmas cards. The man in the street couldn't tell a red nose reindeer from a brown nose moose.

What was even more disconcerting was that, every Christmas, in full view of sweaty shoppers wilting in the 90 degree plus heat of Kingston in December, faux snow would be falling in the display windows of the finest downtown department stores. Ridiculous cutouts of Santa Claus bundled up in his sleigh drawn by reindeer would soar from the ceiling high above the heads of shoppers.

As I grew into self-awareness, I had many unanswered questions about the irreconcilable differences between the Christmas I lived and the one I heard about on the radio or saw in picture books or on display in shop windows.

How *did* Santa Claus get around on a sleigh in Jamaica? How did he land on the roofs of the shaky zinc-topped shacks scattered throughout the Jamaican countryside, some of them so frail they couldn't support the weight of a matchbox-sized sleigh drawn by a team of cockroaches? And here was the kicker: *how* did he slide down the chimney of houses that had none?

Up to that time in my life, I had never seen a house with a fireplace, to say nothing of a chimney. Indeed, the only chimney I'd ever seen was an enormous one on the grinding mill of the Frome sugar plantation in Westmoreland. But that one was narrow, towered over the cane fields, and had no convenient roof big enough to accommodate a sleigh laden down with Christmas gifts and a fat driver. Slide down that chimney, Santa, and you came out the other end as molasses!

The older I grew the more jarringly incongruous Christmas seemed and the more confused and troubled I became. My father was not the kind of man to whom I could go with these misgivings. Moreover, he had just started a new business, which was going so badly that he was beginning openly to fret.

So I turned to his father, my grandfather, who had Santa's waistline and white hair and was always playful and patient with me. He was willing to answer my every question, no matter how ridiculous.

One December day we lay entangled on the bed sheets after a spirited bout of wrestling – just for fun he had held me down and farted in my face, saying, 'Smell your grandfather's gunpowder!' A commercial counting down the shopping days remaining before Christmas was playing on the radio.

'Grandpop,' I asked with all the solemnity of a puzzled seven-year-old, 'how does Santa Claus deliver presents with a sleigh in Jamaica?'

'Oh,' he said breezily, 'I used to worry about that myself when I was your age. He leaves his sleigh in Miami. When he's in Jamaica, he rides a donkey.'

I was very familiar with Jamaican donkeys, saw them practically every day, and knew them to be overworked, downtrodden, miserable brutes who were often yoked to dray carts twice their weight. But I also knew that the donkey was a scheming plodder who never scampered unless employed at a fair or garden party to give rides to children whose necks were still unbroken. Then he became a rampaging monster who would charge headlong into a barbed wire fence if that's what it took to break the unbroken neck – just what a hired thug of a donkey had done to me on my sixth birthday. The image of Santa Claus on a surly, unpredictable Jamaican donkey was too preposterous to picture.

'The donkey flies?'

'It's a special donkey.'

'But,' I pressed, 'how does he get inside the house if there's no chimney?'

'Oh,' Grandpop replied smoothly, 'we leave the door unlocked for him on Christmas Eve.'

He answered my questions with a straight face, giving explanations that seemed to make sense. I wondered, for example, how come the dogs didn't bite Santa – any Kingston homes kept multiple dogs to guard against night prowlers, and there was no way in the world that the dogs I knew wouldn't rip to shreds any fat white intruder dressed in a red velvet suit who landed his special donkey at their front or back door late at night. Grandpop explained this quite simply as the example of the powerful magic of Santa Claus, which could pacify even the most ferocious beast.

Yet my doubts increased as the discrepancies accumulated. For example, all the North American Santa Clauses – from the one who flew on the walls of stores to the ones that populated display windows – were white. But all the Jamaican Santa Clauses I'd ever seen were black. When I'd asked a kindly uncle about this colour difference, he'd glibly explained that Santa got sunburned when he came to Jamaica.

'But he comes to Jamaica once a year and only at night!' I protested.

'Don't you have to go out and play?' he murmured, using that classic dismissal line that adults resort to when children ask too many probing questions.

Finding out the truth about Santa Claus and Christmas is part of growing up. No matter where we live, we all shed our milk teeth just about the same time we dump the fat man from the North Pole. But even though by now I dreaded the truth – that Christmas, as well as Santa Claus, was an adult hoax – I clung with a fierce tenacity to the magical world in which my child's mind dwelled.

You see, I loved the idea of Santa Claus. I was mesmerised by a flying sleigh, whether drawn by reindeer or donkeys. And though the grounds for my belief were being constantly eroded by a tidal wave of inapt images from the US, I simply would not give up Santa Claus no matter how incongruous the North American model was to life in Jamaica.

One day, about a week before my seventh Christmas, my father called us together – me and my two brothers – and did something he'd never done before and never did again. Looking embarrassed, he took us into his office and sat us down in a scruffy circle before his chair. In a faltering voice, he confided in us that the family was near financial ruin. The strain, he said somberly, was so bad that even Santa Claus was affected and had had to lay off an untold number of elves. So weak from reduced rations were the reindeer that they couldn't possibly make the annual global trip on Christmas Eve.

Looking very grave, my brothers and I cringed at my father's feet as he fumbled to explain how the business climate in Jamaica had spread all the way to the North Pole. The solution, he said awkwardly because he was not an emotional man, was that Santa had asked every father to sub for him this year but not to spend more than 10 shillings per child.

We'd never seen our father this way before. He was usually an aloof, hard man, matter-of-fact and unemotional. Hearing him almost pleading with us made us uneasy. When he asked us if we had any questions, we were more than willing to let him off the hook. My older brother, for example, who was far more logical than I and merciless in debunking everything adults said about Christmas, asked lamely if Santa had sent daddy a telegram and could he please see it.

'He didn't send a telegram,' my father said with a serious expression. 'He phoned.'

My brother's reply was a weak 'oh,' though for a blink I saw him clench his teeth as he squashed the urge to argue. With a shrug, he let pass unchallenged the preposterous idea of a phone call from the North Pole to every father in the world.

After an awkward pause during which we fidgeted uneasily, my father asked, 'Is that all right?'

The three of us immediately leapt to our feet and chorused in one voice, 'Of course, Daddy!'

Then we began to babble reassuringly to him that it was more than all right; it would make this Christmas extra special. And my two brothers and I gang-hugged him, the first and last time in our lives.

The next day he drove us downtown and let us off on King Street to find a gift for under 10 shillings. After prowling from store to store, we found it in the Hindu Bazaar. Our choice was a wind-up tank that ran on rubber treads and made a rat-a-tat noise as its turret gun gashed flint sparks. It cost eight shillings and we bought one each.

On Christmas morning that year, each scrawny stocking bulged with a single lump like the belly of a python that had swallowed a mouse: it was the tank we had selected.

Since then, 55 Christmases have streaked by in a translucent blur of past, present and future like Dickens's ghosts. Yet the one that remains most memorable to me is that seventh Christmas when we received only one gift. It was also the Christmas that taught me the truth about Santa Claus.

He existed.

But he did not live in the North Pole nor ride a sleigh drawn by reindeer or donkeys.

He was a Jamaican, lived in Kingston and drove a Morris Minor pickup. His street name was Louis Winkler. He was my father who, during his struggle to support his family, cared enough to try and preserve the myth of Santa Claus for his children while asking for their understanding in a time of desperation.

Counting from that seventh Christmas morning, my father had only nine more Christmases ahead. He would die at 44, his health ruined by too much smoke and rum.

We never got along.

But that Christmas I would not have swapped him for a hundred idealised Santa Clauses huddling with their reindeer in an igloo somewhere in the snowbound wilds of North America.

Escape to Devil's Island

Simon Lee

It was definitely 'the hell in paradise' tag which got me going. I'd surfeited on white sand beaches, dazzling coral reefs and pristine rainforests; suffered architectural indigestion in the oldest city in the New World; climbed Martinique's sleeping Mt Pelee and braved the lower slopes of Montserrat's active Soufriere Hills volcano. True I hadn't yet met a manatee or even Fidel, but Paradise was beginning to pall. It was time to check out hell.

The Islands of Salvation, three outcrops of black volcanic rock lying a few miles off the coast of French Guyana, are the eeriest and furthest flung spots in the Greater Caribbean. During the nineteenth century, Ile Royale, Ile St Joseph and Ile du Diable, France's premier penal colony for the most desperate criminals and political prisoners, acquired the dubious reputation of 'hell in paradise.' They were originally known, in the days before colonisation, as 'The Triangle Islands' and then 'The Devil's Islands,' on account of the dangers they posed to shipping. After the disastrous 1763 expedition to the Kourou river ended in disease and death, the survivors took refuge on the islands, where trade winds create a healthier climate than on the mainland. They have been officially named 'The Islands of Salvation' ever since.

I start my infernal journey imbibing courage in the English Pub in Cayenne, capital of French Guyana. A Saturday morning of enervating humidity finds me at the estuary of the Kourou River, waiting to embark on the one-hour voyage, out across the mud flats and the green Atlantic waters to the infamous islands. A party of weekend vacationers toting fishing rods, baguettes, coolers and beat boxes rushes the ramp leading to the express catamaran, *Soleil Royale*, and we're on our way.

Soon I can distinguish individual coconut trees on Ile Royale, the largest of the three islands in the archipelago. Through the fog of the previous night's carousing, my mind wanders back to March 1895. Momentarily, I am Alfred Dreyfus, captain of artillery in the French army, catching my first glimpse of 'Le Bagne,' my place of exile, from across these green and purple swathes of sea and mud.

Unlike today's passengers aboard *Soleil Royale*, most of the arrivals during the 19th century would have been wearing the red and white striped uniform of the *bagnard*. They consisted of convicts and transportees from the camp at St Laurent on the Surinamese border, who were shipped out here, along with political prisoners, until the Bagne was officially closed in 1946. The last prisoners left in 1952, a year after I was born.

The islands entered the 20th century popular imagination courtesy of *Papillon*, the Hollywood version of the – largely fabricated – escape story of small time pimp and convicted murderer, Henri Charriere, played by Dustin *'is it safe?'* Hoffman. But it was the Dreyfus Affair that first focused international attention on this 'hell in paradise.'

Dreyfus was the son of a wealthy Jewish industrial family who moved to Paris from Alsace when it was annexed by Germany in 1871. In 1894, papers discovered in a wastebasket in the office of a German military attaché made it appear that a French military officer was providing secret information to the German government. Dreyfus came under suspicion, probably because he was a Jew and also because he had access to the type of information that had been supplied to the German agent. He was convicted on the flimsiest of evidence, damned by a wave of anti-semitism and xenophobia, stripped of his rank and disgraced, his sword broken across the knee of a seven-foot tall sergeant of dragoons. Dreyfus was then banished to Devil's Island, without hope of reprieve.

The smallest island in the archipelago, separated by a shark infested sound from Ile Royale and Ile St Joseph, Ile du Diable or 'the Black Rock' had been reserved for political prisoners since the establishment of a penal colony in French Guyana under Napoleon in 1852. When Dreyfus arrived, the island had last seen service as a leper colony. He was held here incommunicado, under constant surveillance, shackled hand and foot to his bed between sunset and dawn, for four years to July 1899. It took the suicide of the colonel who had helped frame him, a one-man campaign by the eminent writer, Emile Zola, whose famous article, 'J'accuse!' fuelled international outrage, and the flight of the real traitor Captain Esterhazy, to liberate Dreyfus. He was not officially pardoned until 1906.

As we berth at Royale, I'm met by a shaven-headed East German French Foreign legionnaire, part of the detachment which guards the Guyana Space Centre at Kourou, site of the Ariane rocket launches. Since 1971, the Space Centre has owned the islands, which fall strategically in the rockets' flight path. It's one of those quirks of fate that St Joseph, known during the Bagne days as 'the man eater' – where failed escapees were punished by solitary confinement and silence – should now become a leisure destination for the Foreign Legion.

In moments we've sped across to St Joseph and I'm clambering up the stone steps to the abandoned 'seclusion cells.' The jungle has largely reclaimed the block, thick sinuous roots entwining the haunted corridors. Wedged between wall and root, a three foot albino iguana with black and white striped tail sleeps, oblivious to the horror that lingers in this heart of darkness.

The cells are windowless, roofed with an iron grid through which the guards kept constant watch on the prisoners from the walkway above. Sentences here ranged from six months to five years. On each block are two 'cachots,' or black holes: solitary confinement cells, with domed roofs, allowing no light, condemning the prisoner to total sensory deprivation. Although the maximum sentence in the cachot was officially 30 days, any new offence meant an extension. 'King of the Dark Cells,' the incorrigble Roussenq, spent a record 3,779 days here, on one occasion receiving 30 days for yelling at the guards 'Another punishment if you please!'

It is not surprising that in the 1930s an international press campaign was launched to abolish the Bagne. Venezuela, Brazil and Colombia had tired of escapees from penal camps on the mainland and possibly a few from the islands finding their way into the underworld, where they formed narcotics and prostitution gangs. A 1932 editorial in the Colombian paper *El Tiempo de Barranquilla* railed: 'This penal colony is a disaster which dishonours both France and the Americas. French Guyana is a horrible cancer which requires urgent surgical inter-vention for the sake of international hygiene and for the honour of the

Americas, which have been soiled by this survival of slavery in its most intolerable form – state slavery.'

Many escapees made their way to Trinidad, where the colonial authorities refused to return them to French Guiana. In April 1931, Trinidad officials announced all convicts arriving from Guiana would be given supplies to continue their escape. By 1937, the number of escapees became an embarrassment and new regulations were introduced, by which nationals other than Frenchmen would be returned to their own countries. Trinidad still maintained that 'under no circumstance will Trinidad return them (French nationals) to Cayenne.'

Infinitely depressed by the seclusion cells, I set off round St Joseph. Turning a corner on the coconut tree lined track I catch my first glimpse of Devil's Island across the spray soaked sound, Dreyfus' first small house clearly visible close to the shore. Among the many unmarked graves in the St Joseph cemetery reserved for guards and their wives, I find a headstone with the stark message: 'Ici repose Madame Colonna. Née à Balogna Corse le 2 janvier 1870. Decedée à l'Ile Royale le 20 Decembre 1899. Priez pour elle.'

In the afternoon my legionnaire speeds me across to Royale, and I make my way to my room in what used to be the guards' married quarters, now the over-priced Auberge Iles du Salut. The next morning, I set out to tour Royale, which during the Bagne days was a thriving community with workshops, prisoners and guards' quarters, hospital, church, school and lunatic asylum. In the1890s, a death row of condemned cells was constructed, leading out to the execution yard where the guillotine would be erected the night before an execution. An almond tree now stands on the spot where the guillotine once stood, and agoutis wander the grounds in search of food, so tame they crouch on their hind legs to nibble, only feet from curious tourists. Many of the buildings are locked, including the church, a listed historical building. As a result, I don't get to see the walls decorated by the master art forger and counterfeiter Francis Lagrange, whose series of paintings so dramatically captures the life of the Bagne.

I have to be content with the beautifully restored pink and blue presbytery in high French colonial style, an indication of what could be if a serious restoration project were undertaken. Many of the buildings, like the cells on St Joseph, are being reclaimed by the jungle, with signs warning of the danger of collapse. Wildlife and the jungle now rule Royale. Small grey sapajou monkeys with orange glove paws and white ringed eyes make bacchanal in the trees. Peacocks strut unconcerned while down by the beach a wild pig and a cock scrabble over foodscraps. Down by the landing stage, a magnificent red and blue Ara macaw peers down from a coconut branch at the lunch party below. Of the 60,000 convicts who came so far to die there is no visible record.

I look through the palms across the narrow strait at Devil's Island itself. My guide follows my gaze and gently reminds me it's off limits. 'Too bad, I'll just have to swim.' I reply, undaunted. 'Ah but the sharks …' Graciously, I concede that although there is indeed hell in paradise, I won't be escaping to Devil's Island.

On the Sea Wall (or 'A Love Affair')

Denise deCaires Narain

In one of our family albums, there's a grainy black-and-white photograph of my parents walking along the sea wall in Georgetown, Guyana, while I, a girl of six or seven, try to keep pace. It's taken from the back and they are both wearing shorts and look tall and sturdy against an early-morning sky. The muddy Atlantic Ocean is just visible along the right-hand side of the picture. I think they are holding hands, as they always did when walking around Canterbury in their latter years. I can't find the photograph to check this detail and I worry that I'm inventing the photograph or worse, inventing the memory.

Most of Guyana's tiny population lives on the stretch of muddy coast, lying below sea level, which borders Venezuela in the north and Suriname in the South. The Dutch, during their stint as the colonising power, built a sea wall along this stretch of coast line, evidence of their dogged determination to get the upper hand of the sea – and to keep their colony in place. In time, the sea wall became a focal point in Georgetown life. In the morning, it provided a place where early risers could go and stretch their legs, walk their dogs and take the sea breeze. In the afternoon it was the children's turn to be walked – by parents or nannies – and buy ice cream, peanuts and soft drinks. On Sundays, in the little canopied pavilion, the Police Band played as the promenaders made their leisurely circuit of the sea wall, or sat in irregular clusters compulsively shelling groundnuts. The bandstand was the usual starting point, followed by a gentle stroll up to the Round House, but hardier walkers headed past this to where the wall became narrow and trickier to negotiate and follow it right out to the groyne. When the tide was in, walking to the tip of the groyne made me cling anxiously to my mother or father and made them both appear amazingly solid – and *tall*. In the opposite direction from the groyne, curving past the Police Barracks and the Pony Club towards Kitty and Subryanville, was the long unbroken length of wall where the runners and stretchers conducted their routines with an intense dedication, as if to distinguish themselves from the promenaders in the opposite direction. As the light faded, children were rounded up and bundled into cars or prams or onto bikes to be taken home.

And then the courting couples appeared. The walking pace would become even more leisurely and eventually peter out as couples settled on suitable sites for whispered intimacies and to make plans inspired by the breeze blowing in off the Atlantic. When it was dark night, and the air thick and velvety, the lovers arrived and occupied the wall in tensely knotted pairs, favouring the flat expanse of wall over the comfort of the benches which dotted the wall. Sometimes, as a treat, or perhaps in desperation as my parents tried to find ways to soak up the boundless energy and random aggression of their nine offspring, we would be taken for a drive in the evening. If the drive included a stop at Brown Betty for ice-creams, then at least the first part of the drive would be relatively quiet as we concentrated on our cones (though one of my younger brothers had a talent for making his last for the duration, however long the drive). I'd spy the lovers on the sea wall, locked in complicated embraces, and think them outrageously *adult*. I remember my eyes stinging against the salty night air as we headed towards Kitty past the discreetly spaced pairs along the wall.

If the noise in the back seat wasn't intolerable to my laid-back father, we would drive further up the coast to Turkeyene, where a sign indicated the road to 'The University of Guyana.' I didn't know what went on there, but I knew I wanted to go there too. I loved the way the air seemed to change as we drove further away from Georgetown and the smell of the sea met the warm smell of vegetation coming off the open expanse of land. I was a child of the 'Independence Generation' and we sang our 'green land of Guyana' anthem with boisterous good will and commitment. We really did think our land was beautiful and that we belonged there and would always belong there.

My parents met in Cornwall and my mother enjoyed telling the story of how, in her job as a postal officer in the WAAF, she'd deliver my father's mail. He was in the RAF, sent to England as a teenager by parents anxious that if he stayed in Guyana (as it then was), he risked becoming a wastrel. When my father died, among his 'personal effects' was a fragment of brown parcel paper with his address on which he'd kept – or she'd kept – as a memento of that time. And there's a photograph, too, taken in Cornwall: they are leaning in towards each other, squinting into the sunlight. Her hands rest lightly on the shoulder strap of her handbag and her right leg is poised behind the left as if, in the next shot, she will have pivoted round to meet the embrace which the angle of his arm suggests. She is tall and handsome and her expression is anxious and open at the same time. He is tall and slim with dark wavy hair and just a hint of West Indian swagger in his rumpled jacket. There's a much later photo of them standing outside the B & B where they had their honeymoon, a huge flowering magnolia tree just behind them. This was her landscape. Only now, as I finally accept that England is where I live and probably will for some time, do I see how much my mother loved my father, to follow him from her familiar landscape of England with its soft greens and clear streams to the wide rivers, humid air and muddy sea of Guyana.

But, as a child, it was *his* landscape that I claimed unequivocally as mine; the stories she told of the flora and fauna of her childhood seemed quaint and irrelevant. We went with him to places further up the East Coast, like Beterverwagting, where he would stand on the sea wall and throw out his castnet with practised ease. The wide brown net with its little lead weights, like a filthy tutu, would settle gracefully for a moment on the surface of the sea before going under, and then my father would wait. I don't remember if he caught much. But I remember the heat of the sun at midday and the way the muddy sand would glitter with spikes of broken shells and the silvery scales of fish. It was easy to run in the shallows of the warm, brown sea, laughing as the four-eye fish leaped in disarray out of our way. Sea spray dried on our skin, leaving us dusted with a layer of crusty salt that burned and tingled as we ran on tiptoe back to the shade of the house. The sea wall, then, would be too hot to walk on barefoot.

As a plump teenager, I remember hot weekend afternoons sneaking out of the house while my parents rested in bed and my brothers vainly attempted silent games of cricket under the house. Posted redundantly in the far outfield, it was easy for my absence to go unremarked. My boyfriend 'Chubby' and I – the irony of his name appears now in retrospect: he was slim, *I* was chubby – would sit on one of the benches on the sea wall and look out to where the brown expanse of Atlantic met the bright blue of the sky. The horizon itself seemed inscribed with all the indeterminate yearning of our young selves. Only now do I wonder why Georgetown's citizens seemed so magnetically drawn to sit on that length of sea wall and gaze out at the sluggish, murky ocean. This wasn't Walcott's 'emerald water'; and there were no crashing waves or see-through blues to catch one's reflection. Guyanese were called 'mudheads': were we revelling in our muddy difference from other West Indian islands or did the lure of the sea wall derive from a desire for bluer seas just out of sight?

But no-one else would be on the wall in the blazing heat just after midday and Chubby and I revelled in our defiant occupation of it. He was 'Indian' and his father had a small shop (above which the family lived) and a stall in Stabroek market. I was 'Portuguese' and my father was responsible for the pharmaceutical line of the (respectable) family business in town. A 'nice' Portuguese girl did not frequent the sea wall with an Indian boy, however 'nice' he was. The rhetoric of our newly independent co-operative republic of Guyana proclaimed us, 'One People, one Nation, one Destiny' but that didn't really wash with my parents' generation. Years of colonial manoeuvring had left its grubby freight of prejudices deeply ingrained in the social fabric of the country and it would take more than an independence motto to erase it. But our teenage capacity for self-dramatisation made Chubby and me stalk the sea wall with defiance, convinced that our liaison was significant to *nation building*. We never thought of extending this defiance by sitting together on the sea wall *at night*. As a 14 year-old rebel, even I could see that that was out of my league. The wall at night was for *lovers* and *sex* and the nuns at my convent school had a whole armoury of powerful metaphors which had honed these words into the equivalents of *hell* and *damnation*. I lost touch with Chubby when we left Guyana (as I did with most of my friends) so I don't know how long it was before that independence motto soured in his mouth too. Inevitably, rumours of our sea wall jaunts reached my parents (some bored brother, fed up with being made to field endlessly without being allowed to bowl, must have spied on me) and Chubby and I were forced to curtail them and find less obvious places to promenade our love.

Early every morning, and again in the late afternoon, my mother and father drove to the sea wall, parked the car and walked along it. We children would be sleeping when they left in the morning and would smell their return because they always brought that day's supply of bread from the bakery around the corner on their way home. At a certain point in my growing-up, I would ask to be woken to join them in their walk. I don't think this lasted long but whether the 5.00 a.m. start was what put me off or another sibling muscling in, I don't recall. But the smell of the bakery and the pleasure they both took in the ritual of going in to select the bread remains. In the early afternoon, the younger children were taken to the sea wall by our nanny, Agnes. The four little ones, with their dazzling blond hair, glowed in the afternoon sun. At the height of my daughter-of-Guyana phase, the photo of my smiling blond brothers in their white shirts and shorts (my mother loved quoting Agnes saying 'dey look like dey bathe in milk') made me cringe and I hated my mother – and Agnes – for being so besotted with all things English. Now I still balk at this embarrassing display of *whiteness,* but also glimpse in it the dogged determination of my embattled mother not to give up on England – despite the way those closest to her moved to the rhythm of calypso and Creole and West Indian cricket. Later, as the country moved towards independence and race determined *everything,* her resolve wavered. I remember the look on her face when the women's branch of the PNC (People's National Congress) marched past our house in sedate Kingston chanting 'sweep them out and keep them out,' brandishing the Party's symbol – the broom – when they caught sight of my mother – ' a whitey pokey,' in the gallery.

In the late afternoon, my mother and my father would do the sea wall walk again, arriving back at sunset in time to orchestrate our supper. I think I imagined the evening walks they shared as intimate spaces in which they nurtured their love for each other – away from our clamorous demands. I didn't think then to wonder whether my mother's thoughts wandered home to England, to her people and her place in Melton Mowbray. And when I thought about it later, it was too late to ask. So I never really knew what my mother's country meant to her in those two decades she spent with my father (and us) far away from it. Now that they have died, I find their sea wall walks appearing again and again in my memory as an emblem of their love.

In 1975, married and with a young son, I returned to live in Guyana. The country was knotted up with shortages and there were restrictions on travel and sending money abroad and prohibitions on what could be imported. Everyone there kept asking, 'Is why yuh come back?' My parents came to visit and I remember my father's pleasure as we took a walk on the sea wall one afternoon. He rarely got involved in the detail of day-to-day family dramas and seldom expressed opinions on personal matters (while we children besieged our mother with our various enthusiasms, he rocked quietly in his hammock reading) but as we walked, he told me how deeply pleased he was that we had returned home to Guyana to make a life. That 'homecoming' didn't last long. Exhausted by the endless shortages and the political tensions which kept the atmosphere palpably tense, we headed back to the solid comforts of England. Now, nearly 30 years later, my eldest son has returned to Guyana to do postgraduate research and I find myself taking the same foolish pleasure that my father took in my brief return home in the Seventies. I imagine myself strolling with him on the sea wall and repeating the benedictions my father so lovingly bestowed on me.

My father died two years ago. He asked that his ashes be scattered in the Garden of Remembrance in the grounds of Canterbury Cathedral, a place he loved to walk in with my mother. When my mother was ill, my Dad would drive out to visit her in the hospital in Margate with me and my two sisters. He always asked to be dropped outside the city wall, some distance from their house, so he could walk through the Gardens of Remembrance. Only now, writing this, do I think about this wall replicating the treasured routine of that other wall. We scattered some of his ashes in the Garden of Remembrance on a warm day in April, the event quickly losing its melodramatic potential as his grandchildren ran around laughing in the sunshine. On a visit to Guyana the following year, I took the remainder of the ashes with me. Early on Sunday morning, my younger son and I took a taxi to the sea wall. Once there, we got out of the car and headed for the wall, me holding the jiffy bag with the ashes close against my heart. But the sea was out and the beach was littered with rubbish and there were *trees* growing on the beach and it wasn't not the place I remembered. We confered and decided that it would be undignified to simply scatter the ashes into this debris. So we got back into the taxi and headed out to the groyne. When the taxi pulled up, my memories were jolted again: what was the strip of muddy beach is now populated with dwellings made from bits of wood, zinc, cardboard and other flotsam. One or two of the people who have made their home here were coming out of the shacks, stooping because the doorways were low and narrow, and headed towards a standpipe with towels and toothbrushes in hand. We felt like intruders – from another country altogether – in this space, sprawling dangerously between mud and sea. We kept our heads down and made doggedly for the end of the groyne. The taxi-driver waited at a respectful distance: he knew the nature of our mission and perhaps knew, too, the danger of intruding into this intensely intimate squatters' camp. It felt like a very long walk to the end of the groyne but we got there and the familiar brown water was slapping gently against the wall. I looked to my left where the water of the Demerara river meets the Atlantic and I lifted the bag high and opened it: the ashes streamed in a graceful arc westwards up towards the river and towards Georgetown. I could see my shadow and that of my son in the muddy water as we quietly watched the last of the grey dust blow away. Then we headed back to the taxi.

Territory of the Heart: Jean Rhys's Dominica

Lennox Honychurch

In the centre of the village of Massacre, on Dominica's west coast, a narrow side road turns sharply off the main highway and climbs through a maze of small scattered dwellings up into the hills behind. We are on our way to the site of the 'honeymoon house' in Jean Rhys's novel *Wide Sargasso Sea*.

Here on the coast at Massacre, not far from the stony beach, we wait as she waited when she was a child, in the final years of the 1890s, to walk or ride on horseback 2,000 feet up the zigzag path, through forest and abandoned gardens, to her father's little hilltop house at Bona Vista; or, later in her life, to the house in the valley at Amelia. She describes these places herself in her unfinished autobiography, *Smile Please*:

> The larger of the two, Bona Vista, was very beautiful wild and lonely, remote. From the windows of the shabby white house you could see a range of mountains; the highest Morne Diablotin, then slightly lower Morne Anglais, Morne Collé Anglais, Morne Bruce.

We wait on the beach, as her protagonist Antoinette waits in *Wide Sargasso Sea* with her new husband, expectantly, for the honeymoon to come.

'I looked at the sad leaning coconut palms, the fishing boats drawn up on the shingly beach, the uneven row of whitewashed huts, and asked the name of the village.
'Massacre.'
'And who was massacred here? Slaves'
'Oh no' she sounded shocked. 'Not slaves. Something must have happened long ago. Nobody remembers now.'

But of course people do remember still. A whole village of Kalinago/Caribs was massacred here on the orders of the English planter, Phillip Warner of Antigua, in bitter revenge against the chief of the village, his native half brother, Carib Warner.

No place in Jean Rhys's novels or short stories is purely imagined. All over Dominica, one drifts in and out of the juxtaposed scenes of her writing, pieced together as a collage of settings upon which her haunting narrative unfolds. She is widely regarded as one of the best women novelists of the 20th century and her books have been reprinted in many languages. Her stories of luckless women taken advantage of by unreliable men have been made into films, television dramas and radio plays.

Ella Gwendoline Rees Williams was born in Roseau on August 24, 1890. It was over 30 years later, in 1923, that she began using the pen name, Jean Rhys. Her father was a Welshman, Dr Rees Williams, who had come to Dominica to take up a government job as medical officer. As a retreat from his work in Roseau, Dr Rees Williams owned, at different times, two small properties in the cool mountains of the island's interior. Her mother was Minna Lockhart, of an old Dominica family which, since the early 19th century, had owned the extensive Geneva Estate at Grand Bay in the south.

In all of Jean's work there is an undercurrent of childhood memories, of blue-green mountains, rushing streams, heat and masquerade, even when she is writing about Paris, Vienna or London. It is through her books that many people first hear of Dominica or become fascinated by the effect that the island had upon the work of this brilliant but temperamental author.

As we climb out of Massacre along the ruins of the old paved stone pathway, the dry scrub of the coast merges into the green tangle of banana plants, mango trees and pawpaw before folding into the steeper more luxuriant forested slopes above. We ride with Antoinette, heroine of Jean's *Wide Sargasso Sea,* and with the character we know to be Mr. Rochester, hero of Charlotte Bronte's *Jane Eyre,* viewing the scene through his eyes:

The road climbed upward. On one side the wall of green, on the other a
steep drop to the ravine below...Everything is too much, I felt as I rode
wearily after her. Too much blue, too much purple, too much green. The
flowers too red, the mountains too high, the hills too near. And the
woman is a stranger.

High up on a ridge among breadfruit and cinnamon trees, we turn
and look back down towards the Caribbean stretching out to the
horizon, framed by the encroaching foliage of the valley walls that rise
above us. In her short story, 'Mixing Cocktails,' Jean lingers over this
view also:

... One looked down the green valley sloping to the sea ... It is a purple
sea with a sky to match it, the Caribbean. The deepest, the loveliest in the
world ...

In *Wide Sargasso Sea*, the honeymoon party reaches the stream that
we now cross:

We came to a little river. 'This is the boundary of Grandbois.' She smiled
at me ... A bamboo spout jutted from the cliff, the water coming from it
was silver blue.

In another short story, 'I Used to Live Here Once,' the stream appears
again:

She was standing by the river looking at the stepping stones and
remembering each one. There was the round unsteady stone, the
pointed one, the flat one in the middle – the safe stone where you could
stand and look around. The next wasn't so safe for when the river was
full the water flowed over it and even when it showed dry it was
slippery. But after that it was easy and soon she was standing on the
other side.

There are no longer any houses at either Amelia or Bona Vista, just
scattered clay bricks and low ruined walls of volcanic stone to mark the
spot where the country retreats of the Rees Williams family once stood.
But she always remembered:

Perched up on wooden stilts the house seemed to shrink from the forest
behind it and crane eagerly out to the distant sea. It was more awkward
than ugly, a little sad as if it knew it could not last.

And it did not last. Today both house sites are fields of dasheen, the green heart-shaped leaves of this edible tuber covering the flat spaces that were once houses and lawns. The estate name of Amelia appears in *Wide Sargasso Sea*, not as a place, but in the name of a person, the maid Amelie, who seduces Mr. Rochester in what she calls 'the sweet honeymoon house'...

She was so gay, so natural and something of this gaiety she must have given to me, for I had not one moment of remorse.

Back down in Roseau, the large rambling wooden house, where Jean lived until she was 16, still stands on the busy corner of Independence Street and Cork Street. It is not certain that she was actually born there. The outside of the house, its clapboard walls, wooden hurricane shutters and steep galvanised roof, has not changed much, but, since being converted into Vena's Hotel in the 1980s, the insides have been completely converted. The garden with the big mango tree and its kitchens and maid quarters, which Jean Rhys recalls in her stories, has been turned into the World of Food Restaurant. The long front gallery which she describes at the end of her novel, *Voyage in the Dark,* and her unfinished autobiography, *Smile Please,* still exists. Though the wooden jalousies have been replaced with aluminum louvres, you can still look through them to the street, as she did during masquerade:

> *I was watching them from between the slats in the jalousies dancing along dressed in red and blue and yellow, the women with their dark necks and arms covered with white powder, dancing along to concertina-music dressed in all the colours of the rainbow and the sky so blue.*

The large cool drawing room where she would watch her father's musical evenings has gone too, all chopped up into little cubicles with a dark passage. Dr Rees Williams's surgery opened onto Grandby Street, later Queen Mary Street, and now Independence Street. The large back yard was the domain of the domestic staff, and here Jean learned patois and began to fear the zombies, soucouyans and lou garous of Dominican folklore, introduced to her through the 'Tim-tim' stories told her by her 'da da,' or nurse, Meta.

Dr Rees Williams was a liberal man who showed concern for the underprivileged. Coming fresh from Wales he did not share, and was impatient of, the petty prejudices which were ingrained in the consciousness of white Creole families like that of his wife. In *Smile Please* Jean remembers:

> *On certain mornings a procession of old men, or women, would come to the house and for some reason my father insisted that I must stand on the pantry steps and hand out the loaf of bread and small sum of money, sixpence or a shilling, I can't quite remember, what was given to each one. My mother objected strongly. She said that they were old and not very well, it wasn't a thing I should be expected to do ... One of them was very different from the others. He bowed, then walked away through the garden and out the gate at the other end with the loaf under his arm, so straight and proud.*

As is common in the larger Roseau town houses, the bedrooms were upstairs. From here, in her short story 'Heat,' from the book *Sleep it off Lady*, she remembers the eruption of Morne Pelée in the neighbouring island of Martinique. The date was May 8, 1902.

> *Ash had fallen. Perhaps it had fallen the night before or perhaps it was still falling. I can only remember in patches. I was looking at it two feet deep on the flat roof outside my bedroom. The ash and the silence. Nobody talked in the street, nobody talked while we ate, or hardly at all. I know now that they were all frightened. They thought our volcano was going up.*

It was from upstairs too that Jean and her brothers and sisters first heard the sounds of the riot mentioned in *Smile Please*:

> *I heard far away a strange noise like animals howling but I knew it wasn't animals, it was people and the noise came nearer and nearer.*
> *My father said: 'They're perfectly harmless.' 'That's what you think,' my mother said.*
> *I half realised that we had dressed to run away from the ugly noise, but run where? We could run as far as Mr Steadman's house on the bay but long before we got there they'd kill us! This strange idea didn't frighten me but excited me. They surged pass the window howling, but they didn't throw stones ... This particular riot was aimed at the editor of the local paper. His house was near ours. He had written an article attacking the power of the Catholic priests in Dominica. The crowd was some of the faithful who intended to stone his house, frighten him and prevent him ever writing about religion again.*

Jean's mother, Mrs Rees Williams, had reason to fear the sound of the mob. In 1844, during the Census Riots, the Lockharts' family house on Geneva Estate had been attacked by a similar band of angry villagers and its contents dragged outside and burnt. There were to be other fires. The estate houses of Geneva have been burned down by arsonists twice more in their history – first in 1930 during a strike of legislators, which was broken when Jean's nephew, Norman Lockhart, accepted a seat as nominated member in the Legislative Council; and, more recently in 1974, when the house of the estate's new owner, Elias Nassief, was torched during disturbances in Grand Bay. Jean Rhys used the 1930 burning of Geneva house and the events of 1844 as the inspiration for a similar episode in *Wide Sargasso Sea*. The links are numerous between these two childhood houses at Geneva and Roseau and episodes in her novels and short stories.

The motorable road to Geneva runs along much the same route as the old bridle path that Jean and her family rode to get from Roseau to the family plantation. Even today, as we drive along its sinuous course, cut deeply into the mountainside, the tree ferns and wild heliconias hang high over the road on one side while huge clumps of bamboo mask the steep precipice that runs along the other.

> *Before I was old enough to ride to Geneva myself ... Aunty B was accompanying me. About half an hour after we left Roseau, she fell off her horse and lay still on the ground. I was very frightened for it was a lonely road and I didn't know what to do. Just as I was fearing she might be dead ... she got up, remounted and we rode on as if nothing had happened.*

The remnants of what was once Geneva Great House sit perched on a narrow plateau overlooking the abandoned estate. Like Jean's childhood home in Roseau, this ruin is being transformed with no sympathy to its past. Cast concrete and cinderblocks now smother what is left of the stone ground floor and its vanished wooden upper storey. Even when she returned in 1936, it was in ruins. '*Geneva was an old place, old for Dominica. I tried to write about Geneva and Geneva garden in Wide Sargasso Sea.*' Here, indeed, is the Coulibri of Jean's novel, although she took the name from the neighbouring estate of Grand Coulibri. Similarly, 'Nelson's Rest', of the book, was another estate in the vicinity of Geneva. We walk from the ruined house into the wild garden:

Our garden was large and beautiful as that garden in the Bible – the tree of life grew there. But it had gone wild. The paths were overgrown and a smell of dead flowers mixed with the fresh living smell. Underneath the tree ferns, tall as forest tree ferns, the light was green ... All Coulibri Estate had gone wild like the garden, gone to bush. No more slavery – why should anybody work? This never saddened me. I never remember the place when it was prosperous.

At the edge of the garden, near a spray of bamboos, we can look down through the trees towards the old main road to Grand Bay. Here on this spot Antoinette's mother stood, brooding, bitter at being ridiculed by the former slaves and abandoned by Spanish Town society in the novel's Jamaican setting:

Standing by the bamboos she had a clear view to the sea, but anyone passing could stare at her. They stared, sometimes they laughed. Long after the sound was far away and faint she kept her eyes shut and her hands clenched.

In the valley below the house we walk through wild gingers, their blossoms tissue white, to the river where, as a child, Antoinette frolicked with her friend, Tia.

... I lay in the shade looking at the pool – deep and dark under the trees, brown green if it had rained, but a bright sparkling green in the sun. The water was so clear that you could see the pebbles at the bottom of the shallow part.

As she makes use of remembered landscapes and dwellings, so too does Jean pick characters from her past and place them upon the stage set of her childhood memories. Years later, Her 'da da,' Meta, and the Bona Vista obeah woman, Anne Tewitt (or Tuitt), were the models for the fearsome character, Christophine, in *Wide Sargasso Sea*:

Our cook at Bona Vista was an obeah woman called Ann Tewitt. Obeah is a milder form of voodoo, and even in my time nobody was supposed to take it very seriously. Yet I was told about her in a respectful, almost awed tone.

Both the real Ann Tuitt and the fictional Christophine come from other islands. Ann Tuitt came from Montserrat to Dominica,

Christophine comes from Martinique to Jamaica. Up at the 'honeymoon house,' Mr Rochester is introduced to Christophine:

> *And here is Christophine who was my da, my nurse long ago … Doudou ché cocotte' the elderly woman said to Antoinette…She was blacker than most and her clothes, even the headkerchief round her head, were subdued in colour. She looked at me steadily, not with approval I thought.*

Later, Rochester is warned about Christophine by Daniel Cosway, Antoinette's half brother:

> *She is the worst. She have to leave Jamaica because she go to jail, you know that? … she is obeah woman and they catch her.*

In January 1905, the year before Jean left Dominica for England, Ann Tuitt was convicted of practicing obeah under the recently promulgated Leeward Islands Obeah Act No. 6 of 1904 and sentenced to six months hard labour.

The British Administrator of Dominica at the time was Henry Hesketh Bell, known to the young Jean Rhys as 'Mr Hesketh.' Bell had an anthropological interest in witchcraft and, as Administrator, would have helped to frame the legislation of 1904. What is more, he got a local photographer to take a picture of Ann Tuitt while she was in jail. This portrait of her in prison garb, holding a slate with her name written upon it, now lies among Bell's papers in the Royal Commonwealth Society Library at Cambridge. This was the same man who danced with Jean at a children's fancy dress party at Government House and it was he who Jean snubbed in a fit of confusion while they rode past each other one evening near Roseau. In this way time and again do the persons and places in both Jean's creative work and her life intertwine with each other, appearing and disappearing like the loose weave of forest vines among the wild jungles of her childhood in the garden at Geneva or on the road to Amelia.

We continue to walk with her up into these hills even after her death, for in one of the last short stories she ever wrote, 'I Used to Live Here Once,' Jean returns to Amelia as her own ghost, an unseen spirit, revisiting her childhood retreat on the road above Massacre:

> *She came to the worn stone steps that led up to the house and her heart began to beat. The screw pine was gone, so was the mock summerhouse*

called the ajoupa, but the clove tree was still there and at the top of the steps the rough lawn stretched away, just as she remembered it. She stopped and looked towards the house that had been added to and painted white. It was strange to see a car standing in front of it.

But today, as we reach the brow of the hill and look across the overgrown provision garden to the hills above, it is nothing like that at all. Everything that she had known is gone. Nature, rather than 'other people,' has reclaimed what had once been hers. And perhaps, in her strange, brooding, possessive way, Jean would have preferred that it be so.

From Queen's Lane to Shit Alley –
A Castries Journey

Hazel Simmons-Mcdonald

At 4.45 a.m., if you were not already awake, it would sometimes draw you out of sleep, that faint peal of the smallest bell in the belfry of the Catholic cathedral on Columbus Square. It was a muted call, but it cut through the thick silence to reach those housewives who wanted to get an early start on the day, and some older men who, perhaps, wanted to get their religious obligations over and done with so they could laze through the rest of the morning, sipping a few 'ti mix' in one of the city's rum shops. It was something of an adventure to step out in the cool dark, the early mist still settled sleepily around the darkened doorways and the uncovered drains, waiting for the shadowy figures to get where they were going before it would give a faint shudder and lift itself above the rooftops where it dispersed in the strengthening light.

Wending one's way to the cathedral for early morning mass, through the dark streets at that hour could be something of a perilous journey. One had to avoid other shadowy figures, in particular, the night soil carriers who, swathed in cloths from their ankles up to their eyes and wearing a thick jacket with the collar turned up over all that, shuffled along the sidewalks with a weighty pail in each hand and perhaps a third balanced on the head. There were disasters sometimes – you could easily tell from either the muted muttering or stream of invective whether it was major or minor. If they were lucky, they could earn an extra shilling for lunch by making two or three trips across the city to the barge at the end of Queen's Lane, more popularly called Shit Alley. The more conscientious ones would return to clean up, but others, perhaps the victims of major disasters, would leave it there for the CTC (Castries Town Council) workers to dispose of.

Walking back after mass, the streets would be pristine, the CTCWs having gone about the task of sweeping down the sidewalks and emptying the drains. On the south side of the cathedral, the green verges of Columbus Square would be startling after the sombre colours of the cathedral walls. All around the square, the dwarf casuarina hedges, trimmed to rectangular perfection, screened the lawns in the inner quadrangle, where, later in the day, the children would be out playing. The massive ficus tree, which everyone called the Masav Tree, sheltered the police bandstand and benches on the east side of the park, its yellow berries carpeting the ground around its roots on either side of the hedge. The story of how the tree got to be called Masav is funny. It is said that a sailor, struck by the massive girth and height of the tree asked a local its name. Responding in French Creole, the dialect spoken in St Lucia, the local said 'masav,' the short form of *'mwen pa sav,'* meaning 'I don't know.' Since then, people have called the tree 'masav,' since most did not know the botanical name.

Lining Brazil Street on the south and Micoud Street on the north side of the square, the wooden two-storeyed Victorian houses huddled like sentinels over this oasis in the heart of the city. The eaves at the front and the awnings of the verandah immediately below were adorned with elaborate fretwork. They were all painted in pastel shades that were gentle on the eyes and contrasted with the brilliant green of the square. On the south side, 100 feet or so beyond the houses, the Castries river ran lazily towards the harbour. In the dry season, it was nothing more than a stream that one could cross with a gigantic leap or by stepping on stones on the riverbed. But in the rainy season, it was a torrent overflowing its banks into the back yards of the gingerbread houses on Brazil Street. Everything was swept away in its fury. Once, Lizzie Popot Bouway leaned too far over the Marchand Bridge and was swept away. Several hundred yards further, she was rescued by a group of men, downstream in the city, just before the river poured into the sea at the south end of the harbour, where the *Lady Joy* and the *Lady Nelson* strained at their moorings, loaded with baskets of fruit and vegetables for Barbados, Trinidad, and the Windward Islands.

Lizzie got the name Popot Bouway, French Creole for stuffed doll, because she was short and plump with rounded features much like that of a doll's. She was one of the town's eccentric characters whom everyone knew. Another was Gaga the tranvestite. On a Sunday morning, Gaga's vermillion shoes, that blended perfectly with the hues of his flowing skirt and lipstick, would signal his arrival on the far side of the square. He would walk quickly, with mincing steps, chignon pronounced at the back of his slicked down, pressed and pomaded hair, hips swirling, left hand clutching a matching vermillion handbag, right hand held out, parallel to the ground, fingers outstretched. When he got to the door of the church he would bless himself with a quick sign of the cross and hurry over to the other side of the road.

Two blocks away, on the north side of the square, the boulevard with its dual carriageway would be fairly quiet, with the odd window-shoppers peering at the varied displays through the glass windows of the stores. During the week, when commerce was at its height, it would be busy but not crowded, with a few cars parked along the street and people greeting each other as they went along doing their business. Because, in those days, the late 1950s, everyone knew everyone else and it was inconceivable that one could walk along a street in the city without greeting or stopping for a chat with almost everyone else along the way. It was nothing like it is now, crowded, with a mass of humanity moving constantly along the sidewalk, jostling each other, pushing through the crowded store doorways and darting between the constant stream of cars circling the boulevard and exiting on Bridge Street at the west end or Laborie Street on the east. There used to be grass, benches, and clean parapets separating the park from the pavements along Laborie and Peynier Streets on opposite sides of the park. One could go there in the heat of the day and sit in the cool shade of the spreading flambouyant trees that were strategically placed so that their branches formed a canopy over the benches. One could pick one's way along the paving stones, sit on the parapet or on one of the benches and look down the boulevard or across Peynier Street at the CDC buildings, which stretched for two blocks eastwards to Coral Street.

Now, not even that small park between the Treasury building and the Court buildings offers refuge from the heat and bustle. Peynier Street, on the east side, is perpetually lined with mini-vans, parked end to end, displaying in large bold lettering different routes to the outskirts and rural villages, revving up their engines, emitting noxious gases and honking their horns to attract passengers. Before, the multicoloured buses, with wonderful names like *In God we Trust*, *Forget me Not*, *Beautiful Dreamer*, and *Ajax*, would come in from the countryside and park behind the market. They would make trips twice a day, once in the early morning to bring in the vendors from Gros Islet in the north and the villages and towns in the south. They would bring sacks of coal, pails of milk, baskets of ground provisions and vegetables, fish lying between green seagrape leaves in large rounded baskets, roasted sea eggs in large wooden trays that the vendors would balance miraculously on their heads. They would arrive in Castries, some setting up in the market on Jeremie Street or spreading their goods on sacks on the sidewalk in front of the market, others fanning out through the streets announcing their wares in lilting tones – *Mamai-la mi lèt; mi pwéson; mamai-la mi fawine, mi mouchas*. Housewives would buy, supplementing the milk in small bottles with round card tops they had bought at Ferrand's Dairy across the river, holding out saucepans into which the vendors measured out the milk with long homemade tin ladles. Somehow, they would get their goods sold by midday. They would then shop in one of the department stores, M&C or JQ or Gidharry's or in the small shops on the ground floor of the CDCs on Jeremie Street. Then the buses would roll out of town by 2.00 p.m., churning slowly up Morne Fortuné to begin what was then a long two or three hour journey to Vieux Fort, across the steep and narrow Barre-de-L'isle range that dissected the island or along the precipitous route to Soufriere, or north to Gros Islet along the lonely road snaking through Vide Bouteille, Choc and Marisule. Now, the mini-vans with their sleek lines and mass-minted patina look have displaced the charming, colourful and trundling boxy fleet. They bolt along the now widened roads, careering round corners, overtaking a snaking line of cars on a crowded two-lane stretch, their horns – if one can call them that – blaring out a bar of some popular refrain. They brought with them a pseudo-sophistication that banished the milk pails, sacks of coal and baskets of vegetables and fish. They stamped their raciness on the way of life that is now a constant bustle, a busy-ness that defines the tenor of the day.

Standing at the west door of the cathedral, I look across at Columbus Square, recently renamed Derek Walcott Square, to honour the Nobel Laureate. The verges are now paved and cars are parked all around in designated spaces for which the patrons have paid a fee. The casuarina hedges have gone and concrete walls, with a locked, gated entrance on each side, allow one only a glimpse of the cenotaph on the western side and the tops of the taller flowering shrubs. The ficus still looms above the bandstand, seeming a little less imposing against the backdrop of three-storeyed concrete buildings that have replaced most of the gingerbread houses. Like the mini-skyscraper on the corner of Bridge Street and Jeremie Street that houses the development bank, they embody the new life of the city, a hub of commerce and industry and hurry. A city filled with strange new faces, many from other places and who now call the island home.

And it is still home for me. I note the changes, the extension of the harbour where container ships with boxy cargoes replace the *Lady Joy* and the *Lady Nelson* with their rustic boxes and sacks; the un-imaginative concrete structures that have sprung up over the foundations of the old-style graceful wooden houses with their artistic fretwork; the streets, lined with cars on both sides and constantly choked by another, slow moving cavalcade easing its way between the stationary rows, horns blaring at all hours muffling the sound of the church bell ringing out the Angelus at midday; the noise; the frenzy; the loss of peace. But I see it still, telescoped through time and memory. I visualise the square as it was then: the cenotaph gleaming white in the early morning sun, churchgoers sitting on the benches, verges still wet with dew, as green as the surrounding hills ... Walcott's 'flock of faiths' that could tell the tale of this city's passage from old world charm to bristling modernity.

Put me down whey yuh pick me up

Marina Salandy-Brown

I jam my body up against the side of the plane and crick my neck forward, anxious not to miss the very first view of Tobago coming up on the left. It is always worth all the hassle with the London travel agents of getting a seat on the correct side of the aircraft. I can take in the intensity of colour of the Tobagonian water, sometimes more green than blue, except at the island's southern tip where the coral reef makes it look like everyone's idea of Caribbean Paradise – tranquil turquoise water and blindingly white sand. Behind Pigeon Point and going north, layers of compact, high hills, dense in vegetation, slip past as the angle of my neck slowly changes from right to left, and right again.

The long strip of Trinidad's northern coast now comes into view. The deep waters of the Atlantic and Caribbean mingle here and curl over in a messy meeting point between sea and land. I try to see as far east as I can, as far as the villages of Toco or Matelot where I spent some of the most memorable times of my childhood.

Our house, a government residence, sat on a clearing high up over a craggy Matelot bay. Adjoining the long kitchen was a breakfast room with two large, rectangular, wooden windows that, fascinatingly, opened down into tables leaving an uninterrupted view of the clear green waters below. It was there that I first witnessed the implacable fury of the sea and learned to fear it. Wave after wave rolled in, smashing, unrelentingly, the rocks below, pounding my eardrums and sending up clouds of white spume while the sea gulls ducked and dived squawking plaintively as if in pain. I can still feel the sticky film of salt on my skin and lips and hear the din.

We didn't live in this house all the time. My father was an agronomist, a civil servant in the Ministry of Agriculture who, wonderfully for us children, ran several of the government Agricultural Experimental Stations around the country. Here new techniques for growing and improving our major crops were developed and implemented. It meant that we got around the island from north to south, east to west. My father's postings would each last two years, on average, but sometimes the stations were too far from Port of Spain to allow my mother to get to work and us children to school every day. So, unusually for a Trinidadian family, especially in the 1950s and 1960s, we lived in the city during the week and spent the weekends, with my father, in the country. Matelot was probably the most remote of the postings.

On Friday evenings we would set off: my elder sister, my much younger brother, my great aunt and me, in my mother's smart, black Austin Prefect, to get to Matelot on the other side of the island. Forty or fifty years ago many rural roads were like tracks, full of potholes of unimaginable breadth and depth. There were few street lights, even when passing through villages and almost no lengths of straight road on which to gain time, except on the absolutely straight three-mile Valencia Stretch which we called the killer strip. My mother always insisted that it was built by the Americans in the war years. And it looks as if it was, not least because it was *properly* built.

The straight and unusually smooth, black, and slightly undulating line through thick forest was guaranteed not to have any potholes. Unlike the roads we locals are more used to, the Americans had laid proper foundations, and as far as we could tell, had used something other than pure asphalt as a surface. When the heat of the sun rose to its vehement heights you could leave your foot prints in the hot tar covering most country roads. Then the torrential rain would come, suddenly, and too fast to drain away, so the surface would cool off quickly and, with time, eventually crack open. The stones in the shallow and inadequate hardcore foundations popped through and danced around in the pools of water, eventually making them the size of small ponds.

But that didn't seem to happen on the Valencia Stretch – and just as well, since every motorist in those days of few cars wanted to belt through that strip to escape the devil behind them. That road was desolate. There were no houses along the way, no clearings with farmers' huts, no tethered animals, or stray dogs even to relieve the air of spookiness. It was good to spot another traveller – safety in numbers. On all of those journeys we made to spend weekends with my father in Matelot, we always felt a sense of trepidation as we neared that highway. It wasn't just the fear of being annihilated by another car driving at high speed but the knowledge that other, stranger things could happen there. Week after week my aunt would have to retell the story of the Spirit who once held up a car on that dark and eerie strip.

Late one night, a driver is on his way to the town of Sangre Grande, situated at the other end of the highway from Valencia. There is little moonlight but the car's headlights catch the figure of a man flagging down the vehicle. The driver screeches to a stop. 'Wah yuh doin' out here a' dis time a' night, man? Get in, get in.' He bends around, opens the door behind him, the man jumps in and the car shoots off.

In friendly mood, the driver tries to engage his passenger in some chat. 'Yuh lucky I come now, yuh know? Dis eh no nice road to be walkin' alone in de night. Whey yuh livin'?' But no response comes from the back seat. He lights a cigarette and tries again, 'Yuh walkin' long?' After a few failed attempts to extract a single word from his passenger, he gives up and settles himself, happy for the physical company, at least. He slackens his speed a bit into Grande.

When they arrive at the centre of the town, the driver pulls up. 'Yuh go have to get out here, man. I eh goin'... ,' but, as he turns to the man in the back of the car, he sees there is no-one there to hear him finish his sentence. The seat is empty. His passenger has disappeared into thin air.

Each time my old aunt told the story I would shiver and nestle up to her as she explained, tirelessly, that by lighting his cigarette the driver had saved himself from the evil spirit who had come to claim his soul. I always felt safe because both my mother and father smoked, so some form of salvation was usually at hand if needed. She assured us that the Socouyants, La Diablesse, Douens and other spirits that fed our wild imaginations all hated fire, some hated salt and none could withstand daylight. What a relief to arrive in bustling, noisy Grande, our journey's mid-way point!

To get to Matelot from Port of Spain you have to drive inland along the bottom of my beloved Northern Range of mountains to Toco at the eastern tip of the island, and then along the coast, going back on yourself but on the other side of the Range, to Matelot. There the road ends. In those days, there was no road between the popular Maracas Bay with its long sandy beach, much further west, and Matelot and, as I stare down from the plane, I am delighted that there is still no northern coastal road.

But things have improved. Much of the 15 or so miles of road between Toco and Matelot used to be unmade. Then it was nothing more than a dirt track with grass growing in the middle. To one side was high mountain, the other deep precipice. The rain would regularly gather in big clouds over the Atlantic and these heavy, grey sacks would empty themselves with a vengeance as the wind drove them into the high ridge. Often, we edged for hours along roads that had been all but carried away by landslides. The thin and low-speed windshield wipers were totally inadequate for the job, the yellowish beam of our headlights hardly lit the middle distance, and the steam from our hot breaths in the airless car made it impossible for my intrepid mother to go any faster than at the speed of a snail. The 53-mile journey from Port of Spain could take up to four hours, so we never managed to arrive before nightfall. A big, bright moon was what we, including my father, always hoped for especially in the last part of the journey.

From the air, I can really appreciate how massive those deep green hills are. They fill the entire view from my window. The canopy reminds me of a head of uncontrollably tight curls, so perfect for all those Spirits to secretly inhabit. I think I would like to reach down and stroke my mountains and, immediately, like a reflex, I remember that I must always be careful in touching anything of great beauty in Nature. Once, just as my child's hand reached out to stroke a most beautiful, large and shiny, velvet-like spider sitting serenely on a mossy wooden wall, I remembered, just in time, what I'd been taught. I ran away, heart pounding and breathless, leaving the tarantula just where I saw it.

My old Aunt Ida would take advantage of our hours of imprisonment on that treacherous journey and use her apocryphal stories to good effect.

One day a man is walking along the edge of the bush to a nearby village. All of a sudden he hears something strange. He stops and pricks up his ears. It sounds like a baby, 'but dah eh possible,' he thinks to himself, 'it eh have no people or house 'round here so ah kyah be hearin' right.' He continues on his way but soon stops again because a little further on he sees a small bundle at the edge of the track and it is stirring. As he approaches it, there is no mistake that what he had heard the first time was a baby's cry.

He picks up the sobbing infant. 'How people could be so wicked, Boy, as to leave a little chile like dis, in a t'in, t'in sheet out here so?' He cradles the baby in his arms and heads off for the village at greater speed. After a little while, he notices that the baby is growing heavier and heavier. His arms soon start to ache. Just when he begins to wonder if he could actually carry on, he hears a big and distinct voice from inside the thin sheet say, 'Put me down whey yuh pick me up. Put me down whey yuh pick me up. Put me down whey yuh pick me up.'

He pulls back the covering from the baby's head and what he sees makes him nearly die of fright. Staring back at him is no baby's face but a fully grown adult, skinning his teeth up at the poor man. 'Well, he dropped the load so fast and ran like hell. You couldn't catch him for greased lightning. You must always mind your own business and don't meddle in what doesn't concern you,' my aunt would counsel.

I want those mountains below to stay dense to protect those Spirits of my island's folklore and of my childhood. I don't know if they are clad in original, virgin forest but, from the air, I imagine my native ancestors might have seen them like this. Well, I used to imagine that. Increasingly, I notice clearings where once there was only a reservoir. As the plane approaches the foothills of the Range and lowers altitude, I can see the city marching up the hills to meet us. On every trip I observe that the homes, many with swimming pools, have encroached farther into the luscious vegetation.

City dwellers used to prefer to turn their backs to the bay, as if bored by its becalmed waters. Now, hugging its length in a curve to the west, is an ever-lengthening string of apartment blocks with large balconies over the water's edge. I try to make out what were once the extremities of Port of Spain – St. Ann's, Cascade, the lower parts of the Maraval Valley. Each time it is more difficult. The urban sprawl has gained pace across the plains too and as far as the eye can see in each direction. As the pilot banks to the left and straightens the plane up for the final run to the airport in the far distance, we glide over what used to be extensive paddy fields of rice. Once they were tilled by yoked oxen, pulling metal and wooden ploughs behind them and geed up by a couple of bare-footed, bare-backed Indian farmers each clad in only a loin cloth or kapra, an item of traditional Indian clothing hardly ever seen nowadays in Trinidad.

The smoke rising up below us could once have been from a funeral pyre on the banks of the Caroni river. There was little difference I came to realise, much later in my life, between what I had seen as a child there and what happens on the banks of the Ganges. Now, this smoke is most likely to be from a bush fire or the burning of sugar cane in the fields through which the Caroni runs.

The feeling that this place nurtured me and several generations of my family intensifies with each trip. I feel grounded in this piece of Earth. I know I want to die here and be buried here, to dissolve into this land like my ancestors, who came from all over the world and are now dust below me. I hope no one can see my lips moving because I am talking to the hills that are now along to my left in the distance. Bits of lyrical poetry come into my head. I can't stop this raw emotion that frequently makes me tearful. It all seems so perfect from up here, but I know that down there is another reality.

The stories of the current breakdown in law and order – the lack of security, violence, drug-abuse and disconnection – have all reached me abroad. All you need to do is get up the *Trinidad Express* or *Trinidad Guardian* website on the Internet to keep informed about goings-on in Paradise. I am told repeatedly by members of my family that I am mad to want to return to Trinidad to live after 30-something years abroad, that things are not what they used to be, that people have changed, the place has changed.

I argue back that change is inevitable, especially in a place like Trinidad. It has been in perpetual evolution not only since I became a conscious human being but throughout its history. Anyone can cite the arrival of the many European tribes, the Arawaks and Caribs before them, the Africans, Indians, Chinese, Arabs and Jews, and everything that's happened since. But on my most recent trip I felt, for the very first time, that the island I knew had indeed passed into history. I was overcome with an acute sense that Port of Spain was well on its way from being the capital of the twin-island nation of Trinidad and Tobago, to being a modern big city. It became evident that the rules of engagement had changed, the community had changed, and an entirely new period of our history had begun.

A lot of this may be entirely personal. There have been a few recent deaths among older members of my extended family, including my own father who passed away just a few years earlier. Also, many relatives have emigrated to the US, they seldom return and their children do not know or have any interest in Trinidad & Tobago. Entire branches of the family have been severed from the family tree. Out of curiosity, on my last visit I got out the telephone directory. There are no entries under Recile or Rosteing – they have ceased to exist – and only one under Whyms, although the Rauceo, Julien, Rostant, Huggins, Romain, Camps and still more related families are very much in evidence. The fact is that all those members of the extended family tree are not known to me, and the abiding sense I have is that, now, they never could be, not to either me or mine, and that it doesn't matter.

As a child growing up in Trinidad, we always knew who was 'family,' even if we didn't socialise. But the clans now operate in much tighter circles. There seems to be much less interest in, or knowledge of, those loose family connections, and a lot more emphasis on the immediate family and the new families of friends. In that sense, Trinidadian families have begun to function much more like the British who do not particularly value or routinely exploit blood ties, prizing self-sufficiency and like-mindedness instead.

Much of this change is driven by the recent economic and social changes in society. Young professionals do not need to know anyone in the family, necessarily, to get a job, buy a house, or secure a place for their child in a prestigious school because their own education and social connections provide the leverage needed. The economic clout that the family used to wield, traditionally, is waning as the economy develops, drawing upon a wider pool of human talent and providing all different types of employment across the entire country. People now are prepared to go anywhere for work and they have the means to do so. The expanded road network has given Trinidad rush hour traffic jams comparable to any big city as thousands of people are sucked from their suburbs and satellite towns into the metropolis, and spewed out again at the end of the day.

The professionalisation and modernisation of many industries – though the public institutions have not caught up yet – have also contributed to my general sense of 'big city' Port of Spain. Take banking. Not so many years ago, getting money out of the bank, or even into it, was a pretty drawn out and stressful affair for most people. But, by adopting a more liberal and commercial approach to the movement of money, banks have changed the way people function, giving them much more self-reliance and independence. Providing cash dispensing machines for the public and direct debit and standing order facilities has depersonalised the entire affair.

Personal relationships must count for something in certain financial transactions, but it would be quite possible to know no-one in a bank and be able to conduct one's financial affairs perfectly smoothly. It is almost like banking in England where you have a telephone account, but no branch, or bank manager and pay all your bills by remote. And this de-personalisation is just as well since it would be almost impossible to know, or know anything about, all the vast array of different sorts of people, many of them from other islands, who are now employed in the service, retail or financial industries in Trinidad.

The degree of social mobility and change is singularly impressive. In the Fiftees and still in the Sixties, only local whites worked in banks, only black men played steel pan, the Chinese ran laundries and restaurants, the Indians were pretty much confined to the south and pockets elsewhere and the Levantine people were well entrenched in their fabric stores and dry goods wholesale shops in Henry, Charlotte and Duncan Streets. Everyone knew how to operate in such a society of clearly defined roles.

During my visits in the years since the end of the Sixties, I have seen the scrambling of all these norms. The racial and economic divides are of a new variety and social mores are sometimes unrecognisable to me. I get the feeling that large sections of society have retreated or emigrated and their space has been filled by groups, ideas, aspects of culture that are evolving into something that is no longer Trinidadian in the sense I once knew. This is inevitable, and in some ways desirable, but we haven't yet made sense of it all. It is work in progress, but the degree of detachment and disconnection that it has engendered is contributing to the impersonal nature of the capital city, particularly.

Of course, the fear of crime is a major factor in this process. Gone is the ease with which one might offer a ride or lift to a stranger, or let them into your house to use the telephone – and that is as true in Port of Spain as in the south. I am constantly being warned to be on my guard. A lot of this is middle-class angst but it is something we now have in common with big cities everywhere. The notion of the stranger has acquired new potency.

In these changing circumstances it would be foolish not to recognise the usefulness of social or family connections. After all, Trinidad may be the size of an English county and Port of Spain the size of a handkerchief, but it is every bit as complex as any other old society where 'who yuh kno' can sometimes do you no harm at all. A few years ago, I took my aunt's dog to the vet. He was perfectly civil and professional but he became distinctly friendly when he discovered who my relatives were. Doctors and other professionals, I would guess, do not necessarily charge less because they know you, but they might see you more quickly – just as in any big city.

Yet there is an inherent downside to these connections in a small society – the loss of anonymity. Once, I arrived at Piarco, was met by a cousin and, before we could get to the Port of Spain suburb of Woodbrook where he lived, 20 or so miles away, someone who didn't know about my visit had already called my aunt's house to give her the news that I had been seen in my cousin's car. The feeling of being free from social coercion is one of the most precious aspects of big city life. Privacy in the midst of the throng is another.

So I want to keep my magical mountains, but I do not mourn the passing of the Trinidad of my youth. In some ways it is a relief to me, the prodigal child, who feared that after some 35 years away I would not know how to live at home again. It is a paradox that, in many ways, I feel better equipped to deal with the new, emerging reality than many of my fellow Trinidadians who are so caught up in the turmoil of change. Lucky me, I left a provincial capital and returned to find a virtual Big City, one I can recognise from the air and from down below too.